THE FEMINISTS

WOMEN'S EMANCIPATION MOVEMENTS IN EUROPE,
AMERICA AND AUSTRALASIA 1840-1920

RICHARD J. EVANS

CROOM HELM
London & Sydney

BARNES & NOBLE
Totowa, New Jersey

©1977 Richard J. Evans
Croom Helm Ltd, Provident House, Burrell Row,
Beckenham, Kent BR3 1AT
Croom Helm Australia Pty Ltd, Suite 4, 6th Floor,
64-76 Kippax Street, Surry Hills, NSW 2010, Australia
Revised edition 1979, reprinted 1984 and 1985

British Library Cataloguing in Publication Data

Evans, Richard John
    The feminists.
    1. Feminism — History
    I. Title
    301.41'2'091812   HQ1121

    ISBN 0-85664-977-5

First published in the USA 1977 by
Barnes and Noble Books,
81 Adams Drive,
Totowa, New Jersey 07512

ISBN 0-06-492044-5

Printed and bound in Great Britain
by Billing & Sons Limited, Worcester.

CONTENTS

For Elín

PREFACE

A comparative history of feminist movements would scarcely have been possible five or six years ago. It is only since the end of the 1960s that scholarly interest in the history of feminism has awakened, and only since 1972-3 that academic studies of women's emancipation movements in the past have become available in any number. We still do not know enough about the history of feminism in most countries; some female emancipation movements have yet to attract the interest of a single historian. Nevertheless, I believe that sufficient work has now been done to warrant a first attempt at a comparative synthesis. Many people have tried to explain why feminist movements emerged, what they wanted and how − or whether − they achieved their aims. Almost invariably they have based their explanations on the example of one country alone, usually England or America. It is only by looking at the development of feminism in a variety of countries, however, that we can overcome the distortion of perspective which this involves, and reach towards a more comprehensive grasp of the history of women's efforts to emancipate themselves through political action.

I first became aware of the need for a comparative study of feminism at the beginning of the 1970s, when working on a history of the feminist movement in Germany. In part, therefore, this book is the outcome of my own need to place German feminism more firmly in an international and comparative context than I was able to do then, limited as I was by the necessity of concentrating on the presentation and interpretation of detailed archival research within the confines of a book devoted primarily to German history. I also felt it would be a useful exercise for a general study of feminism to be written from the point of view of a practising historian, sympathetic to, but not a member of the present-day feminist movement. At the same time, this book also comes out of the personal experiences in which I became involved through my work on Germany. Initially, my work on German feminism was conceived as a case study in German liberalism, and had no connection at all with the Women's Liberation movement, which at that time (1970) was only in its earliest stages. Although the historians and archivists with whom I came into contact in the course of my research could not have been kinder or more helpful, many of them, both in East and West Germany, were unable to conceal their surprise that I had chosen to study feminism, and some of them clearly thought I would have done better to have picked a subject that was more central to the concerns of the historical profession in general and to have left feminism to women. At the same time, my research aroused a good deal of interest in supporters of the Women's Liberation movement, and it naturally brought me into contact with many of them. These two influences forced me to embark on a more general consideration of women's history, the reasons for its neglect, and the problems involved in researching and writing it.

These considerations on the hybrid parentage of this book may help to indicate to some extent where its focus lies. My basic concern is not to analyse the history of women's position in society, nor to discuss the structures and realities of women's everyday life in the past and the variety of techniques used by women to adapt to them, change them or escape from them. These are important subjects, of course, and they are inspiring a great deal of significant and trail-blazing research. But I also believe that there is room for a discussion of the political dimension of women's history, or, in other words, for a history of feminism. It is a curious feature of the present historiographical climate that it should be necessary to justify such an enterprise, but necessary it is, not least because of the tendency for women's history to be subsumed under the category of social history, where the habit is to dismiss active feminists as 'untypical' and to concentrate on rediscovering the lives of the 'average' housewife or working woman. Yet millions of women were involved in feminist movements over the period covered by this book, and this fact alone, quite apart from any relevance their experience may have for the Women's Liberation activist of the present day, surely justifies the attempt to understand them. If this study must be categorised into a sub-branch of the historical discipline (though such categorisations are in my view artificial and constricting), it is to the category of political history that it should be assigned, not to that of social history.

The intention of this book is not to be definitive or comprehensive, but rather to establish a general framework of interpretation tracing the origins, development and eventual collapse of women's emancipation movements in relation to the changing social formations and political structures of Europe, America and Australasia in the era of bourgeois liberalism. It is not primarily an account of personalities, ideas, or literary expressions of feminism. Its focus is mainly on organisations and their development, rather than on the effects which feminism had on the mass of women, though of course objective changes in the social position of women are taken into account in the analysis. The first part of the book discusses the origins of organised feminism and advances a model or 'ideal type' description of the main general features of its development. The second and longest part of the book takes a number of case studies of individual feminist movements to illustrate the main varieties of organised feminism and the differences in its structure and evolution from country to country. Brief accounts are given of the development of feminism in America, Australasia, Britain, Scandinavia and the Nordic countries, the Habsburg Monarchy, Germany, Russia, France, Belgium, Holland and Italy, and in each case there is an attempt to determine the extent to which the feminist movement conformed to or deviated from the model outlined in the first chapter. The third part of the book, which strictly speaking is not in conformity with the book's general title, deals in a similar way to parts one and two with socialist women's movements. Some consideration of these is necessary since their emergence played a crucial role in the further development of middle-class feminism, but I have thought it important to go beyond this and discuss socialist women's movements in some detail since they formed the major, indeed almost the only alternative form of women's emancipation movement to that developed by the feminists of the middle classes in the late nineteenth and early twentieth centuries. The fourth part of the book discusses the reasons for the collapse of bourgeois feminist movements after the First World War. A general conclusion pulls together some of the arguments advanced in all four chapters and tries to explore some of their implications. There is a brief appendix on international feminist organisations. A short note on further reading concludes the book.

The first draft of this book was written during a semester's sabbatical leave granted to me by the University of Stirling in 1976, and I am most grateful to the staff of the University of Stirling library for their unfailing courtesy and helpfulness in dealing with my requests for material. I also wish to express my thanks to the British Library, Reference Division, and the Fawcett Library, for their assistance in obtaining the original sources on which parts of this book are based. I have also made use of some of the documentation collected during my researches on German feminism, and once more I am happy to express my gratitude to the various archives and libraries in whose care the material rests. In a synthesis of this kind, the author is more than usually indebted to the labours of others; I particularly wish to acknowledge the debt I owe to the historians whose work I cite, and to offer my apologies to them for using their hard-won information to support arguments which they might not always accept. My debt to particular works on individual countries is indicated in more detail in the notes; it is to be hoped that some at least of the many important PhD dissertations which have appeared on the history of various feminist movements in recent years, and which I have derived much from consulting, will reach a wider public by appearing in print in the not-too-distant future. I am also grateful to all those individuals who have helped me obtain material, especially Agneta Pallinder, Gunnar Qvist and Anna Sigurdardóttir. Parts of the typescript were read and commented on by David Barrass, Jane Caplan, Elín Hjaltadóttir, Karen Leonard, Stewart Oakley and Neil Tranter, and I am very grateful to them for their critical suggestions and remarks. I would also like to thank Marjan Bhavsa, Pat Jackson and Margaret McCallum for their assistance in preparing the final draft, which was completed in February 1977. Cathleen Catt kindly undertook the task of reading the proofs. Finally, I owe a more general debt of gratitude to Elín Hjaltadóttir, who helped me in many ways, but above all with her constant criticism and encouragement; it is to her that this book is dedicated.

Norwich
February 1977   Richard J. Evans

Preface to the Paperback Edition

For this edition I have mostly confined myself to the correction of misprints and minor errors, and the insertion of a few stylistic improvements. There are two substantial alterations to which I must draw the reader's attention. On pages 168-9 I have recast my account of the Finnish Social Democratic Women's Movement in the light of information kindly provided to me by Dr David Kirby, of the School of Slavonic and East European Studies in the University of London. Secondly, I am grateful to Jill Craigie for pointing out in her generous review of this book in *The Spectator* that the account which I gave on page 191 of the English suffragettes' 'truce' in 1910-11 was misleading, and I have amended the passage accordingly. Neither this nor any of the other points made by Ms Craigie alters my more general views on the political significance of the suffragettes. Finally, a number of important studies on the history of feminism have appeared since the completion of the original manuscript of this book in February 1977, and I have mentioned a few of them in the 'Note on Further Reading' on pages 254-5.

Norwich, 1978   Richard J. Evans

ABBREVIATIONS

AFL	American Federation of Labor
AWSA	American Woman Suffrage Alliance
ICWT	*International Council of Women: Transactions of Quinquennial Meetings*
IWSAC	*International Woman Suffrage Alliance: Reports of Conferences*
IWW	Industrial Workers of the World
NAWSA	National American Woman Suffrage Alliance
NUWSS	National Union of Women's Suffrage Societies
NWSA	National Woman Suffrage Alliance
NZWCTU	New Zealand Woman's Christian Temperance Union
SPD	*Sozialdemokratische Partei Deutschlands* (Social Democratic Party of Germany)
WCTU	Woman's Christian Temperance Union
WSML	*Women's Suffrage in Many Lands*, ed. Alice Zimmern, London, 1909
WSP	*Women's Suffrage in Practice*, ed. C. Macmillan *et al.*, London, 1912
WSPU	Women's Social and Political Union
WTUL	Women's Trade Union League

1 PHILOSOPHERS AND ORGANISERS

Reason, Religion and Revolution

Women have always protested against their oppression in some way, and individual writers and thinkers throughout the ages have often devoted their attention to women's plight; but it was only in the nineteenth century that women began themselves to combine in organisations expressly created in order to fight for the emancipation of the female sex as a whole. The origins of this historically novel development lay in a conjuncture of historical forces operating at three different levels — intellectual, economic and social, and political. These three levels were of course interrelated, but it is convenient for the purpose of analysis to separate them from one another. In order to grasp the nature of the social, economic and political developments which lay behind the emergence of organised feminism, it is first necessary to understand what feminists themselves wanted, and how they justified their demands.

The ideological origins of feminism,[1] with which this first part of the opening chapter is concerned, must be sought in the first place in the eighteenth-century intellectual 'Enlightenment'.[2] The thinkers of the Enlightenment rejected the view that revelation from God was the source of all knowledge. Truth, they argued, could only be found out by free and reasoned enquiry. All obstacles to the discovery of truth, including censorship, should be dismantled. Truth, once discovered, should be applied, and traditional institutions and vested interests which impeded its application should be removed. The triumph of reason was assured, since all human beings were fundamentally rational creatures, and once they were educated, they would perceive the truths revealed by rational enquiry and naturally proceed to implement them. In the face of reason, no received wisdom was sacrosanct. The intellectual ferment of the Enlightenment was expressed in an almost infinite range of theorising and empirical investigation. The curiosity of Enlightenment thinkers was all-embracing.[3] It was natural that one of the many subjects they touched on should be a topic which had exercised the minds of previous thinkers throughout the ages: the nature and role of women.

Many of the leading philosophers of the late eighteenth century devoted at least some attention to the question of women, marriage and

13

the family. Few, however, did so specifically, and none devoted an entire work to the subject. Those who did were generally on the fringes of the movement. The German writer Theodor Gottlieb von Hippel is a good example. Mayor of the East Prussian town of Königsberg and a friend of the philosopher Immanuel Kant, Hippel produced a book which besides being regarded as the beginning of the literary debate on women's place in society in Germany, also has a more general interest and significance: *On the Civil Improvement of Women (1794).* It is a rambling, discursive and somewhat eccentric piece of work, but some of the ideas it contains are important. Hippel argued that women's abilities were the same as men's, but 'they are not simply neglected, they are deliberately suppressed'. Women were coddled into laziness and educated to be ignorant:

> 'Reason' is a gift which Nature has vouchsafed to all human beings to the same extent. The most basic principles of Natural Law, in the implementation of which compulsion may be used without fear of contradiction, is the law 'oppose anything that endangers the full development of all human beings'. This principle resides in the highest material law of morality, 'develop every human being to the fulfilment of its potential'.

Hippel saw his age as the era of female equality. 'For a series of centuries, Europe bore only one face: despotism and slavery, ignorance and barbarism ruled everywhere.' Now, however, Enlightenment had at last triumphed. 'Why should not women be capable of being raised to that rank which belongs to them as human beings after such a long suppression?'[4]

All the themes that Hippel introduced were to recur in feminist propaganda. His own writing was limited in several respects. For example, though he believed women capable of full and equal participation in politics and justice, argued for coeducation, and urged the employment of female physicians, he also thought that women were naturally more peaceful and generous than men, and used this as an additional reason for placing them on juries and in offices of state. He did not seem to sense the contradiction between his belief in the equal abilities and differing natures of the male and female sex. This was a contradiction that was to recur with great regularity in feminist writing. Hippel was attacked and derided by his contemporaries. Nevertheless, his book was an important one, above all for its enunciation of the principle that women should be allowed to develop their abilities and personalities without hindrance.

Hippel was writing in 1794, at a time when the French Revolution had already reached its most radical point. He was a strong critic of the Revolution, because, as he said, it ignored half the nation — the female half. But he did recognise that many women were 'growing weary of the chains which the law paints for them in such a favourable light'[5] and in fact the French Revolution provided an important additional impetus to that of the Enlightenment in the development of feminist ideology. In France, the place of women in society had long been discussed by writers concerned with the morality of marriage, the reform of the law or the restrictive nature of nobility.[6] The leading French writers of the Enlightenment had also considered the question, though usually only in passing; Rousseau was anti-feminist, while Montesquieu, Diderot and Voltaire were sympathetic to women's claims and Condorcet — to whom, incidentally, the German von Hippel's debt was particularly great — was enthusiastically on the side of feminism.[7] The debate was taken up by a host of lesser writers. By 1789 there was a respectable body of literature advocating equal education, equal access to jobs and equal political rights for women, justifying these claims on the grounds that all human beings were equally endowed with reason. These ideas found some political expression in the Revolution which broke out with the calling of the Estates General, the old French Parliament, occasioned by the total collapse of royal finances in 1789. No fewer than thirty-three of the *cahiers de doléances*, grievance lists drawn up by constituents and electors, urged greater educational opportunities for women.[8] In the Estates General itself, and the various constituent and legislative assemblies which followed it, there were always a number of deputies influenced by Enlightenment writings in favour of women's rights, and some of them expressed their views quite forcefully.

More important, perhaps, in the political ferment of the years 1789-93, in Paris and the major provincial cities, women themselves began to organise in the struggle for their rights. They formed women's political clubs, and exerted strong pressure on some of the leading men's political clubs which formed the equivalent of political parties in the Revolution. The leading figures in this movement included Etta Palm, a woman of Dutch origin who petitioned the Assembly and spoke before it in 1791 in favour of equal rights in education, politics, law and employment, and tried to form a national movement of women's clubs; Anne Tervagne, who called herself Théroigne de Méricourt and who also tried to form a women's club; and Marie Gouze (known as 'Olympe de

Gouges'). The last-named of the three, Olympe de Gouges, drafted a
Declaration of the Rights of Women, modelled on the basic document
of the Revolution, the *Declaration of the Rights of Man and Citizen*.
But feminism in the French Revolution did not last long. Olympe de
Gouges was executed as a royalist in 1793; Théroigne de Méricourt
was beaten up by Jacobin women in the same year and ended her days
in a lunatic asylum; and the women's clubs were dissolved by the Convention, at the instigation of the Jacobins, in 1793, after the most
prominent of them, the *Citoyennes Républicaines Révolutionnaires*,
had moved to the far left and involved itself with the ultra-radical
Jacques Roux and the *enragés*.[9]

The feminists in the French Revolution were really a marginal
phenomenon. Most of them seem to have been minor writers, intellectuals or journalists with no solid political backing. The leading figures
of the Revolution were indifferent to women's rights.[10] The legislation
of the Revolution ignored women almost completely. The mass of
women who participated in the great bread riots and street battles of
the Revolution had no time to think of the theories of Enlightenment
feminism; they were too busy simply trying to feed themselves and
their families.[11] Feminism remained a predominantly literary phenomenon in France for many decades. It continued in the Revolution to
concentrate on the theory of education and the conquest of equality
of educational opportunity.[12] The most famous feminist polemic to
owe its inspiration to the Revolution, Mary Wollstonecraft's *A Vindication of the Rights of Woman* (1792), is really an educational tract.[13]
The ideas in Wollstonecraft's work are still those of the Enlightenment;
indeed, in many respects they are identical with those of Hippel or the
Revolutionary women's clubs. Women, argued Wollstonecraft, were
endowed with Reason: therefore man's predominance was arbitrary.
As civilisation progressed, Reason advanced. 'As sound politics diffuse
liberty, mankind, including woman, will become more wise and virtuous.' Women were kept in unnatural subjection; the spread of
Reason and the reform of education would bring them to the full
realisation of their innate rationality. This would then result in an
immeasurable improvement in the state of mankind as a whole, as
women became 'truly useful members of society'.

The limitations of these ideas were as clear as their more bold and
original features. The rationalist assumptions of all these writers would
soon be shown to rest on false premises. Only a minority of women
were capable of responding to the call; few could read at this period,
fewer still could afford books. The optimism which lay behind all the

tracts we have looked at reflected a faith in human progress which was eventually to be belied. But the Enlightenment did assemble a whole battery of intellectual weapons to be wielded in the feminist cause: ideas of reason, progress, natural law, the fulfilment of the individual, the beneficent power of education and the social utility of freedom from restrictions and equality of rights. The French Revolution, in which for the first time women actually tried to band together to fight for their rights, showed that social groups — above all, the middle classes, to whom the feminists belonged — did possess the power to shake off legal and institutional restraints and achieve equality of status. All this, however, was insufficient to bring about feminism on a permanently effective basis. More was needed, and in the intellectual heritage of feminism, the Enlightenment and the French Revolution constituted only two among a number of different elements. Even where their influence can be discerned, it was sometimes more in an indirect than in a direct way.

Equally important in the development and inspiration of feminism as the Enlightenment or the French Revolution was the social ideology of liberal Protestantism. The Protestant religion was founded on the belief that the individual, not the priest nor the Church, was responsible for his own salvation. Like the rationalist individualism of the Enlightenment, the religious individualism of the Protestant faith was, in theory at least, equally applicable to both sexes. In practice, of course, the leading figures of the major Protestant churches in the Reformation era believed firmly in the inferiority of women. Martin Luther thought that women should stay at home and keep house. They were not fit for the priesthood: 'Female government has never done any good.' John Calvin agreed with Luther that woman's submission to man was ordained by God. His disciple, John Knox, published a notorious tract against women rulers entitled 'The First Blast of the Trumpet against the Monstrous Regiment of Women'. Nevertheless, their belief in the priesthood of all believers did explicitly include women. All human beings were held by them to be equally capable of direct contact with God, without distinction of sex; and Luther and the Calvinists went to some lengths to demonstrate the falseness of the Catholic belief that women were unclean and agents of the Devil.[14]

More than this, the Protestant Reformation quickly spawned a whole brood of extremist religious sects whose doctrines went even further than those of Luther and Calvin, attacking conventional marriage and advocating free love and the complete independence of the female sex. Women often took a prominent role in this sectarian activity, above all in the seventeenth century. Many of the leading sectarian preachers of the English Civil War were women, and the Quakers, Ranters and other libertarian religious groups were notorious among contemporaries for the freedom of expression they gave to women.[15] This was perhaps not of any great or lasting importance in the development of feminism. What was crucial was the general principle that lay behind these radical manifestations, a principle shared in essence by the official Protestant Churches, however reluctant they might be to accept its consequences. The Protestant belief in the right of every man and woman to work individually for his or her own salvation was to provide an indispensable reassurance, often indeed a genuine inspiration, to many, if not most, of the feminist campaigners of the nineteenth century.

The rationalism of the Enlightenment and the moral imperatives of Protestantism came together in the nineteenth century and fused in the creed of liberalism. The liberals saw the world as composed of a mass of individual atoms, all competing with one another for their own individual benefit. Competition, free and unrestricted, would benefit society as well, because the most just and the most virtuous would come out on top, and use their power beneficently, while the evil and indolent would inevitably get their just deserts. Only if the interference of the state were reduced to a minimum, all artificialities of status between individuals abolished, all outmoded hierarchical institutions removed and all barriers to the free competition of individuals swept away, would a truly just and equitable society come into being. Liberalism wanted society governed in the interests of the people through institutions accountable to them. Reasonable behaviour, fairness and morality, essential in a society where formal restraints on competition had been abolished, could not however simply be taken for granted as the rationalists of the Enlightenment took them for granted. Education was to be moral as well as rational; reasonable behaviour was to be based on self-discipline and inculcated by religion and conscience as well as by persuasion. There were many expressions of these views in the early nineteenth century, and not a few attempts to apply them to women. The liberal creed was a durable one, and by mid-century it had been subjected to a good deal of elaboration and discussion. But its fundamentals remained unaltered. The classic statement of their application to women was given by one of the greatest of liberal theorists, John Stuart Mill (1806-1873). Mill's essay, *The Subjection of Women*, published in 1869, was the feminist bible. It is difficult to exaggerate the enormous impression which it made on the minds of educated women all over the world. In the same year that it was first published in England

and America, Australia and New Zealand, it also appeared in translation in France, Germany, Austria, Sweden and Denmark. In 1870 it appeared in Polish and Italian and was also being discussed excitedly by girl students in St Petersburg. By 1883, the Swedish translation was forming the centre of discussion for a group of women in Helsinki who founded the Finnish women's movement as soon as they finished reading the book. From all over Europe there are impressive testimonies to the immediate and profound impact of Mill's tract;[16] its appearance roughly coincided with the foundation of the feminist movements not only in Finland but also in France[17] and Germany,[18] and very possibly in other countries as well.[19]

Mill's book was influential because it summed up the feminist case in a way that linked it firmly to the political theory of liberal individualism and tied it to the assumptions about society and politics held by its audience. It is often claimed that the appeal of *The Subjection of Women* is timeless, and that its impact derives from the lack of any markedly 'Victorian' character. Nothing could be further from the truth. Its power derived precisely from the fact that it was in many ways a summary of the prejudices and preconceptions of the age. Its rhetoric is redolent of the optimism and arrogance of mid-Victorian liberalism. Mill presented the society he lived in as an almost perfect example of the liberal ideal. In the liberal and prosperous society of Victorian England, according to Mill, 'human beings are no longer born to their place in life and chained down by an inexorable bond to the place they are born to, but are free to employ their faculties, and such favourable chances as offer, to achieve the lot which may appear to them most desirable'. The solitary exception to this rule, according to Mill, was the position of women. 'In no instance except this', he declared, 'which comprehends half the human race, are the higher social functions closed against anyone by a fatality of birth which no exertions, and no change of circumstances can overcome.' The subjection of women, Mill continued, was no harmless anachronism. It positively impeded the further progress of the human race by denying society the use of the talents of half its members, and by the morally corrupting effect of the unearned power it gave to men. 'The only school of genuine moral sentiment', said Mill, 'is society between equals.' Such a society, he believed, existed in every respect in Victorian England, except in that of the relations between men and women. It was, then, almost as the final stage in the progress towards a perfect human society that Mill demanded full equality for women.

Mill conceived of equality as consisting in the absence of positive legal guarantees of inequality. Thus he defined female emancipation in terms of 'the removal of women's disabilities — their recognition as the equals of men in all that belongs to citizenship, the opening to them of all honourable employments and of the training and education which qualifies for those employments', and the removal of the excessive authority which the law gave to husbands over their wives. Mill's standpoint on this issue was the social counterpart of the liberal doctrine of economic *laissez-faire*. He believed that, should all the legal restraints on the individual freedom of women be removed, women would be completely at liberty to live their own lives as self-sufficient individuals. The removal of legal disabilities was intended to give free rein to the full development of the personality of every woman; but this development was in its turn intended to fulfil the economic and social requirements of a market economy. 'All women', he declared, 'are brought up from their very earliest years in the belief that their ideal of character is the very opposite to that of men; not self-will, and government by self-control, but submission, and yielding to the control of others.' By projecting these submissive ideals onto other social groups, women did untold social harm. For example, he said,

> the great and continually increasing mass of unenlightened and short-sighted benevolence, which, taking the care of people's lives out of their own hands, and relieving them from the disagreeable consequences of their own acts, saps the very foundations of the self-respect, self-help and self-control which are the essential conditions both of individual prosperity and of social virtue — this waste of resources and of benevolent feelings in doing harm instead of good, is immensely swelled by women's contributions, and stimulated by their influence.

Mill presented the achievement of legal equality for women as an integral part of the progress of mankind towards a just society affording equal opportunity to all. He did not, of course, believe that all human beings were equal, or that men and women were the same. On the contrary, while stressing the ignorance of the science of his day concerning the psychology of the sexes, he accepted that it was probable that women's faculties were different from men's. But this was irrelevant for the purposes of his argument. The point was, that women should be allowed the freedom for themselves to discover the limits of their abilities:

What women by nature cannot do, it is quite superfluous to forbid them from doing. What they can do, but not so well as the men who are their competitors, competition suffices to exclude them from; since nobody asks for protective duties and bounties in favour of women; it is only asked that the present bounties and protective duties in favour of men should be recalled. If women have a greater natural inclination for some things than for others, there is no need of laws or social inculcation to make the majority of them do the former in preference to the latter. Whatever women's services are most wanted for, the free play of competition will hold out the strongest inducements to them to undertake. And, as the words imply, they are most wanted for the things for which they are most fit; by the apportionment of which to them, the collective faculties of the two sexes can be applied on the whole with the greatest sum of valuable result.

For example, said Mill, if it was believed that women's natural calling was marriage and motherhood, then there was no need to pass laws to prevent them deserting it for a career in the professions. Nevertheless, he argued, there was considerable evidence that women's mental and creative powers were equal to men's. They should therefore be allowed to exercise them.[20]

Mill's arguments were founded on several general principles which were attractive to liberals in Europe, America and Australasia in the nineteenth century. Belief in the superiority of political constitutionalism on the English model, with its principles of parliamentary government and 'no taxation without representation' was one of them. In an era when liberals everywhere looked to England in admiration of its institutions, Mill's faith in the superiority of Victorian civilisation and the beneficent effects of a policy of social and economic *laissez-faire* was echoed by liberal thinkers all over the world. A second element in Mill's appeal was the legacy of the French Revolution, the principles of equality before the law, career open to the talents, representative government, and the sanctity of property; a legacy which had been taken up by the English liberals in the reforming era of the Whigs and Peelites in the mid-nineteenth century. Finally, optimism about human nature and human progress, derived from the Enlightenment, and trust in the Protestant virtues of 'self-respect, self-help and self-control' as the necessary concomitants of a society largely free of formal legal restraints, completed the liberal synthesis which underpinned Mill's work and which gave the ideology of feminism its theoretical backbone.[21]

Feminism in this sense had a general appeal not least because it formed part of a general intellectual movement which sought to justify the removal of formal legal discrimination against individuals on account of their birth. It was against the restriction of state office and legal and fiscal privilege to the aristocracy that the French Revolution was launched. The period from the late eighteenth to the mid-nineteenth century in Europe saw the gradual or (above all, in 1848) the sudden and violent removal of legal barriers depriving serfs of various rights, including the right to hold property, to enter the professions or to dispose of their own persons freely. Similar barriers operating against Jews were also removed.[22] It was the immediate aim of the feminists to extend this process to women, whose situation was in many respects similar to that of Jews or serfs. In the early nineteenth century, women did not have the right to vote, to stand for election, to hold public office (except in certain countries the Crown itself), or, in many parts of Central and Eastern Europe, to join political organisations or attend political meetings. These disabilities may be broadly described as political in nature. They also suffered economic restrictions, debarring women from holding property, transferring a woman's inherited wealth to her husband on marriage, and preventing women from engaging in trade, running a business, joining the professions, opening a bank account or obtaining credit in their own name, and in general ensuring that they did not become economically independent. In addition to this, there was a third type of discrimination, which overlapped with, and in many instances provided the legal ground for, the deprivation of economic rights. This was the denial of basic rights in civil and criminal law. In most countries, women were not 'legal persons', that is, they could not enter into contracts, and were minors or children in the eyes of the law. Until they married, they were in the power of their father, and required his permission to work, marry, change residence and so on. This was the case even with unmarried women in their thirties or forties. After marriage, these powers passed to the husband, who had complete disposal over his wife's property, income and children. Particularly in Roman Law countries (above all, those governed by the Napoleonic Law Code), divorce was relatively easy for a husband, almost impossible for a wife. In cases of sexual deviance (illegitimate birth, prostitution, adultery), the law punished women but allowed men to avoid all responsibility. In law cases of all kinds, women were treated as inferior witnesses whose word counted for less than that of men.[23] Finally, women were discriminated against in education, where the new secondary school systems of the early nineteenth century generally catered for the education of boys alone, and where, at a lower level, the inadequacies of primary schooling for girls ensured that illiteracy was far more common among women than among men. These were in general the objects on which the feminists concentrated, with the addition of moral reform, to be discussed later in this chapter.

The intellectual justification for the feminists' aims came from liberal ideology, from the individualism of Puritanism and the Enlightenment, from what the American feminist Elizabeth Cady Stanton called 'our Protestant idea, the right of individual conscience and judgment, our republican idea, individual citizenship'. But these ideas did not exert a universal appeal. Intellectual history cannot by itself explain the growth of feminism in the nineteenth century; people do not, whatever the rationalists of the Enlightenment thought, commit themselves to political action and suffer the scorn, contempt, ridicule and hatred which the feminists were forced to endure, merely out of intellectual conviction. We must look therefore to social and economic influences to explain why feminist theorists in the nineteenth century, unlike their predecessors in previous ages, found an eager and ready audience for their message.[24]

Economy and Society

Several theories have been advanced by historians to account for the rise of feminism in the nineteenth century, and a consideration of at least two of these, involving the structure of the family and the ratio of the sexes, is first necessary in order to clear the ground for a more detailed examination of the origins of feminism in the social and political changes of the time.

Many historians have attempted to explain the rise of women's emancipation movements in the nineteenth century as a product of the decline of domestic production and the major changes in the structure of the family which this brought about. The nineteenth century was the age of the Industrial Revolution, which saw the rapid urbanisation of society in Europe, America and Australasia. Massive changes in social structure took place as millions of people moved from the country into the towns and forsook their old rural customs and occupations for new urban ones. Among these changes, it has been argued, were fundamental alterations in the structure of the family. Before the Industrial Revolution, the family was an 'extended' unit, consisting not only of husband and wife and young children, but also of uncles and aunts, grandparents, great-uncles, great-aunts and cousins as well, all living under one roof. All these people worked together, according to the theory, in a common economic undertaking to support themselves as a group. The preindustrial family was a productive unit in which all members, married and unmarried, played a useful role.

The Industrial Revolution replaced this kind of domestic productive unit with the factory and the large-scale industrial enterprise. The members of the extended family were thus forced to work for themselves; and the unmarried female members of the family suddenly found that they were barred, usually by law, from all but the most menial and degrading of employments. The size of the family was now, in the industrial era, much smaller; it consisted solely of a husband and wife and their children, and the best jobs were now reserved for men because they had to support a family that was no longer able to contribute significantly to its own upkeep. With the growth of industrial society, bourgeois living standards improved, and social aspirations were raised so that middle-class men tended more and more to wait until they had amassed property before marrying. The emergent proletariat provided poor girls, driven to prostitution through financial need, for sexual gratification. The middle-class wife came to be treated as a piece of ornamental property, expensive, useless and untouchable.

The feminist movement thus emerged in the first place as unmarried middle-class women began to agitate for admission to the professions, which would alone guarantee them an income and standing corresponding to the social status of the family into which they had been born. The rise of these pressure-groups for admitting women to the professions sparked off a kind of chain reaction, as these women found it necessary to campaign for admission into the universities in order to gain the necessary educational qualifications for admission to the professions, and then began to campaign for the vote in order to gain the necessary political power to force the legislative changes which would entitle them to enter the universities. In other words, according to this theory, the rise of feminism was 'a reaction to structural pressures operating on the family . . . the explanation for the rise and decline of the feminist movement', it is argued, 'should be sought for in the sequence of events by which these structural pressures were relieved and a new family system became institutionalised'.[25] The replacement of the domestic economy by large-scale industry robbed the family of its productive functions. Widows and spinsters who had previously been able to find occupation and support within the family could no longer do so. As the family shed its extended links because it was unable to support them, they were left to fend for themselves.

Propertyless gentlewomen, widowed or unmarried, could retain their middle-class status by writing, or by submitting to the tyrannies of companionship or governessing . . . The remainder, unfitted for, or excluded by competition from the narrow range of respectable occupations, sank into the ranks of needlewomen or domestic servants.[26]

Similar developments, according to this theory, affected married women as a result of the separation of home from work brought about by the Industrial Revolution.

From being a partner with her husband when the family was organised as a productive unit, the housewife had rapidly become dependent in the course of the late 18th and of the 19th centuries upon some other person's earning capacity for the income she spent as the family representative. What the organised feminist movement was concerned with in consequence was the plight of single, widowed, divorced and married women who were exploited as a result of this dependency.[27]

It is certainly correct to say that feminist movements began by addressing themselves to women's economic dependency and the exploitation that resulted from it. And although the extended family was by no means a universal constant in pre-industrial society[28], urbanisation undoubtedly brought with it important changes in family life.[29] Housewives began to buy clothes, food and household goods instead of making or producing them themselves. Middle-class housewives found themselves with time on their hands and nothing to do,[30] and simultaneously other social changes, above all perhaps the professionalisation of many traditionally female jobs, were reducing their opportunities to engage in work outside the home. But this analysis must be qualified in at least two important respects. In the first place, it was often precisely these *married* middle-class women who took the lead in founding feminist movements; at the very least, most feminist movements contained as many married as unmarried members. And in the second place, although feminist movements did enlarge their aims stage by stage, the progressive escalation of feminist demands did not follow a simple, linear course, but frequently went off at what often seemed to be something of a tangent. Moreover, the pace and nature of this escalation differed widely from country to country. By the time women came to demand the vote, they had in most countries already obtained access to the professions and the universities. The case of Britain was something of an exception in this respect.[31]

In contrast to this argument, other historians have suggested that a growing surplus of women over men in advanced societies in the nineteenth century, caused by differential mortality and the mass migration of men to America, was behind the growth of feminism.[32] This view has been advanced by a number of writers, notably the historian Roger Thompson.[33] Where there is an excess of women, he argues, there will be a 'general undervaluing of women, exploitation of the weaker sex by men, and various expedients on the part of the oppressed sex to escape their fate and give their lives some kind of meaning'. These 'expedients' will be twofold in character. On the one hand, they will consist of 'an upthrust of extreme patterns of feminism, emphasis on careers for women, the creation of women's organisations and pressure groups'; on the other hand, they will also comprise an increase in female social deviance, including 'higher divorce rates and love triangles, new folkways bearing on family philosophies, concubinage, lesbianism, polygyny and an increase in extra-marital sexuality (to which might be added a growth in prostitution in certain under-developed urban communities)'. The simultaneous emergence of deviance and feminism in situations of an excess of females over males might (though Thompson does not say this) help explain the obsession of feminist movements with moral reform. Where there is a surplus of men, on the other hand, conditions, it is argued, are very different. If the society is almost entirely devoid of females, then life will be violent and brutal. If there is a reasonable number of women, however, even though it is still a minority, society will be better ordered, and women will be in a favourable position, with strong bargaining powers in marriage and considerable independence in civil law. Thompson suggests that sex ratios were favourable to women in seventeenth-century America and unfavourable in seventeenth-century Britain, because of migration and differential mortality rates. As a result, women in the American colonies were in every way better off than their counterparts in Britain, whether in respect of civil rights, education, professional and economic opportunities or the distribution of power in the family. In the eighteenth and early nineteenth centuries, however, things changed. As the American frontier moved westwards, the Eastern seaboard became civilised and the sex ratio evened out. This explains both why feminism arose in early nineteenth-century America in the East (because of worsening sex ratios) and why, paradoxically, it achieved its earliest and easiest successes in the Midwest (because of favourable sex ratios). In 1865, for instance, there were three men for every woman in California, and similar disparities, it has been argued, account for 'the willingness of western territories like Wyoming (1869) and Utah (1870) to grant the suffrage to women long before other regions where the sex ratio was more nearly equal'.[34]

It is doubtful, however, whether the sex ratio theory can explain the rise of feminism in quite so direct a manner. As we shall see, the granting of female suffrage rarely had any direct origin in the ratio of women to men. In Utah, one of the first states to enfranchise women, polygamy prevailed under the rule of the Mormons, and the sex ratio — unusually for a western state — was not particularly favourable to women. And as far as the enlargement of economic opportunities is concerned, this occurred both in areas where women were in short supply, as in Oregon in 1850, when single women were granted the right to own land, and in places where they were in surplus, as in Stockholm in 1846, when a royal statute admitted them to registration as merchants and craftspeople. In both cases, the sex ratio was the major reason for the granting of wider economic opportunities to women, yet both cases represented opposite extremes as far as the sex ratio was concerned. Certainly, the imbalance of the sexes was a major factor influencing the policy of governments everywhere towards women's rights. As an official promulgation issued by the Prussian government in 1908 declared,

> The excess of female over male population and the increasing celibacy among men in the upper classes are forcing a larger percentage of girls in cultured circles to forego their natural calling as wife and mother. Ways must be opened for them to an occupation befitting their upbringing . . .[35]

And the numerous societies which grew up in Victorian England to provide for the employment of 'single gentlewomen' or to assist their emigration overseas testified to the widespread and growing concern about the problem.[36] When it comes to the emergence of feminist movements on a wide scale, however, we are dealing with the urban middle classes, who were less affected by migration than the peasantry and the rural masses, and were therefore less likely to have a surplus or shortage of women. Finally there is a problem of timing. Feminist movements did not emerge during or immediately after the waves of migration which helped create a worsening balance of the sexes. In most cases, they were already in existence. It might also be noted that

the two most dramatic alterations in the sex ratio, those brought about
by the mass slaughter of males in the First and Second World Wars,
were followed not by an upsurge of feminism, but by a decline. Moreover, unbalanced sex ratios were not unknown before industrialisation.
What was new in fact was the great increase in the *absolute* numbers of
'surplus' women in many industrialising societies because of very rapid
population growth, not any great or dramatic change in the ratio of the
sexes. While the imbalance of the sexes either way certainly caught the
attention of contemporaries and undoubtedly played a role in persuading governments to grant reforms which might help alleviate some of
the ill-effects it was alleged to produce, and while changes in the sex
ratio and a growth in the number of 'surplus' males or females may well
have played a part in unsettling attitudes about sex roles in a more
general way, there seems to be no simple formula by which changing
sex ratios and the growth of feminism can be convincingly linked.

In fact, it was not changes in demographic structure, but changes in
class structure that underlay the growth of feminist movements in the
nineteenth century. The most fundamental social development underlying the rise of feminism was the emergence of the middle classes,
above all in the expansion of trade and industry, administration and the
professions. The eighteenth and nineteenth centuries saw not only a
vast and unprecedented expansion of population in Europe (except
France), Australasia and the New World, but also large shifts of occupational and social structure within this growing population. The movement of population to the towns was bringing with it a rapid growth in
the numbers of the middle classes, partly as part of the growing power
and complexity of government and administration, partly as a consequence of the new opportunities offered by economic growth, partly
in response to the expansion of education, medical services, building
and engineering, and so on, that followed in the wake of urbanisation
As they expanded, the professionals closed ranks and attempted to
regulate standards and entry requirements. In every country, professional organisations were formed which pressed for formal training,
rigorous standards and a system of state licensing. Examinations became the criteria of admission not only to state service but also to
law, medicine, surgery, pharmacy, engineering, architecture and secondary teaching. In more general terms, the professional and industrial
middle classes began to play an increasingly prominent role in political
and social life. Where they found their prospects of wealth and social
recognition blocked by an entrenched aristocracy, they used their
growing power to press for a voice in the nation's government through

the creation of parliamentary institutions based on a property-qualified franchise (to exclude the lower classes) with full ministerial responsibility (to minimise aristocratic power exercised through court intrigue). They pleaded for the liberal principles of representative government, equality before the law and careers open to the talents.[37]

In the eighteenth century, professionals, merchants and industrialists in most countries did not possess any marked consciousness of themselves as a separate class. Instead, they regarded themselves as aspirants for nobility. The most successful among them bought country estates and found their way into the ranks of the aristocracy. By the nineteenth century, this was no longer the case. In the French Revolution, the bourgeoisie had swept away the entire structure of nobility and the feudal privileges and institutions that went with it.[38] Elsewhere, as in England, parts of the middle classes had come to see the titled elite as idle parasites, who had acquired their position through no merit of their own and therefore did not deserve it. Virtue came to be redefined in terms of ability and achievement rather than in terms of heredity and office. The ethic of work and self-sacrifice came to replace the values of leisure and *noblesse oblige*. Feudal paternalism was abandoned as the dominant social mentality. Its substitute was the harsh creed of individualistic meritocracy.[39] These values were increasingly dominant in England and France. In the absence of a native aristocracy, they were unchallenged in Australasia and America. In Scandinavia, Central, Eastern and Southern Europe they were championed by a progressively more vocal and powerful middle class.

The timing of this development varied from country to country; it took place earlier in England than elsewhere, for example; but whenever it occurred, it could not fail to have an effect on women. The growth of the middle classes brought with it a new and rapidly expanding group of women, both married and unmarried, whose pattern of life was quite unlike that of women in the past. The professionalisation of teaching, nursing, business and law devalued the status of governesses and untrained middle-class female employees and forced unmarried women to adjust by seeking higher educational standards with which to qualify for admission to the new professions. Women were forced out of medicine and teaching by the growth of professional qualifications and the increasing sophistication of medical knowledge and educational techniques. Changing patterns of marriage and family life increased these problems of adjustment. The nature of philanthropy also changed, and became itself more organised and professionalised — above all with the emergence of middle-class concern with the new industrial proletariat. Untutored benevolence gave way to sociological investigation. The casual pattern of female charitable activity familiar from the days when it was dominated by the titled ladies of the aristocracy was no longer appropriate. These developments were accompanied by the increasing importance of property and wealth, as opposed to land and title, as the basis of power and status, a development which quickly led to the articulation of middle-class women's desire for formal legal recognition of their right to an independent share in the newly acquired riches of the bourgeoisie. Changing values and social structures were forcing middle-class women to redefine their role in society in terms of work and achievement; if it was becoming reprehensible for the nobility to be idle, then it was also becoming impossible for middle-class women to share the leisured existence of the female aristocracy and still retain their self-respect.

These changes in mentalities and values took place mainly in Protestant communities. Protestantism itself originated not least in the dissatisfaction of early modern urban society with the restrictions placed by Catholicism on its freedom of action, and it gained widest support in the most economically and socially advanced areas of European civilisation.[40] More specifically, in Catholic societies the existence of a female regular clergy on a relatively large scale provided a socially acceptable and spiritually fulfilling life for the unmarried women of the upper and middle classes in a way that was not possible in Protestant societies. The inward-directed piety of Catholic married women similarly discouraged the involvement of women in public life in Catholic societies. As we shall see, even in predominantly Catholic countries such as Italy and France, feminism was overwhelmingly Protestant or anti-clerical in character and composition, just as liberalism in the nineteenth century was almost exclusively Protestant or anti-clerical. As for liberal Catholicism, it was a minority affair forced to exist on the margin of religious and social life and consistently rejected by the Church, and its attitude to the emancipation of women also tended in fact to be less than liberal. Feminism, like liberalism itself, then, was above all a creed of the Protestant middle classes.

The limitations which this imposed on the social application of feminist ideas appear clearly in John Stuart Mill's classic exposition of the feminist case. The equality of women for which Mill was pleading was emphatically the equality of middle-class women. When he wrote of the kinds of employment to which he wished women to be granted access, it was as 'physicians, advocates or members of Parliament' that he saw them. When he wrote of giving married women the right of disposing over their own property, it was, obviously, of the propertied classes that he was thinking: 'When the support of the family depends, not on property, but on earnings,' he wrote, 'the common arrangement, by which the man earns the income and the wife superintends the domestic expenditure, seems to me in general the most suitable division of labour between the two persons.' So narrowly was his vision restricted to the women of the bourgeoisie, indeed, that he even opposed the idea of a woman of 'the lower classes of society' going out to work, which (he wrote) would enable her husband 'to abuse his power, by forcing her to work, and leaving the support of the family to her exertions, while he spends most of his time in drinking and idleness'. In a more profound sense, Mill's prescription for female equality *could* only be applied to the middle classes, since it consisted wholly of the removal of legal and educational obstacles to equality of opportunity, and took no account of economic and social barriers, which for the great majority of women were far more important.[41]

All that we know about feminist movements in the nineteenth century confirms the impression of their overwhelmingly middle-class composition. Investigation of the hundred signatories of the Seneca Falls Declaration of 1848 (a major document of American feminism) has for example shown that the great majority were 'middle-class, of moderate to comfortable circumstances'.[42] The Woman's Christian Temperance Union (despite its title, an important feminist organisation), was run in America in 1885 by the wives of independent professional men (physicians, lawyers and ministers) and small businessmen (retailers, small manufacturers and wholesalers). Together these groups made up about two-thirds of the entire leadership at a national and local level, with wives of highly paid skilled labourers accounting for 23 per cent.[43] Of the fifty-eight leading members of the same organisation in Victoria (Australia) who joined in 1887-9, fifteen were married to professional men, six to shopkeepers, three to merchants or agents, twelve to manufacturers or builders, four to farmers; the Union's leaders in New Zealand were married to members of the political and social élite.[44] In a study of fifty-one leading 'feminist-abolitionists' in mid-nineteenth-century America, Blanche Hersh has found that as many as thirty-three were from New England families reaching back to the seventeenth century. The fathers of seventeen were wealthy businessmen or professionals. Twenty-nine others were from middle-class or upper middle-class homes; the daughters of ministers, teachers, small merchants and other solid middle-class men. Of the thirty-seven named who were married, ten were married to businessmen, sixteen to professionals, including seven to lawyers, four to writers or editors, three to ministers, one to a doctor and one to a teacher, and ten to farmers or artisans. Only seven of the thirty-seven husbands could be considered wealthy, but all of them were clearly middle class.[45] A list of the eighty-two members of the German Union for Women's Suffrage, Hamburg branch, compiled in 1904 by the political police with information supplied by the Suffrage Union itself, shows a similar picture. Six of the members were men — one medical specialist, two factory owners, a pastor, a merchant and a stockbroker. Of the women, twenty-eight were married and listed as housewives. Forty-eight were unmarried. Two of these were described as ladies of private means. Four lived at home with their parents. Ten lived in the suburb of Altona, under Prussian jurisdiction, and so were not investigated. Thirteen were schoolteachers, four were accounts clerks, two were shopkeepers, and there was also a nurse, a painter, a receptionist, a dressmaker, a commercial student and a factory inspector's assistant. There is little in the list about their fathers, but six of these were known to be merchants, five schoolteachers, two stockbrokers, one a dentist and one an agent.[46]

A recent analysis of 379 biographies of women revolutionaries in Russia between 1860 and 1890 has suggested that about 60 per cent came from the noble or merchant class, 15 per cent were Jewish, 7 per cent came from the families of Orthodox clergy, and the rest were lower class in origin.[47] Finally, of the 194 members who joined Léon Richer's French League for Women's Rights in 1882-3, ninety-six were men: twenty-one politicians (thirteen of them were deputies), fifteen journalists (including some of the politicians), three professors, one teacher, two students, two lawyers, one architect, one physician, two merchants, one broker, one distiller, one lithographer, two accountants, one bookseller, six clerks, one inspector of weights and measures, two retired officers, two tailors, one sculptor, one barber, one mechanic and one cab-driver (the only member of the lower classes in the list). Of the ninety-eight female members, two-thirds were married, and only fourteen actually worked for a living — eight as teachers, five in literary or artistic occupations, and one as a physician.[48] These scattered figures of course do not represent any systematic study of the social origins of feminists — much more research is needed on this subject. But, taken together with the feminists' ideology, they are strongly suggestive of the movement's middle-class nature. The social origins of organised feminism therefore have to be sought in the changing position of women within the middle classes, and in the changing position of the middle classes within society and politics as a whole.[49]

Politics and Morality

Middle-class liberalism had many objectives in the nineteenth century, varying widely from country to country. They included national self-determination, parliamentary sovereignty, the ending of serfdom and slavery, the curbing of the power of the Catholic Church, the broadening of the political nation to reduce the power of the aristocracy, and the pacification of the new working classes through social and moral reform. The priority given to different objectives naturally varied according to the political situation of the country concerned, and the stage of social development which it had reached. Common to all the movements formed to achieve these objectives was a concern with the individual. Individualism provided the ideological links between liberal movements of this kind (anti-slavery organisations, nationalist societies, moral crusades, social reform associations, political parties and so on) and the emergence of organised feminism. These links operated in two ways. First, it seems likely — though here again more research is necessary — that many if not most early feminist activists came from families that were closely involved in liberal movements of this kind. Of the fifty-one leading American 'feminist-abolitionists' studied by Hersh, for example, at least twenty-two, and almost certainly many more, were from families active in anti-slavery or other social reform groups.[50] In France, most feminists were married to, or were the daughters or sisters of republican politicians.[51] In Germany, the left-wing liberals provided the family background of many feminist leaders, while in Hungary the most prominent feminists were generally the wives of nationalist politicians and thus presumably came themselves from nationalist backgrounds.[52] An upbringing in a politically active liberal family would give such women not only an interest in and knowledge of politics, but also a belief in the right of the individual to freedom and self-determination. Secondly, these and other women usually played an active part in movements of liberal reform, though this has seldom received much recognition from historians. The common experience of women active in these movements was one of initial enthusiasm, followed by disillusionment with the restraints placed on their activities by the men who led them. The result was generally secession, and the foundation of separate women's organisations dedicated not only to achieving the objectives of the original reform movement but to obtaining equal rights for women as well. A common pattern can be observed in many countries of a progression from the involvement of women in charitable, religious, moral, social, political or cultural organisations to their foundation of or involvement in feminist associations.

Although the aims and objectives of feminism were remarkably uniform in the nineteenth century, feminist movements did not advance them all at one and the same time. In particular, what was conceived of as the ultimate feminist demand, the vote for women, was only raised at a comparatively late stage in the development of feminist movements. There was a characteristic progression from what was generally known in Europe as 'moderate' feminism, which (initially at least) confined itself to demanding more rights for women in the economic, educational and legal spheres, to 'radical' feminism, whose chief distinguishing feature was its concentration on the vote. But while this was undoubtedly the central feature of the 'radicalisation' of nineteenth-century feminism, there were a number of additional nuances. Moderate feminists seldom began by demanding equality across the board even in the spheres to which they initially confined themselves. The history of feminism is in general the history of a progressively widening set of objectives (though there are important exceptions to this rule). When we consider the beginnings of organised feminism, we are considering the formation of a movement whose aims seemed timid and narrow even by the standards of a few decades later, let alone by the standards of the present day. Moderate feminism in its early stages was also in most countries a small-scale affair. The earliest feminist societies, however grand their titles, seldom numbered more than a few hundred members, often indeed only a few score. This apparent narrowness of aims and smallness of scale of early organised feminism was a reflection of the fact that its adherents were pioneers who required great courage to brave male hostility and prejudice and defy social convention in daring to raise their voices for more rights for women at all, however insignificant these rights may have seemed by later standards.[53]

The aims of early moderate feminism were primarily economic in character. Economic independence was fundamental to the personal independence of women, both within marriage and outside it. The control of married women over their own property and the admission of unmarried women to the professions were therefore the two major initial objectives of moderate feminism, along with the improvement of educational facilities for women (or in many cases the provision of educational facilities *tout court*) which were becoming necessary for the pursuit of a profession or the maintenance of middle-class status.[54] The attainment of these objectives was all the more important in view of the fact that economic opportunities for unmarried women were becoming narrowed by professionalisation at the same time as new liberal movements were spreading the values of independence and self-sufficiency throughout society.[55] Similarly, as industrialisation was bringing with it a larger and more wealthy propertied class, so the question of personal control over property became more important. Feminist movements almost invariably began in industrialising societies, in urban centres large and wealthy enough to sustain a sophisticated middle-class culture, in areas where the most advanced sections of the bourgeoisie lived. These were the same social groups which sponsored the reform movements from which feminism emerged.

As moderate feminism developed and became progressively more independent, so it turned gradually towards new objectives. The most important of these was moral reform, which became an integral part of feminism in the nineteenth century, though in most countries it took some time for moderate feminists to penetrate the barriers of convention which prevented women from confronting questions of morality, especially sexual morality, from a feminist standpoint. Feminists aimed in the first place for a formal, legal kind of equality; they sought the removal of legal barriers to the free development of the female personality. But this was only one half of their programme. Almost as much emphasis was placed on the need for morality to replace coercion as the foundation for political and social life. As John Stuart Mill argued, legal restrictions on women's rights prevented women from developing 'the self-respect, self-help, and self-control which are the essential conditions both of individual prosperity and of social virtue'.[56] Mill and the great majority of active feminists saw the emancipation of women as an aspect of social progress from barbarism to civilisation. The growth of social responsibility, they believed, was an integral part of this progress. The more civilised people became, the less need there was for restrictive laws to contain and control their barbarous instincts. Conversely, the more such restrictive laws were broken down and removed, the more need there was for people to be taught the self-restraint essential for the smooth working of a civilised society.

Major dangers to the civilised society were seen by the middle classes in the nineteenth century in drunkenness and sexual licence, both of which they associated with revolutionary upheaval and the collapse of society (the examples of the French Revolution and the fall of the Roman Empire, suitably mythologised, were never far from the bourgeois mind).[57] In coming to support the ideals of temperance or abstention in alcohol and self-restraint in sex which middle-class liberals advocated as the remedy for these two social 'evils', moderate feminists were of course representing the interests of their class, which required a disciplined work-force and an ordered system of sexuality in which property could be rapidly accumulated then passed on by a married couple to offspring which were undoubtedly its own. In addition, drunkenness and sexual freedom were seen as twin dangers to the integrity of the proletarian family, which in turn appeared to the middle classes as a major force in keeping the working man contented with his lot. But the feminists were also using these requirements of bourgeois society to their own advantage as women. Elevated onto a pedestal of irreproachable purity by the bourgeois male, these middle-class women were capitalising on their image of moral superiority and using it to gain a larger role for themselves in the public arena. Moreover, besides being examples of general self-indulgence, alcoholic excess and sexual profligacy were also instances of the exploitation of women by men. Drunkenness led to wife-beating, the neglect of the family, loss of social status or the squandering of hard-earned wages or salaries or carefully accumulated property. Sexual liaisons before or outside marriage were usually disastrous for women in an age of inefficient contraception, double moral standards and non-existent social welfare. The feminists often went on to argue, more explicitly, that prostitution spelled disease and humiliation for thousands of women, while the men who exploited them in turn often neglected their wives or infected them with venereal diseases.[58]

Industrialising societies saw a massive increase in both drunkenness and prostitution, which confronted the emergent middle classes with a stark immediacy that demanded far-reaching solutions. The solution advocated by the feminists was characteristic of their liberal individualist ideology. It consisted in the removal of state influence and the repeal of laws which were held to encourage these phenomena, combined with a propaganda campaign to implant the virtues of self-restraint in society. The state, argued the feminists, was encouraging the belief that sexual and alcoholic indulgence was acceptable in men but not in women. This 'double standard' had to be replaced by a single system of values in which self-indulgence of this sort would be morally condemned in both sexes. The feminists therefore began to work for the repeal of laws which licensed or regulated prostitution and liquor. The removal of these laws was seen as the removal of state interference in society, not as the extension of it. Men were invited to sign a 'pledge' committing them either to abstain from alcohol or to refrain from sexual inter-course before marriage.

The adoption of these policies involved a considerable radicalisation of feminist tactics and aims. Temperance reform and the abolition of state-regulated prostitution were more sensitive and explosive issues than those the feminists had originally tackled. The vested interests which the feminists confronted — the police, the medical profession and the liquor interest — were powerful and well-organised. Moral crusades of this sort, not least because of the furious and often unscrupulous opposition they aroused, had a politicising effect on feminist movements. And the difficulties the feminists experienced in achieving the legislative reforms they desired in these areas often moved them closer to demanding the vote. At the same time, the feminists' moral crusades also usually formed part of a wider political context in which stricter and more repressive moral codes became a desideratum of important political movements apart from the feminists'. The rise of *radical* bourgeois nationalism, for example, often brought with it a stress on the moral regeneration of national life. Similarly, the extension of manhood suffrage which was one of the political consequences of industrialisation and social change in many European countries also created a more repressive moral climate, as the newly enfranchised sought to prove that they were worthy possessors of the vote, and the previous monopolisers of the political suffrage tried to ensure that the new voters would behave in a politically 'responsible' manner. The creation in this way of a system of values in which possession of political rights or power was linked to moral probity gave feminists the incentive and the opportunity to demand the vote for themselves. Their justification for female suffrage was frequently highly moralistic; it was one of the most common of all feminist propaganda devices to point to the fact that drunken or criminal men possessed the vote, while virtuous women did not.[59]

The development of a moral dimension to feminism, and more decisively the creation of female suffrage movements, marked the radicalisation of feminism, but they also led to a split in the feminist ranks. Almost everywhere the radicals (i.e. above all those who demanded female suffrage) were a minority, often strongly opposed by the 'moderate' majority of feminists. The radicalisation of feminist movements helped draw more support to moderate feminist movements by making them appear respectable in comparison with the suffragists, upon whom the odium previously attached to the moderate feminist pioneers now fell. Aided by the expansion of female education and female professions (above all, teaching), feminism now became a mass movement. Its divisions often coincided with wider national political patterns, as politically active feminists — above all, female suffragists — gravitated towards the political parties whose views they found most congenial. In places, feminists were able to link their movement to wider political currents which would help them to gain their objectives. Associations such as these could also weaken feminist movements, particularly where they cooperated with unpopular or unsuccessful political parties or organisations. It was often difficult for the feminists to get the better of the bargain with their allies, who frequently compelled them to adopt their own political creeds without offering much active support to the feminists' objectives in return. The feminists' association with other political movements could often be genuine and deeply felt; and it was not least for this reason that it could also become very divisive. Moderates and radicals in the feminist movement were often divided by far more than a simple disagreement about the way to achieve female equality. The diversification and expansion of feminism was also a fragmentation. Vast new organisations — National Councils of Women, the International Woman Suffrage Alliance, and others — were formed to try to pull the feminist movement together. The only focus they could concentrate on was the vote, which thus became increasingly important even for moderate feminists. In this way, feminism reached its brief, and somewhat precarious apogee. Female emancipation became a major political issue in many countries. But the final campaign for and the achievement of the vote, and what followed it, can all be seen as elements in feminism's decline; discussion of them is therefore reserved for the final part of this book.[60]

At every stage in its development, organised feminism was closely interwoven with the political changes and the shifting balance of social forces that came with economic growth. The actions and beliefs of feminists were not the outcome of a simple passion for female equality; they were a complex mixture of many political and ideological elements, of which the desire for liberation as women was only one. Nineteenth-century feminism had wider political implications, just as it had more general social origins. The feminists were well aware of this. In a similar way, political changes and developments often gave feminists opportunities for pressing or enlarging their claims by linking them to a wider cause. It was in the complex interaction of the feminist movement and its political and social context that the real dynamic of feminism lay, rather than simply within the confines of the movement itself. The nature of this interaction of course differed widely from country to country and from period to period; nowhere did it precisely conform to the rather schematic model outlined here. In the next chapter, therefore, we turn to a series of concrete examples of feminist movements which should help flesh out this rather general and abstract account with some historical detail.

Notes

1. The term 'feminism' is defined in this book in its usual meaning as 'the
doctrine of equal rights for women, based on the theory of the equality of
the sexes'. It first came into English usage in this sense in the 1890s from the
French, replacing the term 'womanism'; its previous meaning of 'the qualities
of women' generally fell into disuse, except in Germany, where *Feminismus*
now means 'effeminacy in a man, particularly in homosexuals'. For most of
the period covered by this book, the term 'feminism' is thus, strictly
speaking, anachronistic, though it is still preferable to 'womanism' on
grounds of common usage; it is also, I believe, superior to 'women's movement', a term which came to be extended to almost every aspect of women's
organised activities, on grounds of clarity and precision. W.L. O'Neill has
devised the term 'social feminists' to denote women not primarily concerned
with equal rights but still active in social reform movements organised by
themselves, and has contrasted it with 'hard-core feminists', a term used to
describe female suffragists. However, the use of these two terms implies a
ᵗatic, permanent dichotomy and obscures the fact that (as I shall show
˙ in this book) feminism *progressed towards* demanding the vote. More-
also breaks down in practice, above all in the case of movements
˙ with equal rights other than the vote (for example, the move-
ᶦˢh state-regulated prostitution). In the present study, the
and 'radical' feminist are employed; their meaning, which
ʰose given to 'social' and 'hard-core' feminist by O'Neill,
ᵈetail in the third part of this chapter. It is also diffi-
ᵒmestic feminism' (the idea that women should
ᵘse its implication, that women's place is in the
The contention of Gerda Lerner that the
ᵉly one aspect of a much larger feminist
ᶦn practice, at least if 'movement' implies
Deutsches Wörterbuch and *Supple-*
ᵗ2 and, for a late usage of 'woman-
ᶦalism in the United States
ᶦal feminism' and 'hard-core
Movement: Feminism
3, and criticised as
ᵉminist-Abolition-
p. 144 n.93. For
ᶦn *Modern*
Lerner,
40 (Spring,
mentioned on

zrung der
430-2. I have
contribution to
because it is not dis-

5. Ibid., pp. 218-19, 432.
6. Léon Abensour, *Histoire générale du féminisme dès origines à nos jours* (Paris, 1921); L.M. Richardson, *The Forerunners of Feminism in the French Literature of the Renaissance from Christine of Pisa to Marie de Gourcy* (Baltimore, 1929); Georges Ascoli, 'Essai sur l'Histoire des idées féministes en France du XIIe siècle à la Révolution', *Revue de synthèse historique*, 13 (1906), pp. 25-57, 161-84; Carolyn Lougee, 'Feminism and Social Stratification in 17th Century France' (PhD, Michigan, 1972).
7. David Williams, 'The Politics of Feminism in the French Enlightenment', in Peter Hughes and David Williams (eds.), *The Varied Pattern: Studies in the Eighteenth Century* (Toronto, 1971), pp. 333-51; Edwin R. Hedman, 'Early French Feminism from the Eighteenth Century to 1848' (PhD, New York, 1954).
8. Elizabeth Racz, 'The Women's Rights Movement in the French Revolution', *Science and Society*, Vol. 19 (1951-2), p. 153.
9. Jane Abray, 'Feminism in the French Revolution', *American Historical Review*, 80/1, Feb. 1975, pp. 43-62; Paule-Marie Duhet, *Les Femmes et la Révolution 1789-1794* (Paris, 1971).
10. Abray, op. cit., pp. 60-1.
11. Graphic details of female poverty and violence in Olwen Hufton, 'Women in Revolution, 1789-1798', *Past and Present*, 53 (1971); George Rudé, *The Crowd in the French Revolution* (Oxford, 1967); Richard Cobb, *The Police and the People: French Popular Protest 1789-1820* (Oxford, 1970); and Richard Cobb, *Reactions to the French Revolution* (Oxford, 1972).
12. Abray, art. cit., pp. 52-3.
13. Carol H. Poston, 'Mary Wollstonecraft's *A Vindication of the Rights of Woman:* A Critical and Annotated Edition' (PhD, Nebraska, 1973), pp. lxvi-xci.
14. Vernon L. Bullough, *The Subordinate Sex. A History of Attitudes towc Women* (Urbana, Ill., 1973), pp. 195-229.
15. Keith Thomas, 'Women and the Civil War Sects', *Past and Present*, 1? April 1958, pp. 42-57; Christopher Hill, *The World Turned Upside I Radical Ideas During the English Revolution* (Harmondsworth, 19⁻ pp. 306-23.
16. Details on the appearance and influence of Mill's book: for Finl May Wright Sewell (ed.), *The World's Congress of Representat 15-22 May, 1893* (Chicago, 1894), p. 523; for Russia, Cathy ¹ *Fathers and Daughters: Russian Women in Revolution* (Lon⁄ p. 181; for Denmark, Gyrithe Lemche, *Dansk Kvindesamfu gennem 40 Aar, med Tillaeg 1912-1918* (Copenhagen, 19? Italy, Società Umanitaria, *L'Emancipazione Femminile i² Secolo di Discussioni 1861-1961* (Florence, 1961), p. 1ᶜ Germany and Austria, Barbara Schnetzler, *Die frühe an Frauenbewegung und ihre Kontakte mit Europa (186.' Frankfurt, 1971), pp. 77-9; for France, Suzanne Grir *Mouvement Suffragiste depuis 1848* (Paris, 1926), ᵣ Ross Evans Paulson, *Women's Suffrage and Prohib⁴ Study of Equality and Social Control* (Brighton, ¹ titles are as follows: *The Subjection of Women (' l'assujettissement des femmes* (Paris, 1869); *Di⟨ dem Engl. übersetzt von Jenny Hirsch* (Berlin. *aus J.S. M.s Unterordnung der Frauen* (Graz, *Kvindernes Underkuelse*, paa dansk ved Geo J.S. Mill, *Qvinnans underordnade ställning⁄ soggezione delle donne* (trad. G. Novelli, ℕ

to locate the Polish title; nor have I found any reference to other early translations; presumably the French version was read in Russia and the Swedish translation in Finland. *The Subjection of Women* has yet to appear in Mill's *Collected Works*.

17. See Léon Abensour, *Histoire générale du féminisme dès origines à nos jours* (Paris, 1921).

18. The translator of the German version, Jenny Hirsch, also founded a women's rights magazine (*Der Frauen-Anwalt*, 'The Women's Advocate') and helped found a women's education society, the *Lette-Verein*, in the same year. See Hugh Wiley Puckett, *Germany's Women Go Forward* (New York, 1930), p. 145.

19. E.g. Switzerland, where the *Association Internationale des Femmes* was also founded at the same time. See below, pp. 247-8.

20. *The Subjection of Women* is available in a number of editions, some of them bound with Mary Wollstonecraft's *Vindication of the Rights of Women*.

21. Cf. Anne Tatalovich, 'John Stuart Mill, *The Subjection of Women:* An Analysis', *Southern Quarterly* 12/1 (1973), pp. 87-105; and further discussion in Alice S. Rossi (ed.), *Essays on Sex Equality: John Stuart Mill and Harriet Taylor Mill* (Chicago, 1970).

22. C.A. Macartney, *The Habsburg Empire 1790-1918* (London, 1968), pp. 108-9; Hugh Seton-Watson, *The Decline of Imperial Russia 1855-1914* (London, 1952), pp. 33-4.

23. See below, pp. 44-5, 47, 51, 63-4, 93-5, 124-5.

24. Carlo M. Cipolla, *Literacy and Development in the West* (London, 1969), Tables 28-29, pp. 121-5, and pp. 34-5; Aileen S. Kraditor, *The Ideas of the Woman Suffrage Movement 1890-1920* (New York, 1965), p. 46.

25. J.A. and Olive Banks, 'Feminism and Social Change: a case study of a social movement', in G.K. Zollschan and W. Hirsch (eds.), *Explorations in Social Change* (London, 1964), p. 563. This version should be read in preference to the less coherent second edition (1976).

26. O.R. McGregor, 'The Social Position of Women in England, 1850-1914: A Bibliography', *British Journal of Sociology*, VI (1955), pp. 48-60.

27. Banks, loc. cit.

28. See Peter Laslett (ed.), *Household and Family in Past Time* (Cambridge, 1972), Introduction (though overstating the case).

29. See Edward Shorter, *The Making of the Modern Family* (London, 1976), and Jean-Louis Flandrin, *Familles: Parenté, Maison, Sexualité dans l'ancienne Société* (Paris, 1976).

30. Patricia Branca, *Silent Sisterhood. Middle-Class Women in the Victorian Home* (London, 1975), argues that middle-class housewives played an important and time-consuming part in household management. But this refers to *lower* middle-class women; most feminists came from the more leisured *upper* middle classes, where an array of servants managed the household.

31. See below, pp. 63-9.

32. For the predominance of men in nineteenth-century migrations, and its effect on sex ratios, see Roger Mols, 'Population in Europe 1500-1700', in Carlo M. Cipolla (ed.), *The Fontana Economic History of Europe, Vol. 2: The Sixteenth and Seventeenth Centuries* (London, 1974), p. 70; André Armengaud, 'Population in Europe 1700-1914', in Carlo M. Cipolla (ed.), *The Fontana Economic History of Europe*, Vol. 3: *The Industrial Revolution* (London, 1975), pp. 70-1; A.S. Milward and S.B. Saul, *The Economic Development of Continental Europe 1780-1870* (London, 1975), p. 158; Constance Rover, *Women's Suffrage and Party Politics in Britain 1866-1914* (London, 1967), p. 14; G. Hohorst, G.A. Ritter, J. Kocka,

Sozialgeschichtliches Arbeitsbuch. Materialien zur Statistik des Kaiserreichs 1870-1914 (Munich, 1975), p. 23; Gunnar Qvist, *Kvinnofragan i Sverige 1809-46. Studier rörande Kvinnans näringsfrihet inom de borgerliga yrkena* (Göteborg, 1960), pp. 312-15.

33. Roger Thompson, *Women in Stuart England and America. A comparative study* (London, 1974), pp. 22-4, 260-3.

34. Carl N. Degler, 'Revolution Without Ideology: The Changing Place of Women in America', in Robert Jay Lifton (ed.), *The Woman in America* (Boston, 1965).

35. Hugh Wiley Puckett, *Germany's Women Go Forward* (New York, 1930), p. 179.

36. Cf. McGregor, loc. cit.

37. See *International Encyclopaedia of the Social Sciences, Vol. 12*, p. 536; W.J. Reader, *Professional Men. The Rise of the Professional Classes in Nineteenth-Century England* (London, 1966); Georges Dupeux, *French Society 1789-1970* (London, 1976), pp. 19-21 (with statistics of the huge increase in the numbers of professionals and civil servants); R.M. Hartwell, 'The Service Revolution: The Growth of Services in Modern Economy 1700-1914', in Carlo M. Cipolla (ed.), *The Fontana Economic History of Europe, Vol. 3: The Industrial Revolution* (London, 1973), pp. 358-96; Peter N. Stearns, *European Society in Upheaval. Social History since 1750*, 2nd ed. (New York, 1975), p. 124; and Juliet Mitchell, Ann Oakley (eds.), *The Rights and Wrongs of Women* (London, 1976), pp. 17-58.

38. Georges Lefebvre, *The Coming of the French Revolution* (New York, 1947), pp. 35-44; Albert Soboul, *The French Revolution 1787-1799, Vol. I: From the Storming of the Bastille to the Fall of the Girondins* (London, 1974), pp. 43-51; Pierre Goubert, *The Ancien Régime. French Society 1600-1750* (London, 1973), pp. 232-60; Colin Lucas, 'Nobles, Bourgeois and the Origins of the French Revolution', *Past and Present*, No. 60 (1973).

39. Cf. Lucas, art. cit.; George Lichtheim, *A Short History of Socialism* (London, 1970), pp. 3-18; and Walter E. Houghton, *The Victorian Frame of Mind 1830-1870* (New Haven, 1957), pp. 4-5, 46, 186-7, 239-40, 242-62, on attacks on the 'Idle Aristocracy' by adherents of 'the Victorian gospel of work'.

40. A.G. Dickens, *The German Nation and Martin Luther* (London, 1975); R.H. Tawney, *Religion and the Rise of Capitalism* (Harmondsworth, 1938).

41. J.S. Mill, *The Subjection of Women* (Everyman ed.), pp. 263-4.

42. Ross Evans Paulson, *Women's Suffrage and Prohibition: A Comparative Study of Equality and Social Control* (Brighton, 1973), p. 36.

43. Joseph R. Gusfield, 'Social Structure and Moral Reform: A Study of the Woman's Christian Temperance Union', *American Journal of Sociology*, 51, No. 3, (1955-6), p. 231.

44. Anthea Hyslop, 'Temperance, Christianity and Feminism: The Woman's Christian Temperance Union of Victoria 1887-97', *Historical Studies: Australia and New Zealand* (1976), p. 34 n. 43.

45. Hersh, op. cit., pp. 266-7, 389 (cited in note 1, above).

46. Staatsarchiv Hamburg, Politische Polizei, S9001: Bericht, betr. Feststellung des Vorstandes und der Mitglieder des deutschen Vereins für Frauenstimmrecht, 21.11.1904.

47. Robert McNeal, 'Women in the Russian Radical Movement', *Journal of Social History*, Vol. 5, No. 2 (1971-2), pp. 143-63. For the connection of these women with the feminist movement, see below, pp. 115, 177-83.

48. Patrick Bidelman, 'The Feminist Movement in France: The Formative Years 1858-1889' (PhD, Michigan, 1975), pp. 276-7.

account with some historical detail.

Notes

1. The term 'feminism' is defined in this book in its usual meaning as 'the
doctrine of equal rights for women, based on the theory of the equality of
the sexes'. It first came into English usage in this sense in the 1890s from the
French, replacing the term 'womanism'; its previous meaning of 'the qualities
of women' generally fell into disuse, except in Germany, where *Feminismus*
now means 'effeminacy in a man, particularly in homosexuals'. For most of
the period covered by this book, the term 'feminism' is thus, strictly
speaking, anachronistic, though it is still preferable to 'womanism' on
grounds of common usage; it is also, I believe, superior to 'women's movement', a term which came to be extended to almost every aspect of women's
organised activities, on grounds of clarity and precision. W.L. O'Neill has
devised the term 'social feminists' to denote women not primarily concerned
with equal rights but still active in social reform movements organised by
themselves, and has contrasted it with 'hard-core feminists', a term used to
describe female suffragists. However, the use of these two terms implies a
static, permanent dichotomy and obscures the fact that (as I shall show
later in this book) feminism *progressed towards* demanding the vote. Moreover, it also breaks down in practice, above all in the case of movements
concerned with equal rights other than the vote (for example, the movement to abolish state-regulated prostitution). In the present study, the
terms 'moderate' and 'radical' feminist are employed; their meaning, which
is *not* the same as those given to 'social' and 'hard-core' feminist by O'Neill,
is explained in greater detail in the third part of this chapter. It is also difficult to accept the term 'domestic feminism' (the idea that women should
be paid for housework), because its implication, that women's place is in the
home, is in effect anti-feminist. The contention of Gerda Lerner that the
women's rights movement was merely one aspect of a much larger feminist
movement also seems to break down in practice, at least if 'movement' implies
'organization'. See *Petit Robert, Wahrig Deutsches Wörterbuch* and *Supple-
ment to the Oxford English Dictionary, 1972* and, for a late usage of 'womanism' (1910), Mari-Jo Buhle, 'Feminism and Socialism in the United States
1820-1920' (PhD, Wisconsin, 1974), p. 193. 'Social feminism' and 'hard-core
feminism' are defined in W.L. O'Neill, *The Woman Movement: Feminism
in the United States and England* (London, 1969), p. 33, and criticised as
concepts in Blanche G. Hersh, ' "The Slavery of Sex"; Feminist-Abolitionists in Nineteenth-Century America' (PhD, Illinois, 1975), p. 144 n.93. For
'domestic feminism', see the Preface to Lois Banner, *Women in Modern
America: A Brief History* (New York, 1974). See also Gerda Lerner,
'Women's Rights and American Feminism', *American Scholar*, 40 (Spring,
1971), pp. 235-48; and the brief discussion of the theories she mentioned on
pp. 243-4 of the present work.
2. Kate Millett, *Sexual Politics* (London, 1971), p. 65.
3. Jack Lively, *The Enlightenment* (London, 1966).
4. Theodor Gottlieb von Hippel, *Ueber die Bürgerliche Verbesserung der
Weiber* (Frankfurt/Leipzig, 1794), pp. 30, 235, 348, 389, 430-2. I have
chosen this book as an example of the Enlightenment's contribution to
feminism not only because it is representative, but also because it is not discussed in other general works or anthologies.

5. Ibid., pp. 218-19, 432.
6. Léon Abensour, *Histoire générale du féminisme dès origines à nos jours* (Paris, 1921); L.M. Richardson, *The Forerunners of Feminism in the French Literature of the Renaissance from Christine of Pisa to Marie de Gourcy* (Baltimore, 1929); Georges Ascoli, 'Essai sur l'Histoire des idées féministes en France du XIIe siècle à la Révolution', *Revue de synthèse historique*, 13 (1906), pp. 25-57, 161-84; Carolyn Lougee, 'Feminism and Social Stratification in 17th Century France' (PhD, Michigan, 1972).
7. David Williams, 'The Politics of Feminism in the French Enlightenment', in Peter Hughes and David Williams (eds.), *The Varied Pattern: Studies in the Eighteenth Century* (Toronto, 1971), pp. 333-51; Edwin R. Hedman, 'Early French Feminism from the Eighteenth Century to 1848' (PhD, New York, 1954).
8. Elizabeth Racz, 'The Women's Rights Movement in the French Revolution', *Science and Society*, Vol. 19 (1951-2), p. 153.
9. Jane Abray, 'Feminism in the French Revolution', *American Historical Review*, 80/1, Feb. 1975, pp. 43-62; Paule-Marie Duhet, *Les Femmes et la Révolution 1789-1794* (Paris, 1971).
10. Abray, op. cit., pp. 60-1.
11. Graphic details of female poverty and violence in Olwen Hufton, 'Women in Revolution, 1789-1798', *Past and Present*, 53 (1971); George Rudé, *The Crowd in the French Revolution* (Oxford, 1967); Richard Cobb, *The Police and the People: French Popular Protest 1789-1820* (Oxford, 1970); and Richard Cobb, *Reactions to the French Revolution* (Oxford, 1972).
12. Abray, art. cit., pp. 52-3.
13. Carol H. Poston, 'Mary Wollstonecraft's *A Vindication of the Rights of Woman:* A Critical and Annotated Edition' (PhD, Nebraska, 1973), pp. lxvi-xci.
14. Vernon L. Bullough, *The Subordinate Sex. A History of Attitudes toward Women* (Urbana, Ill., 1973), pp. 195-229.
15. Keith Thomas, 'Women and the Civil War Sects', *Past and Present*, 13, April 1958, pp. 42-57; Christopher Hill, *The World Turned Upside Down. Radical Ideas During the English Revolution* (Harmondsworth, 1974), pp. 306-23.
16. Details on the appearance and influence of Mill's book: for Finland, see May Wright Sewell (ed.), *The World's Congress of Representative Women, 15-22 May, 1893* (Chicago, 1894), p. 523; for Russia, Cathy Porter, *Fathers and Daughters: Russian Women in Revolution* (London, 1976), p. 181; for Denmark, Gyrithe Lemche, *Dansk Kvindesamfunds Historie gennem 40 Aar, med Tillaeg 1912-1918* (Copenhagen, 1939), pp. 17-19; for Italy, Società Umanitaria, *L'Emancipazione Femminile in Italia. Un Secolo di Discussioni 1861-1961* (Florence, 1961), p. 19; for America, Germany and Austria, Barbara Schnetzler, *Die frühe amerikanische Frauenbewegung und ihre Kontakte mit Europa (1863-1869)* (Bern/Frankfurt, 1971), pp. 77-9; for France, Suzanne Grinberg, *Historique du Mouvement Suffragiste depuis 1848* (Paris, 1926), pp. 51-60; for Poland, Ross Evans Paulson, *Women's Suffrage and Prohibition: A Comparative Study of Equality and Social Control* (Brighton, 1973), p. 109 n.15. The titles are as follows: *The Subjection of Women* (London, 1869); *De l'assujettissement des femmes* (Paris, 1869); *Die Hörigkeit der Frau, aus dem Engl. übersetzt von Jenny Hirsch* (Berlin, 1869); Alex Reyer, *Auszug aus J.S. M.s Unterordnung der Frauen* (Graz, 1869); John Stuart Mill, *Kvindernes Underkuelse*, paa dansk ved Georg Brandes (Copenhagen, 1869); J.S. Mill, *Qvinnans underordnade ställning* (Uppsala, 1869); J.S. Mill, *La soggezione delle donne* (trad. G. Novelli, Naples, 1870). I have been unable

to locate the Polish title; nor have I found any reference to other early translations; presumably the French version was read in Russia and the Swedish translation in Finland. *The Subjection of Women* has yet to appear in Mill's *Collected Works*.

17. See Léon Abensour, *Histoire générale du féminisme dès origines à nos jours* (Paris, 1921).

18. The translator of the German version, Jenny Hirsch, also founded a women's rights magazine (*Der Frauen-Anwalt*, 'The Women's Advocate') and helped found a women's education society, the *Lette-Verein*, in the same year. See Hugh Wiley Puckett, *Germany's Women Go Forward* (New York, 1930), p. 145.

19. E.g. Switzerland, where the *Association Internationale des Femmes* was also founded at the same time. See below, pp. 247-8.

20. *The Subjection of Women* is available in a number of editions, some of them bound with Mary Wollstonecraft's *Vindication of the Rights of Women*.

21. Cf. Anne Tatalovich, 'John Stuart Mill, *The Subjection of Women:* An Analysis', *Southern Quarterly* 12/1 (1973), pp. 87-105; and further discussion in Alice S. Rossi (ed.), *Essays on Sex Equality: John Stuart Mill and Harriet Taylor Mill* (Chicago, 1970).

22. C.A. Macartney, *The Habsburg Empire 1790-1918* (London, 1968), pp. 108-9; Hugh Seton-Watson, *The Decline of Imperial Russia 1855-1914* (London, 1952), pp. 33-4.

23. See below, pp. 44-5, 47, 51, 63-4, 93-5, 124-5.

24. Carlo M. Cipolla, *Literacy and Development in the West* (London, 1969), Tables 28-29, pp. 121-5, and pp. 34-5; Aileen S. Kraditor, *The Ideas of the Woman Suffrage Movement 1890-1920* (New York, 1965), p. 46.

25. J.A. and Olive Banks, 'Feminism and Social Change: a case study of a social movement', in G.K. Zollschan and W. Hirsch (eds.), *Explorations in Social Change* (London, 1964), p. 563. This version should be read in preference to the less coherent second edition (1976).

26. O.R. McGregor, 'The Social Position of Women in England, 1850-1914: A Bibliography', *British Journal of Sociology*, VI (1955), pp. 48-60.

27. Banks, loc. cit.

28. See Peter Laslett (ed.), *Household and Family in Past Time* (Cambridge, 1972), Introduction (though overstating the case).

29. See Edward Shorter, *The Making of the Modern Family* (London, 1976), and Jean-Louis Flandrin, *Familles: Parenté, Maison, Sexualité dans l'ancienne Société* (Paris, 1976).

30. Patricia Branca, *Silent Sisterhood. Middle-Class Women in the Victorian Home* (London, 1975), argues that middle-class housewives played an important and time-consuming part in household management. But this refers to *lower* middle-class women; most feminists came from the more leisured *upper* middle classes, where an array of servants managed the household.

31. See below, pp. 63-9.

32. For the predominance of men in nineteenth-century migrations, and its effect on sex ratios, see Roger Mols, 'Population in Europe 1500-1700', in Carlo M. Cipolla (ed.), *The Fontana Economic History of Europe, Vol. 2: The Sixteenth and Seventeenth Centuries* (London, 1974), p. 70; André Armengaud, 'Population in Europe 1700-1914', in Carlo M. Cipolla (ed.), *The Fontana Economic History of Europe*, Vol. 3: *The Industrial Revolution* (London, 1975), pp. 70-1; A.S. Milward and S.B. Saul, *The Economic Development of Continental Europe 1780-1870* (London, 1975), p. 158; Constance Rover, *Women's Suffrage and Party Politics in Britain 1866-1914* (London, 1967), p. 14; G. Hohorst, G.A. Ritter, J. Kocka,

Sozialgeschichtliches Arbeitsbuch. Materialien zur Statistik des Kaiserreichs 1870-1914 (Munich, 1975), p. 23; Gunnar Qvist, *Kvinnofragan i Sverige 1809-46. Studier rörande Kvinnans näringsfrihet inom de borgerliga yrkena* (Göteborg, 1960), pp. 312-15.

33. Roger Thompson, *Women in Stuart England and America. A comparative study* (London, 1974), pp. 22-4, 260-3.
34. Carl N. Degler, 'Revolution Without Ideology: The Changing Place of Women in America', in Robert Jay Lifton (ed.), *The Woman in America* (Boston, 1965).
35. Hugh Wiley Puckett, *Germany's Women Go Forward* (New York, 1930), p. 179.
36. Cf. McGregor, loc. cit.
37. See *International Encyclopaedia of the Social Sciences, Vol. 12*, p. 536; W.J. Reader, *Professional Men. The Rise of the Professional Classes in Nineteenth-Century England* (London, 1966); Georges Dupeux, *French Society 1789-1970* (London, 1976), pp. 19-21 (with statistics of the huge increase in the numbers of professionals and civil servants); R.M. Hartwell, 'The Service Revolution: The Growth of Services in Modern Economy 1700-1914', in Carlo M. Cipolla (ed.), *The Fontana Economic History of Europe, Vol. 3: The Industrial Revolution* (London, 1973), pp. 358-96; Peter N. Stearns, *European Society in Upheaval. Social History since 1750*, 2nd ed. (New York, 1975), p. 124; and Juliet Mitchell, Ann Oakley (eds.), *The Rights and Wrongs of Women* (London, 1976), pp. 17-58.
38. Georges Lefebvre, *The Coming of the French Revolution* (New York, 1947), pp. 35-44; Albert Soboul, *The French Revolution 1787-1799, Vol. I: From the Storming of the Bastille to the Fall of the Girondins* (London, 1974), pp. 43-51; Pierre Goubert, *The Ancien Régime. French Society 1600-1750* (London, 1973), pp. 232-60; Colin Lucas, 'Nobles, Bourgeois and the Origins of the French Revolution', *Past and Present*, No. 60 (1973).
39. Cf. Lucas, art. cit.; George Lichtheim, *A Short History of Socialism* (London, 1970), pp. 3-18; and Walter E. Houghton, *The Victorian Frame of Mind 1830-1870* (New Haven, 1957), pp. 4-5, 46, 186-7, 239-40, 242-62, on attacks on the 'Idle Aristocracy' by adherents of 'the Victorian gospel of work'.
40. A.G. Dickens, *The German Nation and Martin Luther* (London, 1975); R.H. Tawney, *Religion and the Rise of Capitalism* (Harmondsworth, 1938).
41. J.S. Mill, *The Subjection of Women* (Everyman ed.), pp. 263-4.
42. Ross Evans Paulson, *Women's Suffrage and Prohibition: A Comparative Study of Equality and Social Control* (Brighton, 1973), p. 36.
43. Joseph R. Gusfield, 'Social Structure and Moral Reform: A Study of the Woman's Christian Temperance Union', *American Journal of Sociology*, 51, No. 3, (1955-6), p. 231.
44. Anthea Hyslop, 'Temperance, Christianity and Feminism: The Woman's Christian Temperance Union of Victoria 1887-97', *Historical Studies: Australia and New Zealand* (1976), p. 34 n. 43.
45. Hersh, op. cit., pp. 266-7, 389 (cited in note 1, above).
46. Staatsarchiv Hamburg, Politische Polizei, S9001: Bericht, betr. Feststellung des Vorstandes und der Mitglieder des deutschen Vereins für Frauenstimm-recht, 21.11.1904.
47. Robert McNeal, 'Women in the Russian Radical Movement', *Journal of Social History*, Vol. 5, No. 2 (1971-2), pp. 143-63. For the connection of these women with the feminist movement, see below, pp. 115, 177-83.
48. Patrick Bidelman, 'The Feminist Movement in France: The Formative Years 1858-1889' (PhD, Michigan, 1975), pp. 276-7.

49. For further considerations on the social origin of feminists, see below, pp. 51-2, 99-101, 115, 121, 127.

50. Hersh, op. cit., pp. 266-7, 389. It should be noted that the Russian feminists were not, strictly speaking, 'middle class'; the point remains, however that they came from the middle ranks of society.

51. Theodore Zeldin, *France 1848-1945: Vol. I. Ambition, Love and Politics* (Oxford, 1973), p. 348.

52. For Hungary, see below, pp. 98-102. For Germany, see for example biographies of Gertrud Bäumer, Anita Augspurg, Helene Lange, Lida Gustava Heymann, in *Lexicon der Frau* (Zürich, 1953), biographies of Auguste Kirchhoff, Ottilie Hoffmann, Rita Bardenheuer, Eleonore Drenkhahn in W. Lührs (ed.), *Bremische Biographie 1912-1962* (Bremen, 1969), and biographical sketches of numerous feminist leaders in Deutsches Zentralinstitut für Soziale Fragen, Berlin-Dahlem, Archiv des Bundes Deutscher Frauenvereine, 2/I/2-4.

53. It is this *progression* from economic to political aims that invalidates O'Neill's division of feminists into 'social' and 'hard-core' (see above, p. 39 n.1.) For some membership figures of moderate feminist organisations see below, pp. 61. 76, 129.

54. For these aims, see below, pp. 44-6, 50-1, 63-4, 82, 99, 104-5, 107, 111, 114, 116, 125-6, 128-9, 131.

55. See below, pp. 44-5.

56. *The Subjection of Women* (Everyman ed.), p. 304.

57. Eric Trudgill, *Madonnas and Magdalens. The Origins and Development of Victorian Sexual Attitudes* (London, 1976) pp. 27ff.

58. For some general insights into the social context and meaning of drunkenness and prostitution, see Trudgill, op. cit.; D. and J. Walkowitz, ' "We Are Not Beasts of the Field": Prostitution and the Poor in Plymouth and Southampton under the Contagious Diseases Act' in M. Hartman and L. Banner (eds.), *Clio's Consciousness Raised: New Perspectives on the History of Women* (New York, 1974), pp. 192-225; Brian Harrison, *Drink and the Victorians. The Temperance Question in England 1815-1872* (London, 1971); Joseph R. Gusfield, *Symbolic Crusade: Status Politics and the American Temperance Movement* (Urbana, 1963); Charles van Onselen, 'Randlords and Rotgut, 1886-1903: an essay on the role of alcohol in the development of European imperialism and southern African capitalism', *History Workshop Journal,* 2 (1976), pp. 33-89.

59. For more detailed examples, see below, pp. 60, 205-6.

60. See below, pp. 211-28.

2 MODERATES AND RADICALS

The United States

The feminist movement in the United States began earlier than elsewhere; and by the end of the nineteenth century, the Americans' domination of international feminism was unchallenged. European feminists looked to America for a lead. They envied the enormous scale on which the American movement for the emancipation of women was organised, and wished that the obstacles to success were as few and as weak in the Old World as they seemed to be in the New. Every other feminist movement, however deep its roots in its own national politics, was to a degree an imitation of the American one.

Women in the United States were from the beginning in a better legal and economic position than their sisters in many European countries.[1] But in some ways they suffered under similar if less extreme forms of oppression. In the areas with which the feminists themselves were particularly concerned, women's rights and opportunities were very limited. At the beginning of the nineteenth century, there was no higher education for women; secondary education, available only to the wealthy, was confined to music, embroidery, French and the inculcation of polite manners. Women played no part in the professions. In law, married women could not sign contracts or retain their property or earnings. Though it was possible for women to gain legal redress against their husbands, at least in New England, it was difficult in the South, where divorce was effectively impossible. Women had no political rights save those of assembly and association.[2] And women's position in American society was actually getting worse in the late eighteenth and early nineteenth centuries. The rough equality of frontier society, with its shortage of women and its wide range of female occupations, including the production of clothing, printing, silversmith work and even the management of farms, was being replaced by the increasing sophistication and expanding social hierarchy of urban America.[3] Women were changing from producers into consumers in East-coast society. Education and professionalisation were progressing apace, but for the male sex only. Midwifery was becoming obstetrics, for example, and by mid-century most American babies were being delivered by male physicians rather than by female midwives. The ideal of the frontier woman, in partnership with men in many spheres of life, was gradually superseded by the 'cult of true womanhood', in which the 'true' middle-class woman was depicted as pious, delicate, submissive, domesticated and pure.[4] As Alice Rossi has pointed out, this development was occurring at precisely the same time, in the Jacksonian era, as the values of education and professionalism, success at work and participation in political life were becoming dominant in American society.[5] The decline of female status had not been arrested by the American Revolution,[6] though women had played a part in the revolutionary events, signing petitions, organising in societies such as the 'Daughters of Liberty' and suggesting that the new law codes framed by the revolutionary state should give greater freedom to women than those they replaced.[7] The women who advanced such proposals, the most eminent of them being Abigail Adams, were isolated theorists in the manner of the feminist writers of the Enlightenment and the French Revolution, many of whose basic assumptions they in fact shared.[8] They had little or no immediate impact on society or legislation.

It was not the American Revolution, but the religious revival that followed it, the so-called 'Second Great Awakening', that provided middle-class American women with the opportunity to recover lost ground. The American churches were democratised by this revival, and ministers and parishioners converted to an active gospel of moral regeneration and social reform. In the wake of the Second Great Awakening came a rapid proliferation of voluntary organisations aimed at moral revival, social reform, education or general humanitarian objectives. In this way, Protestantism in America reoriented itself to the changing conditions of social life as the town replaced the frontier as the basis of American society. Moral regeneration accompanied national independence in a way that was to become familiar in European experience later in the century. A prominent feature of the revival was the part played in it by women. Public speaking by women spread from its Quaker origins to prayer meetings and revivals in other Protestant denominations. Despite some resistance from ministers, women were able in this way to capitalise on the premium laid by the 'cult of true womanhood' on female piety and translate it into a means of emancipation from restrictions on their public activities. Correspondingly, women took an equally prominent part in the social movements connected with the revival, notably the anti-slavery movement, which began in the mid-1830s, just as the Second Great Awakening was coming to an end. Anti-slavery petitions invariably contained large numbers of female signatures, and soon women were also participating in canvassing and organising their own societies in support of the petitions.[9]

By the 1840s, therefore, the idea was fairly widespread among the middle classes in America that women had an active role to play as the moral guardians of the home and, by extension, of society.[10] In the middle of the decade, however, the petitioning campaign came to an end and the focus of the anti-slavery movement's efforts shifted to Congress. The anti-slavery movement thus became by implication one of voters instead of one of citizens. That women had no role to play in the political lobbying and pressurising through which the movement was now attempting to secure its ends was soon made clear. Indeed, already in 1840, women had been expressly excluded from a world anti-slavery convention held in London.[11] Their gradual loss of function in the anti-slavery movement turned their attention to matters of more direct concern. Throughout the 1840s, they fought a campaign in New York State for a Married Woman's Property Bill then under consideration. It became law in 1848. Possession of their own property was almost invariably a major demand advanced by feminists at the very earliest stage of their movement, and the American feminists were no exception.[12] The culmination of these activities was the celebrated Women's Rights Convention held at Seneca Falls, New York State, in 1848. The Convention passed a 'Declaration of Sentiments' which adapted the language and forms of the American Declaration of Independence to the case of women: 'We hold these truths to be self-evident', it began: 'that all men *and women* are created equal'. It detailed the 'long train of abuses and usurpations' to which women had been subjected. The first three items in this list referred briefly to women's lack of voting rights. The next seven items, considerably longer and more detailed, criticised women's subjection and lack of property rights in civil law, their economic subordination and their exclusion from advanced education and from Church office. Finally, there were some general statements about the moral aspects of discrimination against women. The Declaration was accompanied by two resolutions, one justifying female equality, the other urging 'the zealous and untiring efforts of both men and women, for the overthrow of the monopoly of the pulpit, and for the securing to women an equal participation with men in the various trades, professions, and commerce'.[13]

The Seneca Falls Declaration subsequently achieved the status of myth. It did so not because of its general content or tenor, but because of its endorsement of the principle of votes for women. Remarkable though this may have been, it was perhaps inevitable once the decision had been made to use the Declaration of Independence as a model.

Later in the century, the main proponent of the Declaration, Elizabeth Cady Stanton, used the Seneca Falls Convention to legitimise her claim to leadership in the female suffrage movement. In 1848, however, the focus of attention was on women's economic rights, which took up the largest amount of space both in the Declaration and in Stanton's introductory speech.[14] The reason for the convention itself was the Married Woman's Property legislation passed in New York earlier in the year, an issue which had already been discussed at a state constitutional convention in 1846.[15] And indeed, the centrality of economic issues to American feminism in this formative period is attested by the passage of Married Women's Property laws through the great majority of state legislatures in the years 1839-50; often, petitioning and campaigning had begun much earlier, as in New York, where the first petition was submitted in 1839.[16]

Seneca Falls initiated a long series of women's rights conventions in the United States. A second meeting took place only two weeks later, in Rochester, New York. A third, the first to lay claim to the title of a national women's rights convention, was held in 1850 in Worcester, Massachusetts. Further conventions were held every year up to 1860 except 1857. At these conventions the moderate nature of early American feminism emerged even more strongly than in 1848. Little interest was shown in the vote.[17] No permanent organisation was formed. Instead, the women, led by Elizabeth Cady Stanton (1815-1902), Susan B. Anthony (1820-1906) and many others associated with the anti-slavery movement, including Lucy Stone (1818-1893) and Lucretia Mott (1794-1880), continued to concentrate on the petitioning which had first brought women into political life in the 1830s. Instead of slavery, the target of these petitions was now the parallel one of women's economic subjection in civil law. Anthony's first petition contained three demands: the control by women of their own earnings, possession of their children on divorce, and the vote. Six thousand signatures were collected in 1854 on behalf of this petition, and Stanton spoke before the New York state legislature on it as a result, concentrating on the first two items. Further petitions followed. The culmination was a law passed in 1860 giving women in New York the right to collect their own wages, to sue in court, and to inherit their husbands' property. Until the Civil War, these issues, and to a lesser extent the educational question, formed the focal point of the American feminist movement's campaigns. The reason is not hard to see; economic independence was a primary need if women were to achieve full emancipation. Moreover, behind the mobilisation of American women lay the onset of industrialisation in the 1840s and above all the 1850s, which brought with it a new emphasis on the importance of property rights and individual self-help for the rapidly expanding middle classes of the North. It was precisely in the areas most affected by the Industrial Revolution that the emergence of the feminist movement occurred. Where industry did not develop rapidly, where there was no burgeoning middle-class society, as in the American South, there was no women's rights movement.[18]

The impetus to organise on a formal basis came from the experience of the Civil War, and more particularly from the expectations it aroused. The feminists themselves suspended women's rights activities for the duration of the war, and rallied to the support of the Union in a number of ways. They believed that they would be rewarded for their support after victory was won. But they were to be disappointed. When the Republican Party, with which the feminists had for long been closely identified, introduced the Fourteenth Amendment to the Constitution in Congress in 1866, the Amendment explicitly denied the vote to women by insisting that only the freed *male* slaves should be granted the suffrage. The feminists saw the Fourteenth Amendment and the widening of the franchise which it entailed as an opportunity for pressing their claims to the vote. Such an opportunity might not recur at the federal level for decades.[19] They were outraged by the refusal of the Republicans to accede to their demands. They had expected the anti-slavery movement to support their claim to the vote as they themselves had supported the abolition of slavery and the victory of the Union. Nothing of the sort occurred. The black leader Frederick Douglass had seconded Elizabeth Cady Stanton's motion in favour of female suffrage at Seneca Falls in 1848, and he was to renew his support for it in the 1870s. But in the vital years of 1866-9 he withheld his support. Giving freedmen the vote was more vital than giving women the vote, he believed, and the Amendment should not be endangered by adding to it another controversial measure such as votes for women.[20] The speech in which he put this view, delivered in 1869, effectively marked the end of the identity of feminism and anti-slavery in America. The failure of a women's suffrage amendment in Kansas (1867) and the rejection of female suffrage by Congress and by a New York state constitutional convention, convinced Elizabeth Cady Stanton and Susan B. Anthony that the fight for women's rights now had to be waged by women alone.[21]

Stanton, Anthony and their followers in New York formally withdrew from the Anti-Slavery Equal Rights Association and founded a

National Woman Suffrage Association (1868). 'I protest', said Stanton, 'against the enfranchisement of another man of any race or clime until the daughters of Jefferson, Hancock and Adams are crowned with all their rights.' Despite this hostility to the black vote, the NWSA was in most ways radical feminist in character. It was anti-clerical, it stood for social purity and moral reform, and it believed in women's independence in family life. Above all, it was individualist to the core. In 1892 Stanton put forward the arguments with which it justified votes for women with unparalleled clarity and force:

> The point I wish plainly to bring before you on this occasion is the individuality of each human soul; our Protestant idea, the right of individual conscience and judgement; our republican idea, individual citizenship. In discussing the rights of woman, we are to consider, first, what belongs to her as an individual, in a world of her own, the arbiter of her own destiny, an imaginary Robinson Crusoe with her woman Friday on a solitary island. Her rights under such circumstances are to use all her faculties for her own safety and happiness.
>
> Secondly, if we consider her as a citizen, as a member of a great nation, she must have the same rights as all other members, according to the fundamental principles of our government.
>
> Thirdly, viewed as a woman, an equal factor in civilisation, her rights and duties are still the same: individual happiness and development.
>
> Fourthly, it is only the incidental relations of life, such as mother, wife, sister, daughter, that may involve some special duties and training.

This argument was at the ideological basis for radical feminist claims in the nineteenth century. The moderates too, of course, had aimed to give women more independence and more control over their own destiny, but their reasoning had seldom been as explicit or as all-embracing as this. Nevertheless, the middle-class character of the feminist appeal was as clearly evident in Stanton's ideology as it was in that of the moderates; woman might be a Robinson Crusoe on a solitary island, but she also had her woman Friday to act as a domestic servant and do all the chores.[22] Many American feminists less bold than Stanton and Anthony were not prepared to follow their lead. Under the lead of Lucy Stone, they seceded in 1869 to form the American Woman Suffrage Association. It represented the more conservative, Bostonian wing of the movement. Its aims differed from those of the New Yorkers under Stanton and Anthony in several respects. It concentrated on the vote, and paid no attention to many issues such as the condition of working-class women, which Stanton and Anthony considered important. It was not anti-clerical. It considered that the correct way to win the vote was in a gradual state-by-state campaign. It thus rejected the Stanton-Anthony policy of a direct assault at the federal level. More than this, it believed that it was wrong to put the female vote before the black vote. By supporting the Fourteenth and Fifteenth Amendments as they stood, Stone and the AWSA believed they would earn the gratitude of abolitionist and black leaders and thus induce them to lend their support to female suffrage later on. In placing a premium on respectability and on 'indirect' ways of winning through to its objectives, the AWSA was behaving in a way that subsequent European experience was to reveal as wholly characteristic of moderate feminists drawn into the campaign for the vote by more radical spirits. The division of the American female suffrage movement was further accentuated by the activities of the feminist adventuress Victoria Woodhull, who was for a time associated with Stanton and Anthony. When Woddhull publicly advocated free love, and became involved in a sensational sexual scandal, some of the mud that was slung inevitably stuck to the NWSA, thus reinforcing the suspicions of its rival that it was perhaps not as respectable as it might be.[23]

Nevertheless, it is doubtful whether the affair set back the feminist cause to any significant degree. Far more important was the gradual expansion of the social and political base of moderate feminism after 1860. In education, a number of women's colleges were opened after the Civil War, and more and more male colleges opened their doors to women as well. By 1880 there were 40,000 American women enrolled in institutions of higher education, constituting over a third of all students. Many of these institutions were not of a very high standard, of course, and the admission of women did not take place in the south; but still, the best universities, such as Harvard and Cornell, did admit women to take degrees, and female equality in education had certainly gone much further in America than it had in Europe by the 1880s. In the professions, the pioneer woman physician, Elizabeth Blackwell, founded a hospital in New York staffed entirely by women in 1857.

Admitting women to the medical profession was one of the major aims of moderate feminism everywhere. Many male physicians lacked a proper understanding of female physiology, and many middle-class women felt too embarrassed to submit to medical examination by a man. In America the lead in opening the profession was taken, characteristically, by voluntary associations, above all the Female Medical Education Society (1848). Based in Boston, the bastion of moderate feminism, the Society opened a medical college which began as little more than a school for nurses and midwives but nevertheless gave many female physicians the first training in their chosen profession. Similar institutions opened in other cities in the 1860s and 1870s. By 1890 there were no fewer than thirteen scattered across various urban centres in the United States.

Even more remarkably, women in America were also entering other professions as well in the 1870s and 1880s. In 1870, Myra Bradwell applied to the Supreme Court of Illinois for a licence to practise law. The Court objected. But in 1873 the state legislature passed a law ordering that 'no person shall be precluded or debarred from any occupation, profession or employment (except military) on account of sex (provided that this act shall not be construed to affect the eligibility of any person to an elective office)'. Illinois was not the first state to pass legislation of this kind, nor was it the last. By 1880 a woman had been admitted to practise at the bar of the United States Supreme Court. Women were also gradually admitted to the ministry in a number of religious denominations. By 1890 there were 250,000 women teachers and 4,500 women physicians of varying qualifications. The growing numbers of professional women were accompanied by the proliferation of societies to cater for their needs. The astronomer Maria Mitchell, elected to the American Academy of Arts and Sciences in 1848, founded an Association for the Advancement of Women in 1873. In 1882 women graduates led by Marion Talbot founded the Association of Collegiate Alumnae later to become the American Association of University Women. This was an elitist organisation which attempted to bring about the improvement of academic institutions for women by admitting only graduates of a limited number of 'recognised' colleges. In 1868, the first professional women's club was founded; by 1890 these institutions existed in sufficient number to warrant the formation of a General Federation of Women's Clubs, which boasted a membership of 20,000 in 1892, 150,000 in 1900 and nearly a million in 1910. Primarily social, the clubs nevertheless supported, both financially and actively, many moderate feminist activities.[24]

The significance of these developments was twofold. First, they drew an increasing number of women into the wider orbit of the feminist movement; and second, they constituted for the feminists themselves evidence of progress and success. In certain limited areas — teaching and nursing, for example, and university education — women gained a new independence and entered the realm of public activity on a large scale. These developments helped feminism prepare to expand into a mass movement. They were not simply the result of feminist pressure; but they also provided the basis for the further application of feminist pressure in other, more controversial areas. Unless large numbers of women took the opportunity offered to them by the opening of new careers, however, the breaking of a barrier such as that of the admission of women to the legal profession did not in itself have any great significance for the emancipation of women even in the sense of liberal individualist feminism. Nevertheless, it did have an important symbolic meaning. Even if thousands of women did not rush across the fallen barrier into the new field of activity that lay beyond, the mere destruction of the obstacle reassured feminists that the road to final victory lay open before them, and confirmed their hope that they would eventually get to the end. That is why feminist histories are full of lists of such apparently trivial events as the appointment of the first woman police commissioner or the first woman tax inspector. The equality thus conferred on women was symbolic evidence of equal status in a more general sense. Even if women did not choose to enter the professions newly opened to them, at least now they had the right to choose. That meant a great deal to the mind of the nineteenth-century liberal individualist.

The entrance of women into certain of the professions was only one of the social changes underlying the growth and diversification of the American feminist movement in the two decades after the Civil War. Another was the increasing involvement of married women in movements of moral and social reform, above all in the rapidly developing and newly colonised areas of the West and Mid-west. The need to impose an ordered social system on the disorderly towns of the West came together with a more general wave of moral reform in the 1870s, partly directed against corrupt administrators and 'carpet-bagging' businessmen, partly reflecting the widely felt need for national regeneration on a strong moral foundation after the ravages of the Civil War. The moral and political concerns of the anti-slavery movement in which so many feminists had been active before the war found a new and more explicitly feminist object of attention once the primary aim of the anti-slavery movement had been achieved. The new area of concern lay in the growth of opposition to the state regulation of vice, which was introduced in many American towns in the early 1870s to cope with the spread of prostitution which accompanied the urban and industrial expansion of these years. The new movement called for the ending of 'white slavery'. Its adherents termed themselves 'New Abolitionists'. They organised an American Committee for the Prevention of Legalising Prostitution in 1877. Leading members included the ubiquitous Susan B. Anthony, who had led campaigns of this sort in New York in 1867 and 1871. By the 1880s the movement was gaining many of its objectives; the medical profession had been converted to its views, and state regulation had been removed or prevented in a number of towns.

For much the same general reasons, the same decade (1870-80) also saw the rise of a feminist temperance movement in the United States. The leading feminists had long been active temperance reformers. In the 1850s they had been refused permission to speak in a number of temperance conventions run by men. But it was not until the 1870s that the women's temperance movement was really launched. In 1873-4 a 'women's crusade against alcohol' swept across the American Midwest, and bands of middle-class women entered saloons, praying, singing hymns and sometimes smashing bottles, glasses and windows and wrecking furniture. Many hundreds of bars were closed, but most of them opened again later, and the women soon realised the need for a more sustained campaign. The result was the Woman's Christian Temperance Union, founded in 1874 and led by Frances Willard (1839-98), its founding secretary, from 1879 to 1898. Willard quickly overcame the forces within the WCTU that favoured a cautious approach, and her election as President in 1879 set the seal on the movement's commitment to getting women the vote. The movement always remained moderately feminist in the sense that female suffrage was seen mainly as a means to achieving prohibition. It is quite erroneous to claim, as some historians have done, that Willard saw temperance agitation simply as a means of recruiting conservative women to the feminist cause. But the WCTU nevertheless played a major part in the struggle for the vote. It was important to the feminists not least because of its size. By 1879 it had 25,000 members, rising to 200,000 by 1900, and a quarter of a million by 1912. Even though its leaders did not intend it as such, it was indeed a means by which women could be won over to the feminist cause.[25]

All these developments laid the social and organisational foundations for the development of feminism into a mass movement. They were necessary preconditions for changes in the more radical wing of American feminism, the suffrage movement. In the 1870s and 1880s the NWSA, led by Stanton and Anthony, developed a radical campaigning style which included speaking tours and mass meetings, the scattering of handbills at American Centennial celebrations in 1876, repeated attempts to secure legal backing for the claim that women already had the vote by virtue of the fact that the Constitution referred to 'persons' (including the illegal casting of votes at elections by women), and the almost annual introduction of a Constitutional Amendment in favour of female suffrage into Congress from 1878 to 1896. The NWSA concentrated on federal politics; the moderate AWSA focused its energies on state-by-state women's suffrage referendum campaigns, of which there were seventeen between 1870 and 1910. Many gains were made in the field of municipal suffrage and voting rights for school boards and similar bodies. But these state campaigns were almost uniformly unsuccessful, save in a handful of exceptional cases (to be discussed in a later chapter of this book). Moreover, municipal suffrage was also seldom successful, since women proved reluctant to vote, and those who did attend to cast their ballot had to brave election officials puffing smoke in their faces, jeering loiterers outside the polling booths, and even (on occasion) stone-throwing mobs. The common and frequently unexpected difficulties faced by both wings of the suffrage movement helped bring them together. More decisive by far, however, was the influx of professional women into the movement. Pressure from below was probably the main impulse behind reunification, which took place in 1890 after three years of negotiation. Similar influences were behind the formation of a National Council of Women in 1888. Frances Willard's WCTU also played a major part in bringing about these new organisational developments.

Initially, the reunified suffrage movement, the National American Woman Suffrage Association, was dominated by the Stanton-Anthony wing, which was numerically preponderant. Stanton was the NAWSA's first President. When she retired in 1892 she was succeeded by Anthony. But most of the new rank and file opposed their views. Stanton was obliged to withdraw from the movement because of her anti-clericalism. The tactic of concentrating on a federal amendment was abandoned, and none was debated in Congress between 1896 and 1913. The 1890s also saw the growing separation of the WCTU and NAWSA as professional women found the small-town attitudes of the former increasingly distasteful. NAWSA membership did not grow significantly for nearly a decade. In 1893 the NAWSA counted some 13,150 members. By 1905 the number had risen only to 17,000. Though this made the NAWSA the largest female suffrage organisation in the world, it was disappointing in terms of its own rate of growth. Moreover, the organisation was increasingly torn by internal dissension. In 1900, when Anthony retired, a fierce election battle for the presidency resulted in the election of

Carrie Chapman Catt. Catt (1859-1947) was essentially an organiser. She favoured a federal amendment. In 1904 she was ousted in favour of Anna Howard Shaw (1847-1919), a preacher whose talents lay in the field of oratory. Catt's centralised leadership was widely resented, and Shaw, a state suffrage campaigner, was thought to favour greater decentralisation. Constantly on speaking tours, Shaw neglected even the day-to-day administration of the movement however; in addition to this she was completely without tact and quarrelled constantly with her subordinates. In the early years of her Presidency, the expanding western branches of the NAWSA resented her identification with the East, which supplied most of the money. They sought to gain increased representation in the controlling bodies of the movement. Shaw rejected their claim. Tension between East and West led to constant quarrels about the location of the headquarters, which first found an unsatisfactory home on neutral territory, in the NAWSA Treasurer's house in Warren, Ohio, then moved to New York in 1909. To these difficulties were added political differences which Shaw proved altogether incapable of controlling. When in 1912 she presided over the NAWSA's endorsement of the Western-backed Progressive Party, the Easterners tried to vote her out, and in a bitter fight she was re-elected by a greatly reduced majority. Under Shaw, too, the State referenda were proving uniformly unsuccessful. The American suffrage movement seemed to be in the doldrums. Only the onset of a rapid and spectacular growth in membership, which rose to 75,000 in 1910 and reached 100,000 by 1915, for which Shaw's spellbinding oratory was in good measure responsible, hinted that beneath the surface yet another phase in the movement's development was in the process of gestation.[26]

The problems faced by the American female suffrage movement, and the decades that passed without any major advances being made, may seem at first sight surprising. The suffragists themselves put the blame on the liquor interests and big business trusts. These indeed were firm opponents of female suffrage.[27] But there was more to the problem than this. Aside from the sheer immensity and complexity of the task that faced them in a country so vast, so rapidly changing and so politically decentralised as the United States, the main problem facing the suffragists was probably the fact that votes for women affected other more immediately controversial issues such as votes for immigrants and votes for blacks. Only in a very few states was this advantageous to women's suffrage. In the great majority of states, above all in the South, it prevented the contemplation of any extension of the suffrage at all, for while universal suffrage was unthinkable in practice, limited suffrage was intolerable in principle. The 1880s, 1890s and early 1900s saw the gradual *de facto* restriction of the franchise in many areas, above all in the South, as incumbent elites sought to preserve their hegemony over blacks and immigrants. Elsewhere, in the burgeoning urban centres of the East, this was indeed the age of machine politics, and given the moral reformism of the female suffragists, few party bosses could have deemed the introduction of votes for women an advantage. The problem that faced the American suffrage movement after it had overcome the internal disunity that dogged it for most of the latter half of the nineteenth century was therefore how to link its cause to a wider and more successful movement of political and social reform in such a way as to make female suffrage not only acceptable to it but also desirable in a positive way.

This linkage, which began to take place from the turn of the century onwards, was only achieved at the cost of crucial and ultimately damaging alterations to the feminists' political programme and ideology.[28] Still, it did bring the suffragists ultimate success. The rise and fall of the Populist movement, a moralistic political crusade whose ideas corresponded closely to those of the feminists on many issues, in the early and mid-1890s, had brought swift results for the feminists in areas where Populism was (for a time) the dominant political force. By the end of the 1890s the Populist tide had ebbed, and it was not until 1910 that a similar, more widespread movement, Progressivism, became sufficiently powerful in the midwest to resume the series of feminist laws, above all the enactment of female suffrage at state level, which had come to a temporary halt with the collapse of the Populists. The hiatus of the 1900s, as Progressivism (of which the feminist movement eventually came to be a part) was in the process of forming itself into a mass movement, was the general political factor behind the failure of female suffrage campaigns in this decade. The growth of NAWSA membership from 1905 onwards can in turn be regarded as part of a more general mustering of Progressive forces as the movement gathered momentum.[29]

It is possible, then, to explain the development of American feminism in terms not only of the changing position of women in American society, but also as part of more general processes of social and political change. The stages through which the American feminist movement passed will be encountered again in the history of other feminist movements, but there were also some unusual features in the American example. The emergence of organised feminism began with the participation of women in middle-class religious revivals (to the mid-1830s) and led on through a major middle-class movement (anti-slavery, to the mid-1840s) to the organisation of an independent moderate feminist movement (mid-1840s to late 1860s). An exceptional feature of moderate feminism in the United States was its early commitment to votes for women; even more distinctive perhaps was the lack of any formal organisational structure beyond the holding of periodic congresses. The commitment of moderate feminism to the vote was due perhaps to the pervasive influence of the democratic principles enunciated in the Declaration of Independence, in which the suffrage was generally seen as the foundation on which political legitimacy was based — a very different situation from that which obtained in most European nations. Until 1869, however, the vote was in general fairly low on the feminists' list of priorities. The expectation that the anti-slavery movement, which frequently reiterated its belief in women's suffrage, would enfranchise women on achieving its final victory, dissuaded feminists both from pressing hard for the vote and from forming separate organisations which the anti-slavery movement might see as divisive. It was because they did not enjoy such powerful allies that most other feminist movements (with the exception, as we shall see, of those in Australia and New Zealand) began almost immediately with the formation of separate organisations on a permanent basis.

The transition to radical feminism in America took place in stages, again reflecting a common pattern. Exceptionally, however, the formation of a female suffrage movement in 1869 was *followed* in the mid-1870s by the emergence of moral reform movements, in a reversal of the usual pattern. The early formation of the women's suffrage movement, while in part a reflection of the advanced state of the suffrage cause in the United States, was mainly a response to the prominent place taken by other suffrage issues in national politics in the late 1860s, after the Civil War. In other countries too (e.g. Britain, Norway) the occurrence of a national debate about the extension of *manhood* suffrage stimulated feminists to advance *their* claim for the vote as well, and to back this up by founding an organisation specifically devoted to fighting for it. Women's suffrage organisations formed in this way were often short-lived, and collapsed once the national crisis over manhood suffrage was resolved. They were premature, artificial and *ad hoc*, formed in advance of the social and political conditions necessary for a permanent radicalisation of the feminist movement, and owing their existence mainly to outside political conditions which were in their very nature ephemeral. The foundation of the AWSA and NWSA in 1869 can to a large extent be regarded as an example of this 'premature radicalisation'. Full transition to radical feminism did not occur until twenty years later, with the uniting of the suffrage movement after two decades of moderate feminist and moral reformist expansion. The AWSA and NWSA successfully survived the intervening period in the first place because, for reasons more or less unconnected with their foundation, women were enfranchised in two Western Territories, Wyoming and Utah, in 1869-70, thus giving the suffragists' hopes a timely boost; and in the second place because there were fewer disincentives to the advocacy of female suffrage than there were in other countries. Further gains in the West followed quickly on the union of the two suffrage societies. These successes, and in a more general sense the rapid progress made by the feminist movement in winning equal rights for women in many other spheres, justly gave American feminism the reputation of being the most successful in the world in the late nineteenth century. But perhaps its most remarkable feature was its sheer size, above all the scale on which the suffrage movement was organised. In few other countries could its numerical strength come to rival that of the moderate feminist societies, as it did in the United States in the years after 1905.

Australia and New Zealand

North American society, though rapidly expanding in the nineteenth century, with the great migrations from Europe and the advance of the Western frontier, had roots going back several centuries, and particularly in the East and South it was highly developed and well established. Society was complex enough for the achievement of equal rights not only in politics but also in other spheres to present the feminists with some difficulties. The development of feminism in the United States, particularly if it is seen as a movement of moral reform, can be interpreted in terms of the dialectic of urban-frontier relationships: the feminist movement emerged in the East, but enjoyed its earliest successes in the West. Middle-class women migrated from the settled communities of the Eastern seaboard and, in attempting to impose their own standards of morality and order on the turbulent society of the frontier, they also secured the acceptance of many points on the feminist programme, including (in places) the suffrage. Once successful, they turned their attention to the East once more, where the expanding cities and industrial towns seemed now to harbour evils far worse than the frontier had known even in its wildest days. Both Populism and Progressivism can be viewed to some extent as movements through which rural and small town society in the West attempted to impose its own standards and values on the great cities of the East. In the development of feminism in the other new European societies of the nineteenth century, Australia and New Zealand, only the first part of this process was operative, reflecting the fact that these were societies of far more recent vintage, and on a far smaller and simpler scale, than the United States. It was only from the middle of the nineteenth century that Australia really began to escape from its origins as a (predominantly male) penal colony and to develop the institutions of a modern society. There were no entrenched elites or traditional social institutions. Australia in the second half of the nineteenth century was a society in the throes of creation.

It was in this period that the pattern of emigration to Australia became more middle class with the growth and gradual industrialisation of coastal towns such as Sydney and Adelaide. The rise of feminism can be seen in large measure as a feature of the struggle of these urban middle classes to impose their values and ideals on the men of the outback and the labourers of the new cities. The pioneer Australian feminist was Caroline Chisholm (1808-77), who started a home for destitute immigrant girls and prostitutes in Sydney in 1841. Chisholm pursued the same objective of the reform of morals in the cities with her Family Colonisation Loan Society and her Ladies' Female Emigration Society, based in London. Both organisations aimed to help the creation of an ordered family life as the basis for a morally and socially stable existence in Australia.

Chisholm set the pattern for many other female philanthropists who sought to temper the 'rough masculinity of Australian society'. By the 1860s and 1870s, the social balance in the cities had shifted sufficiently to ensure that her successors were extending the scope of their activities to urge that the primary and secondary school systems then in the process of being established provide for girls as well as for boys. Male middle-class migrants from Britain tended to be men of radical liberal opinions not far removed from those of John Stuart Mill. They saw in emigration to Australia the quickest means of effecting those social reforms which tradition and conservatism were making so difficult to introduce in England. It is not surprising, therefore, that these efforts met with a good deal of success. By the late 1870s there was a generous provision of both public and private schools for girls with a high standard of 'serious' education, and in the 1880s the universities gradually opened their doors to women students as well. All these reforms took place in the virtual absence of an organised feminist movement.[30]

The history of feminism in Australia is complicated by the fact that until the turn of the century the different states — South Australia, Western Australia, New South Wales, Tasmania, Queensland and Victoria — were not federated into a single political entity, but formed separate colonies each with a government and legislature of its own. In consequence, reform movements were obliged to constitute themselves separately in each state. Conditions did not differ markedly from state to state, however. In every case the roles usually filled by a whole range of feminist societies were all taken by the Woman's Christian Temperance Union, which continued the philanthropic tradition begun by Caroline Chisholm and developed it further in the direction of feminism. The origins of the Australian WCTU lay in a visit in 1885 by an emissary of the American WCTU, Mary Clement Leavitt (1830-1912). In Victoria the WCTU really began life in 1887. Its leaders had had experience in women's temperance movements in Britain and America. In all the Australian states the WCTU followed closely the example of its American mentors. As Frances Willard swung the American WCTU round behind the demand for votes for women, the Australian WCTU followed suit. By 1890, for example, the Victorian WCTU's members were describing female suffrage as 'a weapon of protection for their homes from the liquor trade and its attendant evils'. They further believed that 'woman's self-reliance' would lead to 'a higher tone of social purity'. Like the American WCTU, the Australian WCTU had a Social Purity Department, which agitated against the medical inspection of prostitutes and fought for a higher age of consent. In 1891 the Victorian WCTU gathered 30,000 signatures for a women's suffrage petition. It persistently lobbied government ministers throughout the 1890s and arranged for candidates to be questioned on the suffrage at election meetings. In 1894, with the Women's Suffrage Society, a much smaller and only nominally separate group founded in 1884, the Victorian WCTU set up a Victorian Women's Franchise League to coordinate female suffrage work. Despite all this activity, however, the WCTU never really desired votes for women as anything more than a means to the end of liquor prohibition, a fact most tellingly illustrated by its continued opposition to the idea that women should be allowed to stand as candidates in elections even though they should be enabled to vote in them.

In South Australia the WCTU was established in Adelaide in 1886. It inspired the formation of a Women's Suffrage League in 1888, and in 1894 it gathered 11,000 signatures for a female suffrage petition. In Western Australia, the WCTU established a Women's Suffrage League somewhat later, in 1899. In Tasmania the WCTU, founded in 1892, did not trouble to form a Suffrage League and waged the brief struggle on its own until the very eve of victory in 1893. In Queensland the WCTU set up a suffrage department in Brisbane which led to the formation of a Women's Equal Suffrage League in 1894. Only in the oldest and most advanced of the states, New South Wales, with its large and (by Australian standards, anyway) sophisticated capital city, Sydney, was there a divergence between the WCTU and the suffragists. Supporters of votes for women sabotaged the attempt of the WCTU to form a suffrage league in Sydney in 1890 by refusing to accept temperance leadership. They believed that the association of female suffrage with temperance would make enemies and hold back the cause of votes for women. When a Women's Suffrage League was formed in Sydney in 1891, it was under non-temperance leadership. This did not, however, prevent the liquor interest from financing an anti-suffragist movement in the city later in the decade.[31]

In New Zealand, the pattern of events was very similar. Here, as in Australia, the construction of the institutional elements of a modern society in the later nineteenth century — schools, a university, a medical service, a legal profession and so on — took place on the basis of equal opportunities for women. So much so, in fact, that women constituted over half of all New Zealand university students by 1893, at a time when they were not even admitted to universities as full-time students in countries such as Germany. Married Women's Property Acts were passed in 1860 and 1870. Women ratepayers voted in local elections from 1867, all women from 1885. The emergence of a moderate feminist movement along European lines was thus hardly possible, since most of its goals had been achieved before the formation of a middle-class society was advanced enough to allow one to be founded. The origins of feminism in New Zealand, as in Australia, lay in moral reform. In 1869 the passage of a Criminal Diseases Act to regulate prostitution in Auckland met with little opposition. But a movement to repeal it began in the early 1880s. At the same time, the temperance movement grew to be more or less the only large-scale extra-Parliamentary pressure group in the country. In May 1885 Mary Clement Leavitt, the American who founded the Australian WCTU, also founded the New Zealand Woman's Christian Temperance Union in Christchurch. By August 1885 it had ten branches. Another seven opened early in 1886, bringing the total membership up to 600. Like other organisations run by women, the NZWCTU established an elaborate structure which one writer described as 'the most perfect organisation the world has ever known', thus demonstrating that women's administrative abilities were at least the equal of men's, if not superior. The NZWCTU developed a wide range of activities, including meetings to encourage abstinence, canvassing for temperance candidates at elections, petitions and letters to Members of Parliament, provision of temperance refreshments at fairs and other occasions, rescue work for prostitutes, domestic science lessons for working-class women and pre-school classes to keep working-class children off the streets. The attempt to reduce social disorder among the working classes which many of these activities represented was compounded by a deliberate and largely successful effort to enlist the support of working-class women in the campaign for the vote. These developments culminated in a campaign against the Criminal Diseases Act and in the struggle for the vote, which were both run entirely by the NZWCTU without the interference of any separate suffragist or Abolitionist associations such as had made their appearance in other countries.[32]

The small scale of Australasian society can only serve as a partial explanation of the concentration of virtually all feminist activities into a single organisation, for other small societies (for example, Iceland) had a whole range of feminist organisations, including separate ones for female suffrage. What the monopoly of Australian and New Zealand feminism by the WCTU signifies is rather the overriding predominance of the moral imperative in the development of a feminist movement in these two countries. The parallel here is with the American Midwest, where the WCTU was also the only feminist organisation in most towns and cities until after the turn of the century. In both areas, society itself was in the process of formation, and there were no established institutions against which the feminists had to fight, as they did in Europe. Indeed, as we have seen, most of the usual objectives of moderate feminism had been gained well before the feminist movement came into being, for Australasian politics were dominated by what in European terms would count as extreme left-wing liberals, often indeed men who had migrated to Australia and New Zealand precisely in order to give their liberal principles the chance of being put into action. Australasian feminism was thus a peculiarly narrow movement with limited objectives: moral reform and the vote. Once these were gained, the probability was that it would collapse. The Australasian case provides a good illustration of the way in which moral reform could lead to the demand for the vote. But the transition to radical feminism stopped there, for it was only in the largest city, Sydney, that the female suffrage movement managed to take on a life of its own. Elsewhere, it never escaped from the clutches of the moderates in the

Sandra Dee Sandra Dee
Dee Sandra Dee
Sandra Dee Sandra Dee

WCTU. Feminism therefore never really succeeded in striking roots in Australasian society. It gained its objectives (including the vote) very early, thus providing its envious European counterparts with an inspiration and an example. Then it faded away. When urban society in Australia and New Zealand reached a stage of development in which a permanent feminist movement would have been a real possibility, there was no one to launch it, nor any objective, such as the vote, around which women might have rallied. Because it had from the beginning conceded so many legal rights to women, Australasia became a society without feminism.

Great Britain

Although the major part in bringing feminist organisations into existence in many countries — not only Australia and New Zealand, but also Germany, for example — was played by the Americans, British feminism also had an influential if less direct role. As we have already seen, Mill's *Subjection of Women* had an incalculable influence on feminism almost everywhere. And in the crusade against the state regulation of prostitution, the American movement was largely brought into being by its British counterpart, which supplied the 'New Abolitionists' everywhere with the major elements of their programme and ideology. British feminism was chronologically the second after the American movement to emerge in an organised form. It really dates from the 1850s, though a few organisations were founded earlier for purposes whose implications, if not their overt aims, were feminist in character. The 1850s in Britain saw a number of social reforms affecting women. In 1852 an Act of Parliament removed a husband's right to enforce cohabitation on his wife by issuing a writ of *habeas corpus* against anyone who sheltered her. In 1857 a Divorce Act was passed. These were of course only beginnings: until 1891 a husband still had the right to kidnap and imprison his wife, and the Divorce Act of 1857, while allowing a husband to divorce his wife on grounds of adultery, required her to prove him guilty of rape, sodomy or bestiality, or of adultery *in conjunction* with incest, bigamy, cruelty or desertion. Nevertheless, the various measures of the 1850s clearly marked the beginnings of a new attitude towards women, one which was prepared to allow them greater freedom than had been possible before. Before 1857, for example, divorce was only possible through the costly process of obtaining a private Act of Parliament. And at the same time as these reforms were in progress, opportunities were also expanding in the field of education. At the end of the 1840s, secondary schooling for girls began a new era with the foundation of Queen's College and Bedford College in London, and during the 1850s informally organised groups of women began to press actively for further educational reforms. This activity culminated in a Royal Commission Report in 1858 which recommended the establishment of a national system of girls' secondary schools, to educate middle-class girls in the new and complex tasks of household management facing the bourgeois housewife in the expanding society of Victorian England.[33] These educational changes, however, also incidentally benefited unmarried women whose economic opportunities were being reduced by the increasing professionalisation above all of teaching and medicine.[34]

It was out of the involvement of middle-class female philanthropists in the debates over these measures that organised feminism emerged. A committee of women formed to petition for a Married Women's Property Bill in 1855 subsequently transformed itself into the Society for the Employment of Women, and also acquired a magazine, the *Englishwoman's Journal*, which allowed its members to express their views on a wider range of topics. This concentration on economic questions, with an added concern for improved educational opportunities, was a characteristic of moderate feminism in its formative stages in many countries other than Britain. So too were the general political links which students of early British feminism have so neglected: the 1850s in Britain were a time when the forces of reform were realigning, when middle-class concern with social questions was growing after the fright of Chartism in the 1840s, when middle-class radicalism was on the upsurge. The disasters of the Crimean War (1854-6) inspired a growing concern with ability and professionalism as the criteria of administration, expressed among other ways in widespread demands for the abolition of the purchase of office. This not only had the particular implication for women of demanding higher professional qualifications in medicine, nursing and other fields, but also in a more general way spawned a whole series of associations dedicated to social reform, of which the National Association for the Promotion of Social Science, the parent body of the early feminist movement, was perhaps the most important. Women were active in many of these associations, sometimes — as with Octavia Hill in the voluntary poor relief movement in London — at the very centre of them. These developments were part of a general transition from the small-scale, élitist Whig politics of the 1840s to the popular liberalism of the 1860s. In this process, the decline of extreme radicalism among the working class after 1848 and the conversion of skilled labour to liberal attitudes played an important part, as did the integration of non-conformist Protestant groups into the political system, from which they had previously been excluded by various discriminatory measures. In a way that will become familiar as we look at the experience of other countries, this expansion of the political system to embrace larger sectors of the new middle class stimulated active women to demand their share in it as well. For although the initial demands of moderate feminism were modest and apparently non-political in character, the formation of extra-Parliamentary pressure groups for social reform led by and composed of women was political in its very essence.[35]

The female suffrage movement in Britain began in 1866 with the presentation to Parliament of a petition signed by 1,499 women demanding that the suffrage reform then under consideration include votes for women. The organisers of the petition, which was presented in the House of Commons by John Stuart Mill and Henry Fawcett, were mainly drawn from the moderate feminists of the Society for the Employment of Women. It is clear that they would not have demanded the vote but for the debate that raged about the proposed extension of the franchise to classes of men other than those enfranchised by the great Reform Act of 1832. Once the petition had failed, the organisers, joined by various groups outside London, proceeded to form a permanent movement in the form of the National Society for Women's Suffrage (1867). The leading figure in the Society until 1890 was Lydia Becker (1827-90), a Manchester liberal, and the closest ties of the movement were with the free trade liberals of Lancashire. In comparison to the difficulties that confronted her American counterparts, the task that faced Becker seemed simple enough. All she had to do was to drum up enough support in Parliament for the passage of a single Women's Suffrage Act; whereas the federal constitution of the United States made pressure on a large number of state legislatures necessary. Accordingly, leading left-liberals such as John Stuart Mill, Jacob Bright and Richard Cobden, were encouraged to present private bills for women's suffrage. Such bills were presented every year from 1870 to 1878, and from 1884 onwards (save 1899 and 1901). In general, they sought a limited suffrage (i.e. the extension of existing voting rights to women). These measures invariably received considerable support. In 1870 one female suffrage bill passed the House of Commons with a majority of 33. In 1884 another one passed by 21 votes and in 1897 another received a majority of 71. In 1904 the majority in favour was 114, and in 1908 it was no less than 179.[36]

Such a wide measure of support was impressive indeed. Few legislatures in the world, and none in Europe, could boast a record of such early, repeated and sizeable majorities. But although the Houses of Parliament were sovereign in Britain, these votes failed to produce any tangible result, for several reasons. In the first place, the Conservatives, strongly influenced by the aristocracy and the landed interest, were adamantly opposed to female suffrage, and although they were sometimes in a minority in the House of Commons, from the mid-1880s onwards they possessed a permanent majority in the House of Lords. Even more important was the fact that for two decades after 1885 the Conservatives were seldom out of office. The few Liberal Governments to hold power in this period were invariably short-lived. Thus the vast majority of female suffrage bills were either suppressed procedurally without a vote, or 'lost' by Conservative Governments during their passage through the House of Commons, even if (as in 1897) they had received a majority vote at an earlier stage. Then again, in 1867 and 1884, when the franchise was being extended to include the men of the lower middle classes and labour aristocracy, many Members of Parliament considered that to 'tack on' votes for women would endanger the original bill. Other issues, such as the Irish Question, also forced women's suffrage into the background in this period.

In addition to all this, the female suffrage movement itself was almost perpetually in difficulties in the 1870s and 1880s. In 1871 the London National Society for Women's Suffrage broke with the National Society and only rejoined the parent body in 1877. For two decades after the 1867 Reform Act, despite the further extension of manhood suffrage in 1884, the political climate was unfavourable to the female suffrage movement. Like its American counterpart, British feminism had undergone a 'premature radicalisation', and the suffrage movement formed under the stimulus of a national debate about manhood suffrage in 1867 was constantly in difficulties in the following two decades, kept going perhaps mainly by the continued support its cause won in the House of Commons. It was precisely in this period however that the social and organisational foundations for a full transition to radicalism were being laid. Educational and professional opportunities widened; women were admitted to Oxford and Cambridge and in 1876 gained the right to register as physicians. Teaching, nursing and other professions expanded rapidly in the 1870s and gave employment and economic independence to increasing numbers of women. Moreover, the same years saw the launching of female movements of moral reform which further contributed to the extension of the feminist movement in a radical direction. The most important of these moral reform organisations was without doubt the movement to combat the state regulation of prostitution, founded in 1869 by Josephine Butler (1828-1906). Like the American movement which it inspired, Butler's organisation won some spectacular successes, particularly in the Colchester by-election of 1870, when a pro-regulation candidate was defeated after a massive Abolitionist campaign against him. Butler won over the Protestant Churches and the Trade Unions to the cause in the 1870s, and the advent of a Liberal Government in 1880 paved the way for the suspension of state regulation in 1883 and its abolition in 1886.

The English Abolitionists were helped by a number of factors. While the Americans had to mount a whole series of local campaigns because regulation was not sanctioned federally but at state or municipal level, the English Abolitionists were able to concentrate all their energies on influencing one single institution, Parliament, and the fact that regulation was by Act of Parliament (the Contagious Diseases Acts) meant that its repeal was relatively straightforward once the right amount of public support was gained. Besides enjoying the backing of powerful institutions such as the churches and the unions, Butler's campaign also benefited from (and of course also in part reflected) a growing trend towards moral repressiveness in the wake of the Reform Acts of 1867 and 1884. The enfranchisement of the petty bourgeoisie and labour aristocracy, both of them aping, and exaggerating, the moral postures of the established middle classes; and the fears aroused in the existing electorate for the stability of the social and political order by the extension of the franchise from three million to a total of five million voters in 1884 — both these developments helped create a moral climate in which notorious London nightspots were closed down, eminent politicians hounded out of public life for moral peccadilloes, and a National Vigilance Association formed to combat pornography, which it did through propaganda and parliamentary action, to the general applause of the Press.

These developments paved the way for the full transition to radical feminism in Britain. The political background lay in an important reorientation of liberal politics in Britain, beginning in the late 1880s. This laid the foundations at the grass-roots level for the dramatic Liberal resurgence in the landslide election victory of 1906. As they shifted their ground to more radical views, many Liberals began to see the question of votes for women in a fresh light. While the Liberal leaders, Gladstone, Harcourt and later Asquith, remained firmly opposed to votes for women, the reorientation of Liberal politics at the base

produced an increasingly favourable mood towards it among the rank
and file. As part of this process, Liberal women began to take a more
active interest in female suffrage. Initially, they ran up against some
opposition from the established suffrage society, which — like many
moderate feminist groups — felt that it was important to preserve its
own political neutrality, even if most of its members belonged to one
particular part of the political spectrum. In 1888 those suffragists who
believed in admitting Liberal women's groups seceded from Becker's
society and formed the Central National Society for Women's Suffrage. 1889 saw the foundation of the Women's Franchise League,
which was closely connected with the Liberal Party. It was very critical
of the 'want of courage and faith' of the established suffragists in confining themselves (in classic moderate feminist fashion) to asking for
the enfranchisement of propertied widows and spinsters. The Women's
Franchise League asked for the enfranchisement of married women as
well. In 1890 Lydia Becker died and was replaced as president of the
National Women's Suffrage Society by the more radical and determined
Millicent Garrett Fawcett (1842-1929). These developments culminated
in 1897 with the union of all the various female suffrage societies in the
National Union of Women's Suffrage Societies. Its programme was
much broader than that of its predecessors, its membership larger, its
base wider, and its willingness to employ vigorous and inventive tactics
greater. There were sixteen member societies in 1897; after 1903 a
rapid expansion began, taking the number of organisations in the
NUWSS to seventy in 1909 and over 400 in 1913. This rapid growth
was not the result of the NUWSS's efforts alone; but without the foundations laid in the 1890s, it would hardly have been possible.[37]

Britain's importance in the development of world feminism was
exceeded only by that of America. The most important theorist of
feminism, John Stuart Mill, and the most influential figure in international moral feminism, Josephine Butler, were both British. Origi-
nating in the 1850s, radicalising prematurely in the 1860s then more
thoroughly in the 1890s, British feminism followed a course not
dissimilar to that of feminist movements elsewhere. Viewed in a European perspective, the British feminist movement was by the 1900s not
only large and vigorous but also radical and successful. By 1910 its
suffrage movement had become one of the biggest in the world. Its
tactics, which included frequent marches through the streets and mass
demonstrations in the open air, were more daring than those of any
other feminist organisation outside the United States. It had long
enjoyed a degree of support in the legislature unparalleled even in

America. On the question of full suffrage rights for women, however, it proved unable to translate this support into practical results. For European feminist movements which succeeded in doing that, we have to look elsewhere.

Scandinavia and the Nordic Lands

The only European countries where conditions were really comparable to those existing in Britain, America and Australasia, were the Nordic states — Denmark, Finland and Iceland, and the Scandinavian countries of Norway and Sweden. All these nations were predominantly Protestant in culture and enjoyed constitutions which gave a varying though always significant measure of power to the legislature. Nordic feminism was probably the most successful in Europe before the First World War. Sweden, Denmark, Norway, Finland and Iceland were neither very populous nor very powerful countries, but the participation of women in feminist movements was proportionately very high in relation to the size of the female population as a whole, and the degree of success which they could claim by 1914 was very considerable. The only European countries to grant women equal voting rights before the First World War were Finland (1906) and Norway (1913), and the other Nordic lands came closer to enfranchising women in this period than any other European countries, closer indeed than either Britain or the United states. Organised feminism developed in the Nordic countries rather late, even measured by European standards. Feminist movements emerged in America in the 1840s, Britain in the 1850s, Germany in the mid-1860s and France in the late 1860s; but it was not until the 1870s that the feminist movement was formed in Sweden, until the 1880s that it came into being in Norway and Finland, and only in the 1890s that a women's emancipation movement finally emerged in the North Atlantic society of Iceland. However, as we shall see, the Nordic feminists made up for their late start by achieving early successes.

In Sweden, as in the other Nordic countries, legislative reforms had already brought women a number of important rights even before a feminist movement was formed. But these reforms were on a much narrower and smaller scale than their counterparts in Australia and New Zealand. They were primarily economic in character. Although they coincided to a certain extent with the beginnings of literary feminism in Sweden, in the writings of Fredrika Bremer (1801-65), recent research has shown that they owed their enactment to factors that had little to do with Bremer's work. The reforms consisted mainly in the granting of equal inheritance rights (1845), freedom to engage in trade and other occupations previously barred to women by restrictive guild regulations (1864), and legal majority for unmarried women (1858). Women were admitted to the teaching profession in 1853 and 1859, and this was quickly followed by the establishment of an increasing number of secondary schools and teacher training colleges for girls. These reforms were the by-products of the social and political conflicts of the 1850s and 1860s. The right of equal inheritance for women was backed by the peasantry and bourgeoisie and opposed by the nobility because it would, under the prevalent system of partible inheritance, cause the break-up of the great landed estates of the nobility and at the same time in a situation of a large female surplus in the population assist the retention of peasant holdings and bourgeois property within the family. Legal majority for women was a necessary precondition of this reform. The granting of occupational freedom to women was designed to augment the incomes of middle-class families, provide a socially acceptable livelihood for unmarried middle-class women and (to a lesser extent) to alleviate the problems of pauperism and 'immorality' which increasingly beset the surplus female population of the urban masses. Wardship stipulations, which tied up increasingly large amounts of capital as the numbers of unmarried women increased, were therefore abolished. In the debate over these questions, scarcely any mention was made of the rights of women; discussion centred instead around questions of economics. The 1850s and 1860s were a period of rapid population growth and early industrial expansion, and it is these factors that really underlay the reforms in the status of women.[38]

In the 1850s, during the reaction following the failure of the 1848 revolution, the political climate in Sweden was not favourable to the emergence of a feminist movement. Sweden was in many ways a conservative country dominated by aristocratic landowners. But the policies of the large landowners were comparable to those of the English Whig aristocracy rather than (say) the more reactionary Prussian Junkers. In 1865 they agreed to a reform of the constitution which abolished the old four-house Estates and substituted something like a modern bicameral Parliament, the Riksdag. The reform in fact *reduced* the size of the electorate, which constituted only 6 per cent of the entire population for the Second Chamber even as late as 1889 (the First Chamber was elected indirectly). Not only were there property qualifications, but there was also no real ministerial responsibility or parliamentary government. But at least the institutional framework for a more liberal system had now been created. As industrialisation really gathered pace in the 1870s, middle-class liberalism began to emerge along with trade unions and a widespread temperance movement as a significant political force. It was out of this organisational ferment in the 1870s that the feminist movement emerged, though it also perhaps had roots in the religious revival of the free church movement which had appeared in the previous decade. Early Swedish moderate feminism was primarily economic and charitable in orientation. The first expression of organised feminism in Sweden was the Association for Married Women's Property Rights, founded in February 1873. This organisation was mainly female, though it included men on the board. It mobilised considerable support, sponsoring bills in the Riksdag throughout the 1870s and 1880s, though with little success. Women in Sweden had enjoyed the municipal suffrage since 1862 on a property franchise, but few of them had made use of it. The Association mounted a campaign to register women and to get them to vote in local elections in Stockholm, and by 1894 it was reporting that a measure of success had rewarded its efforts. It also secured the eligibility of women to school boards and poor law boards (1889) and claimed responsibility for persuading the Riksdag to raise the minimum marriage age for girls from fifteen to seventeen (also 1889). These efforts were all directed towards exerting pressure on influential bodies such as the Stockholm Town Council to press for the introduction of property rights for married women. Their effect was bound to be in the direction of a politicisation of women that would not long restrict itself to the narrow reform which was the Association's primary objective.

Nevertheless, the next feminist group to appear in Sweden, the Fredrika Bremer Society, founded in 1885, continued the primacy of economic goals, describing as its aims 'procuring and allotting endowments to women' and 'the bettering of the salaries paid to women', followed at some distance by more general educational and charitable causes. Clearly, then, the emergence of the Swedish feminist movement was conditioned by the concentration of debate and reform on the enlargement of economic opportunities for women. It remained in this moderate phase of its development — though increasingly concerned with issues of moral reform, above all temperance — until the turn of the century.

That it took so long for Swedish feminism to develop a more radical programme was primarily due to the conservative nature of Swedish society and politics. Even in the 1890s, the old ruling classes were still firmly in control, though by now they had been forced to bury the differences that had once divided them and make common front against the challenge from below. But as the country industrialised, radical liberal and social democratic movements began to organise mounting pressure for an extension of the suffrage. The 1890s were a decade of great petition campaigns, 'people's parliaments' and increasing political tension, culminating in a general strike held in 1902 to back the demand from oppositional groups for a reform of the suffrage. It was at this point, in 1902, that the Swedish Women's Suffrage Association (*Landsföreningen för Kvinnans Politiska Rösträtt*) was founded. The emergence of radical feminism thus followed a familiar pattern — preparation through decades of moderate feminist activity, economic expansion and widening opportunities for women, followed by the immediate stimulus of a national political crisis centred on the extension of the suffrage to wider groups of men. The Swedish Women's Suffrage Association soon eclipsed the old moderate feminist groups. Led from 1903 to 1913 by the journalist and educationalist Anna Whitlock (1852-1930), it already had 10,173 members organised in 127 branches by 1907. In 1908 these numbers had grown to 11,065 and 142 respectively, by 1911 there were 12,022 members in 170 branches, and at the end of 1912 there were no fewer than 13,000 members organised in 187 local associations. This rapid growth was in part due to Whitlock's evident organising abilities, but it also owed a great deal to the prolonged and increasingly bitter national crisis over the extension of the manhood suffrage, as the entrenched agrarian ruling classes dug their heels in, backed by the King.

Behind all this lay the continuing social and economic influences of the industrial transformation which reduced the rural population of Sweden from nearly 70 per cent in 1880 to under 50 per cent in 1910. These changes and tensions produced a realignment of the social basis of political life culminating in the formation of a Liberal Union party in 1900 and the rapid growth of Social Democracy on the left. The Liberal Union united the progressive middle-class parties behind a programme of universal manhood suffrage and fully-fledged parliamentary government. In 1905 it became the largest party in the Riksdag, with 106 seats to the conservatives' 99. The Social Democrats had 13 seats. The alignment of political parties in Sweden by 1905 was thus very similar to its counterpart in Britain at the same time, and very different from the multi-party systems of France, Germany or Italy; though the lack of parliamentary government in Sweden meant that even a Liberal election victory did not resolve the crisis. This situation favoured the women's suffrage movement in two ways. First, it helped keep it united, and second, since in Sweden as in most other countries it was the Liberals who (with the Social Democrats) gave the most support to women's suffrage, it greatly simplified the movement's task. The suffragists were mostly identified with the Liberal Union, and gained the bulk of their support from that party. Their success or failure was therefore in practice largely dependent on the fortunes of the Liberal Union, however much they protested their political neutrality or tried to win over the support of Conservative deputies.

Female suffrage legislation had first been introduced in Sweden in 1884, when Frederick Borg's bill to give women full voting rights had been rejected amid laughter, despite the fact that taxpaying women had enjoyed the municipal franchise since 1862. Women's suffrage could still be regarded as absurd perhaps because very few of these women had exercised their rights. In 1887 only 4,000 out of the 62,000 women electors had actually cast their vote, a rate of 6.5 per cent. This was a familiar pattern in most countries where women possessed formal voting rights before the great upsurge of organised feminism when the transition from 'moderate' to 'radical' tactics and ideology took place. Improved standards of secondary education only had a slight impact on women's political consciousness; and male prejudice had not yet been modified by the influence that radical feminists came to exert through the press. The suffragists mobilised women to use their municipal voting rights, helped by the effect on public opinion of the agitation of the suffragists and the prolonged political controversy over the franchise in the mid-1900s. In 1908, the proportion of enfranchised women voting in municipal elections was only 15.2 per cent in a sample of twenty-five towns. By 1910 it was 36.9 per cent in a sample of fifty towns — not far below the percentage poll of male electors. The high female poll of 1910 was perhaps helped by the fact that women candidates, admitted by a law passed in 1909, were standing for the first time. In 1902, in conjunction with the formation of the women's suffrage movement, a second female suffrage bill was introduced in the Riksdag. It was defeated, by 111 votes to 64. So too were subsequent bills in 1904 and 1905. In 1905 the Liberals formed a government and introduced a bill for universal manhood suffrage. A bitter and extremely complicated political crisis followed. It resulted in a Conservative government passing a compromise measure giving all male taxpayers the vote for the Lower House in 1908-9, with Liberal support. This prolonged controversy over the franchise drew progressively more attention and support to the feminists' demand for the vote, as the nation was gripped by furious debates on the principles on which the right to vote should be based. In 1906 four women's suffrage bills were introduced by individual members, in 1907, six. In the autumn of 1907 the Liberal Union adopted women's suffrage into its official programme.

This steady crescendo of activity was very encouraging for the suffragists. Although they might well have been alienated by the backing
given by the Liberal Union to the manhood suffrage bill in 1908-9, this
was prevented by the Liberals' decision to introduce a separate female
suffrage bill. The failure of this bill, by 110 to 93 votes, convinced the
suffragists that they should abandon their politically 'neutral' tactics of
sending deputations to the King and submitting petitions to the
Riksdag. In 1907 one petition had contained over 142,000 signatures.
But clearly this kind of approach was ineffective as long as the Conservatives remained strongly represented in the Riksdag. In the elections
of 1908, the suffragists admitted that their 'object was in the first place
to bring about the defeat of the Conservative Party, which had shown
itself hostile to their interests'. A token gesture in the direction of neutrality was made by their declaration of intent

(1) to cooperate with the existing men's political organisations, both
Liberal and Conservative, whenever that was possible; (2) to accept
posts on the committee of these organisations if they were offered;
(3) to take part in all election meetings; (4) to question all the candidates as to their attitude towards woman suffrage; (5) to do everyting feasible to prevent the re-election of pronounced opponents to
the cause; (6) to oppose any new candidates who declared themselves against woman suffrage; (7) to leave constituencies alone where
both candidates were in favour of it; (8) to prepare the ground
thoroughly before the election and arouse interest among women by
arranging for lectures and meetings and also by a wholesale distribution of woman suffrage literature.

In view of the fact that the Conservatives were solidly opposed to votes
for women — their leader remarked in 1910 that 'nothing can be done
until further light has been thrown upon the question of the effect
woman's suffrage is likely to have on the marriage-rate and birth-rate' —
this programme amounted in effect to a declaration of active support
for the Liberals.

The programme soon reaped its reward. In 1909, as we have seen,
women gained the right to stand for municipal office. Already in the
same year a bill giving women full equality of voting rights (a principle
long supported by the Social Democrats) passed the Second Chamber,
though not the First, and in 1911, after the Liberals triumphed at the

elections and formed a government, the energetic work of the suffragists for the return of Liberal and Social Democratic candidates elicited the response of an official Government Bill, which passed the Second Chamber in 1912 but failed in the First by 86 votes to 58 (cf. the House's composition: 86 Conservatives, 52 Liberals, 12 Social Democrats). In Sweden, as in Britain, therefore, it was the First Chamber which proved the main obstacle to female suffrage. In Sweden, however, relations between suffragists and liberals remained good, in contrast to Britain (and also in sharp contrast to Germany). The reason perhaps lay in the polarisation of Swedish politics that underlay the prolonged political crisis of the first decade of the twentieth century. By the eve of the First World War the determining factors in the situation were the continued refusal of the King, backed by the Conservatives, to accede to parliamentary government on the one hand, and the spectacular growth of Social Democratic membership and representation in the Riksdag on the other. With politics divided into two camps, the suffragists came down inevitably on the side of the Social Democrats and the more radical of the Liberals. The Liberals' support for the suffragists was in turn conditioned by their own need to compromise with the Social Democrats, whose support they required in the Riksdag to secure a majority for their legislation. In this situation, all the progressive groups managed to stay together without undergoing harmful splits. But the penalty for the Liberals was a dramatic loss of electoral support as the middle classes, frightened by growing labour unrest, abandoned them for the Conservatives. In 1914 the Liberals lost half their seats in the Riksdag, a Conservative government took office, and the enactment of female suffrage was put off indefinitely.[39]

The development of Swedish feminism, from its moderate beginnings in 1873 through its radicalisation in 1902 to complete domination by the suffrage movement on the eve of the First World War, was relatively simple and straightforward, though the slow pace of change in the first thirty years of its existence contrasted strongly with the rapid and complex changes of the first decade or so after radicalisation. In Denmark, the evolution of the feminist movement took a rather more convoluted course, even if much the same social and political factors were at work.

In Denmark, as in Sweden, the first half of the nineteenth century was characterised by a struggle for power between the absolutist monarchy and the landed aristocracy. Unlike in Sweden, however, there was an early involvement of the peasantry in this political struggle. By the time of the 1848 Revolution, the peasants and small farmers had swung round to ally with the emerging middle classes in Copenhagen. The constitutional reform of 1848 and its consolidation in a conservative direction in 1866 confirmed the defeat of the monarchy and aristocracy in a number of crucial areas of the liberals' political programme — a remarkably wide suffrage, freedom of expression, assembly and association, and a number of other civil rights. But ministerial responsibility and parliamentary government were still not conceded. After the crisis of 1866, which followed on Denmark's defeat by Prussia in the Schleswig-Holstein War, the middle-class and small farmer political groups rallied in the 'United Left', formed in 1870 to press for the further reform of the constitution. It was against this political background that the Danish feminist movement was founded, although it owed its existence in a more immediate sense to the growth of an international feminist movement, based on Switzerland. The foundation of The Danish Women's Association (*Dansk Kvindesamfund*), by Fredrik Bajer (1837-1922) and his wife Mathilde Bajer (1840-1934), in 1871, was also influenced by the publication of a Danish version of Mill's *Subjection of Women* two years earlier, though the translator, Georg Brandes, in common with other Danish exponents of literary feminism such as Mathilde Fibiger, rejected the Bajers' invitation to join the new movement.

The Danish Women's Association, which still exists today, was a characteristic example of a continental European moderate feminist organisation. It began by concentrating primarily on economic questions. Women already possessed equal inheritance rights (since 1857), occupational freedom (also since 1857) and the right to attain legal majority if unmarried (since 1858), for much the same reasons as they had been granted these rights in Sweden. Measures such as these mainly affected unmarried women. The Danish Women's Association therefore began by campaigning for a law to grant married women economic independence. It also established a women's trade school in Copenhagen in 1872. Fredrik Bajer soon ceased active participation in the Association when he entered Parliament, though he continued to take an interest in women's rights and played a role in the final passage of the law giving economic independence to married women in 1880. The Association stagnated and failed to gain a significant degree of support until the 1880s. At the end of its first twelve years of existence it numbered only 124 members. Bajer had also launched another association for women, this time based on a similar society set up in Sweden in 1867; the Women's Reading Society (*Kvindelig Laeseforening*), founded in 1871. The aim was to found a library and reading room for women. The Society was very limited as a feminist association; men generally took their chair at meetings, subscription fees were high, and the library's catalogue contained virtually nothing on the women's question in Denmark. Only 48 of the first 150 members were married women; and perhaps in view of this a careful moral censorship was exercised over the books purchased; one periodical which alluded (albeit very vaguely) to population control was excluded as 'irreligious'. Nevertheless, the society, like the many similar organisations founded in other countries in the late nineteenth century, clearly played a useful role in helping unmarried middle-class women to broaden their horizons and perhaps to give themselves the beginnings of an advanced education.

It was the 1880s that saw the beginnings of a transition to radical feminism in Denmark, against the national political background of a severe constitutional conflict between the left-liberals and Social Democrats on the one hand, and the Upper Chamber of the legislature on the other. This conflict culminated in a sweeping victory for the left-liberals in the elections of 1884. The catalyst of radicalisation in Denmark as in other countries was the emergence of a moral dimension to feminism. In 1880, a branch of Josephine Butler's International Abolitionist Federation was founded by some of the more active feminists in Copenhagen. This was not welcomed by the Danish Women's Association. Tension within the Association grew until in 1883 the journalist and teacher Caroline Testmann, the Association's President since 1872, was ousted and replaced by Marie Rovsing. Under the new leadership the Association's membership quadrupled within a few months, reaching 500 by the end of 1883. In 1885 the Association founded a magazine, *Kvinden og Samfundet* (Women and Society), edited by Elisabeth Grundtvig (1856-1945). By this time, the Association had 546 members. Its failure to continue expanding as it had done in 1883 suggested that, despite all the new activity, all was not well. Two major controversies were in fact tearing the Association apart. The first was over state-regulated prostitution and sexual morality. Led by Grundtvig, the group within the Danish Women's Association which wanted the abolition of the state control of prostitutes argued forcefully against the call issued by Georg Brandes (translator of Mill's *Subjection of Women*) for women to enjoy the same sexual freedom as men. It was unfair to expect women to indulge in loose and changing sexual relationships, said Grundtvig, if they were unable to find satisfaction in real love and permanent marriage. In the absence of foolproof methods of contraception — so went the unstated argument behind this view —

sexual freedom would not be in women's interest. Instead of women indulging in greater freedom, argued Grundtvig and her supporters, men must adopt stricter codes of sexual morality and learn to restrain their sexual urges. As a token of this, regulated prostitution should be abolished. This 'morality controversy' in Danish feminism was fought with considerable bitterness and gave rise to a celebrated libel suit between Grundtvig and Brandes. This aroused widespread public interest. At the same time as the rise of anti-prostitution 'Abolitionism', a growing minority within the Danish Women's Association, led by the Association's founder, Mathilde Bajer, felt that the movement was not doing enough about votes for women. It is more than likely that the growing need felt by the moral reformers for the vote in order to effect the legislative reforms they desired, played a major role in encouraging this feeling, much as it was to do in the German feminist movement at the end of the century.

These developments culminated in the foundation of the Danish Women's Progress Association (*Dansk Kvindelig Fremskridtsforening*), led by Bajer, in 1886, and the Danish Women's Suffrage Society (*Dansk Kvindelig Valgretsforening*) in 1888. Like radical feminist societies in other countries, these new organisations paid especial attention to moral reform and to the working and living conditions of the women of the proletariat. They helped push the Danish Women's Association to the left, and by 1890 it was endorsing the moral objectives of temperance and social purity and giving at least qualified support to the idea of votes for women by petitioning the Danish Parliament for the municipal suffrage in 1888 — a characteristic response of moderate feminism to the radicals' charge of neglecting women's suffrage. At a more general level, these developments were associated with the growth of radical or left-wing liberalism and signified the entry of new social groups into the political arena, a further shifting of political power in favour of the middle classes.

Although the radicalisation of the Danish feminist movement in the 1880s was in some respects a classic example of this process, involving both the long-term effects of the widening of economic opportunities for women since the 1850s and the more immediate impact of the rise of female moral reform crusades, it ran into difficulties in the early 1890s. The moderate Danish Women's Association was still the dominant force in Danish feminism, and in a manner characteristic of moderate feminist societies everywhere, it limited itself to supporting the work of other, more active groups fighting for the vote, and refused to work for the full suffrage itself for fear of jeopardising its political neutrality. In addition, it could never agree with the radicals' insistence on the exclusion of men from feminist organisations. And despite the emergence of radical feminist groups, the moderates gained a good deal of prestige from their connection with the International Council of Women (founded 1888). They also profited from a temporary swing of Danish politics to the right in the early 1890s. The female suffrage society founded in 1888 never managed to recruit more than 200 members and dissolved itself into the Danish Women's Association in 1897. The Women's Progress Association was torn by internal dissension and fell apart at about the same time. The radicals seemed to have made a false start. What transformed the situation was the introduction of an electoral reform bill in the Danish Parliament in 1898, a bill which made no mention at all of female suffrage. When the Danish Women's Association hesitated before making a protest, its more radical members joined with other feminists in founding a new female suffrage organisation in 1898, the Danish Women's Associations' Suffrage Federation (*Danske Kvindeforeningers Valgrets Forbund*). The new female suffrage society remained closely associated with the Danish Women's Association despite the initial reluctance of the latter to support its aims. In 1903 the Danish Women's Association asked its members to withdraw from the suffrage movement and found a women's suffrage section within the Danish Women's Association, but this section itself proceeded to join the suffrage society as a group, so little was gained by the reorganisation. What these links did show was that the Suffrage Federation was still in many ways a moderate feminist organisation, reflecting the leftward shift of moderate feminist policies in a time of rapid political change and liberalisation. Beyond this, the Federation was also connected with the moderate Liberal party in Danish politics. It continued to remain under the tutelage of the Danish Women's Association. It was hardly surprising, therefore, that the feminists who supported the more left-wing Reform Liberal Party accused the Danish Women's Association of holding back the struggle for the vote. In 1900 the radical feminists broke away to form their own society, the National League for Women's Suffrage (*Landsforbundet for Kvinders Valgret*). This campaigned directly for full voting rights at all levels, whereas the more moderate Danish Women's Associations' Suffrage Federation concentrated its attention on the municipal suffrage.

What happened in Danish feminism therefore seems to have been radicalisation in two distinct stages, the first beginning in the second half of the 1880s, getting into difficulties in the early 1890s, then recovering at the end of the century; and the second beginning in earnest in 1900. The retarding factor here was the temporary resurgence of the Conservative Party in national politics, achieved by including an alliance with the right wing of the liberals in 1894. After the turn of the century, however, things proceeded more rapidly, as the social development of Denmark finally reached a stage where left-liberals and Social Democrats became strong enough to go over onto the offensive. The moderate liberals formed a government in 1901; in 1905 the party split, and its left wing joined in an alliance with the Social Democrats which eventually came to power in 1913. During this period, which was beset by constant political debates and crises over the extension of the suffrage, the female suffrage organisations increased rapidly in size. By 1910 their radical wing, the National League for Women's Suffrage, had 11,000 members in 160 branches, while the moderate Danish Womens' Associations' Suffrage Federation had 12,200 members in 144 branches. By 1910, however, the old Danish Women's Association, the main moderate feminist organisation since the beginning of the 1870s, had only been able to bring its membership up to the 7,000 mark.

The existence of a female suffrage movement with at least 23,000 members in a country with a female population of less than one and a half million was a remarkable indication of the strength of feminist sentiment among Danish women, at least when these figures are compared with those for other countries. The fact that the suffrage associations outnumbered the moderate non-suffrage campaigners to such a degree was an even more remarkable measure of the extent and thoroughness of the radicalisation which Danish feminism had undergone. The suffragists' first reward came in 1908 with the granting of the communal suffrage for women on a property qualification with special provision for wives with no income in their own right. The possibility of securing full franchise rights under a left-liberal government was undoubtedly a major factor in swelling the ranks of the two main suffragist associations with new supporters after 1908. In addition the gaining of the municipal suffrage in 1908 effectively forced the moderates to put their full weight behind the demand for the parliamentary franchise. Already in 1906 the Danish Women's Association had voted to give equal attention to both kinds of suffrage, municipal and parliamentary. From 1908 the Association held an annual Women's Suffrage Day on 20 June, in which nationwide 'demonstrations' (i.e. meetings and speeches) for the vote were mounted; in some years the Suffrage Day formed the focal point of an entire week of 'demonstrations'. These 'demonstrations' stopped short of mass marches and lobbyings, since these were associated increasingly in the minds both of

the Danish press and of the moderate feminists with the English suffragettes, whose radical methods the Danish Women's Association considered 'inappropriate for Denmark'. But they were nevertheless a
powerful propaganda device. In 1912, the government introduced a
suffrage bill which included the enfranchisement of all men and women
over the age of twenty-eight for the Lower House. Despite their previous
insistence that female suffrage should be a separate measure, the suffragists supported this bill, which passed the Lower House of the Danish
Parliament by a majority of 100 to 14. In a manner that might have
been predicted from the experience of other countries, the Upper
House proceeded to reject the bill in the course of 1913, partly because
the conservatives who dominated it objected to the changes it proposed
in the composition of the Upper House itself. The resulting constitutional crisis was still unresolved when war broke out in 1914. However,
it seemed clear that votes for women in Denmark would come within
a fairly short space of time, given the existence of a left-liberal and
Social Democratic majority in the Lower House of Parliament.[40]

In both Sweden and Denmark, then, the rise and later radicalisation
of feminism, while reflecting of course many social changes in the
position of middle-class women, going back to the economic reforms of
the 1850s, was also closely related to the prolonged constitutional
struggles which accompanied the growth of middle-class liberalism, and
later of Social Democracy, and their assaults on conservative, semi-
parliamentary aristocratic constitutions. The prominence which the
suffrage issue took in these struggles perhaps helps explain the way in
which feminism in these two countries eventually became identified
with the fight for votes for women to an extent almost unparalleled
elsewhere. The experience of the other Nordic countries was somewhat
different, partly because there were fewer and weaker obstacles in the
way of a liberal constitutional system within these countries, but above
all because all three of them — Norway, Finland and Iceland — were
throughout the late nineteenth century under the control of foreign
powers, only gaining full independence in the twentieth century. The
dominant political movement among the middle classes was therefore
nationalism, the struggle for national self-determination and freedom
from foreign control. Nationalism was above all the political ideology of
professional, administrative and intellectual classes and their allies, businessmen and industrialists. More important for the history of feminism,
the ideology of nationalism was rooted in the concept of the sovereignty
of the people, which implied parliamentary government and the extension of the franchise.[41] Significantly, it was in the two Nordic countries in

which nationalism played a major role (Norway and Finland) that women gained the vote before the First World War.

In Norway, parliamentary government, though subject to checks by the Swedish Crown, under which the country stood, was achieved earlier than in Sweden or Denmark. The Norwegians had their own political institutions, even if the influence of the Swedes on the administration remained strong. Led by the dominant politician of the late nineteenth century, Johan Sverdrup, the left-liberals in Norway managed to secure responsible government in 1884 after a bitter struggle against the Swedish Crown and the bureaucracy. The nationalist and anti-Swedish agitation which lay behind this achievement had mobilised women as well as men in the national cause, and politicised them in the process. As soon as victory was gained, the women went on to form the Norwegian Association for the Promotion of Women's Interests (1884). These developments in general reflected the emergence of a national bourgeoisie, based above all on a massive expansion of Norway's mercantile marine, which by the 1880s made Norway the third largest shipping nation in the world. The women involved in the early feminist movement were drawn essentially from this social class. As in the other Scandinavian countries, they had already been granted a number of economic rights, including admittance to the teaching profession (1869), legal majority for unmarried women (1863), equal inheritance rights (1854) and occupational freedom (1866). Literary feminism was also strong, above all in the works of Henrik Ibsen (1828-1906), which had a European distribution and impact. But early Norwegian feminism remained largely moderate, economic, charitable and educational in character. This has been obscured (rather like the nature of the early feminist movement in the United States) by the very early creation of a Women's Suffrage Society (*Kvinnestemmeretsforeningen*) which was founded in 1885 under the leadership of Gina Krog (1847-1916), the dominant figure in Norwegian feminism before the First World War. This was something of a flash in the pan. The occasion for the society's foundation was the extension of manhood suffrage in Norway, which Krog felt unable to pass over without demanding at least some voting rights for women as well. Her society had only twelve members. It confined itself to working for the municipal suffrage. Once manhood suffrage had been extended and the issue was dead, the society collapsed. It was a temporary expedient, which in no way represented a genuine transition to radical feminism. Krog herself was the leader of the moderate feminist movement in Norway, which she had only founded in 1884, a year before she created the Women's Suffrage Society. There is no doubt that her main interest lay in the first and larger of the two organisations, nor that it took up the bulk of her time and energy. With Krog in control, in other words, the Norwegian feminist movement remained effectively moderate in composition and outlook.

The transition to radicalism in Norway really began towards the end of the 1880s, against the background of deepening divisions in Norwegian political life between the conservatives on the one hand, and the Radical Liberals on the other. The Radical Liberals wanted to quicken the pace of liberalisation and hasten the break with Sweden, whose king was also ruler of Norway. Their nationalism was closely allied with a desire to secure the moral regeneration of the country. This alliance of nationalism with respectability was symbolised in 1887 by a sensational speaking tour by the nationalist writer Bjørnstjerne Bjørnson (1832-1910). Addressing packed and enthusiastic audiences on the subject of 'monogamy and polygamy', Bjørnson denounced the double standard and advocated a stricter, unitary code of sexual morality for both sexes. In 1892 the WCTU-sponsored White Ribbon society was established in Norway by the social purity campaigner Birgitte Esmark. At the same time, the Radical Liberals, whose support was increasing rapidly throughout the country, took up the causes of social purity, temperance and women's suffrage in the Norwegian Parliament, the Storting, from 1890 onwards. These developments culminated in a qualified reorientation of Norwegian feminism, the most important feature of which was the foundation of a women's suffrage movement in 1895. Nationalism was the catalyst which fused together moral regeneration and female suffrage and prodded the feminists to the left, away from the economic and educational concerns of the moderates and towards the political and moral concerns of the radicals.

Female suffrage became a real issue in Norway when the Radical Liberals, a nationalist political group which split from the Liberals in the late 1880s and advocated complete independence from Sweden, emerged as the dominant political party. In 1890, a full female suffrage bill, supported by the Radical Liberals, secured 44 out of 114 votes in Norway's unicameral Parliament, the Storting. In 1893 another bill got 58 votes, a majority, though not the two-thirds required for a constitutional change of this sort. This spurred the nationalist women to create a new National Women's Suffrage Association (*Landekvinnestemmerets-foreningen*) in 1895. It was led by Gina Krog, who was also the dominant figure in the moderate feminist movement. Krog believed in a property-qualified franchise. When universal manhood suffrage was introduced in 1898, she complained that 'the struggle for our national cause has forwarded the extension of suffrage to men and has distanced the claims of women'. Nevertheless, Krog's continued adherence to the principle of limited suffrage in a situation where men possessed universal suffrage indicated how determined the bulk of the suffragists were to stick to the tactic of gradualism. It also showed that in Norway the moderates kept an unusually firm grip on the suffrage movement. In 1894 the Association secured 12,000 signatures for a petition on female suffrage, and in 1901 it successfully persuaded the Storting to write in women's suffrage to a municipal suffrage bill. It was significant that according to the provisions of this Act, while men needed no qualification save age and residence, women had to own, or be married to a man who owned, 300 kroner in property in the country, or 400 kroner in the town. Clearly, while the political opinions of the women of the urban and rural lower classes were still such an unknown quantity, the middle-class political parties that dominated the Storting only felt safe in enfranchising the women of their own social group. This of course was what Krog and her supporters were counting on. Meanwhile, tension with Sweden grew as the swelling wave of nationalist sentiment failed to achieve independence for Norway from the Swedish Crown on a negotiated basis. The unilateral declaration of independence which eventually came in 1905 was to bring Norwegian women the vote within a few years. Even before then, the extension of the municipal suffrage suggested that things were moving in the direction of the enfranchisement at least of the women of the propertied classes.

The growth of feminism in Norway, and the relative rapidity with which it radicalised, can therefore be balanced by the peculiarly 'moderate' nature of the female suffrage movement. Whether or not to demand the vote for *all* women was a burning issue in a number of feminist movements; in Germany and Holland, indeed, it split the movement apart. It does not seem to have been an issue in Norway. The foundation of the first permanent women's suffrage organisation, after all, came only a decade or so after the formation of the feminist movement itself; the gap between these two events was usually much wider — nearly thirty years in Germany, over twenty years in Britain, twenty-nine years in Sweden, forty in Russia. This suggests that the transition to radicalism in Norway, although real, was only partial. Events, however, were to vindicate its gradualist tactics from a feminist point of view, for once a property qualified female suffrage had been secured, universal female suffrage was not long in following it. This gradualism was a characteristic of Norwegian politics, in which social antagonisms had long been muted, as a result of the almost complete absence of a landed aristocracy and the very early involvement of popular movements in political affairs. It was less inevitable elsewhere, although many moderate feminists saw in the Norwegian case a demonstration of their argument that the right way to reach the feminists' goal was step by step, not (as radicals argued) all in one go.[42]

A major role in the rise of feminism was often played, as the Norwegian case shows, by the growth of nationalist movements. Perhaps the best illustration of this close connection between nationalism and feminism is to be found in the case of Finland. Finland had formed part of Sweden for most of its history. It derived many of its institutions from Sweden, including the system of government, which consisted of a Diet, elected by a restricted franchise, and a Senate, based on the example of the Swedish Council of State. Some 12 per cent of the population were Swedish-speaking, and they predominated in the upper classes. Swedish was the official language for legal, governmental and business purposes. In 1809, however, Finland came under Russian rule. Finland was not incorporated into the Russian Empire but remained a separate Grand Duchy and retained its institutions. In the same way that parts of the Habsburg Empire were united principally by the fact that they shared the same monarch, so Finland and Russia were only joined in so far as the Tsar of Russia was also Grand Duke of Finland. Though the Finns were ultimately controlled by a Governor-General appointed by the Tsar, there was also a State Secretariat for Finland in St Petersburg headed by a Finn with the rank of Minister. This autonomy was important for the Finns in pressing their claims against the dominant Swedish-speaking minority. As Finnish nationalism became more vocal, it secured a series of concessions from the Russians, culminating in the achievement of complete official equality for the Finnish language with the Swedish in the 1880s. Under Tsars Alexander II and Alexander III, the Finnish Diet met regularly, and the Finns looked to the Russian bureaucracy for help in their struggle for equality of their language with the Swedish. This situation, in which a colonial administration used internal divisions to attack the existing elites, was a familiar feature of imperial rule; but it also invariably sowed the seeds of its own ruin, as the upwardly mobile groups backed by the colonisers moved on from demanding equality with the old élite to seeking independence from the imperial power.

Nationalism in the nineteenth century was primarily linguistic. The characteristic progress of a nationalist movement — exemplified in the struggle of the Finns for official recognition of their language — could be charted through literary revival to educational and institutional equality. It generally began with the renewal of the publication of poetry and literature in the vernacular and the rediscovery of native folk and literary traditions, then proceeded towards organised pressure for the recognition and teaching of the native language and literature in the schools. Women − that is, the educated women of the new indigenous middle classes which almost invariably formed the social basis for national movements − played a role at every stage, but above all they were important at the point where nationalist activity moved from literary revival to educational reform, not least because of the formal and informal role they played in the education of the young. Finland was a classic instance of the involvement of women in a nationalist movement. Describing the awakening of Finnish nationalism in the 1840s and the growing political pressure for the equality of the Finnish language in the 1860s and 1870s, Baroness Alexandra Gripenberg (1859-1913), a leader of the Finnish Women's Association (*Finsk Kvinno-förening*), gave an account of the association of feminism with liberal nationalism which could well serve as a model description of the experience of a large number of European countries in the nineteenth century, from Hungary to Serbia, Iceland to Bohemia.

> The leading men appealed to the mothers, through whom the idea was to go to the coming generation by the education of the children in their native tongue . . . Women participated in the work for the improvement of the language and the starting of schools and newspapers. Women managed large sales of their work and gave the money to the national party . . . The homes of the more prominent women became headquarters for many of the leaders, and women learned through their discussions the value and importance of organised work and associated powers. This happened at the same time that our country was reached by the echoes of the great movement for the enfranchisement of women which was going on in England and Sweden in the sixties. Thus it is natural that the nationality work became an important means of development for the women of Finland . . . The language movement became also an indirect means of awakening the women to a sense of their rights and responsibilities.

The crucial transition from nationalism to feminism occurred in Finland in the early 1880s. The date was significant: it was precisely at that moment that the primary objective of the nationalist movement, linguistic equality, was gained. In 1863 a decree announcing a twenty-year programme for the achievement of full equality between Swedish and Finnish in public affairs was promulgated. In May 1884, shortly after the completion of this programme, the Finnish Women's Association was founded.

The immediate origin of the Association lay, as we saw in Chapter 1, in a study group organised in Helsinki around the reading of John Stuart Mill's *The Subjection of Women*. The publication of this book, together with the works of Fredrika Bremer, constituted in fact what Gripenberg meant by the suffrage movement of the 1860s. The programme of the Finnish Women's Association, drawn up under the guidance of its leader Elizabeth Löfgren, bore the stamp of Mill's ideas. It demanded the same right for women as for men to higher and professional education, to university matriculation and examination, to hold municipal office and to gain political suffrage. The legal age for marriage was to be raised from fifteen to a higher age, and married as well as unmarried women were to attain majority at the age of twenty-one and to hold property in their own right. Unfaithfulness, ill-treatment or extreme drunkenness were to constitute legal grounds for divorce. Women were to receive equal pay for equal work. Finally, the programme demanded 'the same moral restrictions in law and custom for men as those which now prevail for women'. The Association campaigned in the press and by petition for the abolition of state-regulated prostitution, for admittance to university examinations and for property and majority rights for married women. The moral, political and economic content of its programme revealed a clear bias towards middle-class liberalism. Less immediately apparent, however, was the focus of its activities, which continued to concentrate on the areas in which women were involved as a part of the Finnish nationalist movement. As Gripenberg remarked in 1894, 'Where freedom is the foundation for the development of the people, there the work for the enfranchisement of women usually is concentrated upon suffrage work. But in countries which do not enjoy political liberty, and where even men's suffrage is limited, one must concentrate the work upon questions concerning higher education, professional training, and general enlightenment for women.'

The economic and social background to the emergence of Finnish feminism reveals clearly the nature of some of the problems with which the leading activists had to contend. Finland was a backward agricultural country where as late as the 1860s a series of epidemics and harvest failures had brought an absolute drop in the Finnish population. This shock sparked off a diversification of agriculture and a determined effort at economic growth. Between 1871 and 1914 Finland increased in population from 1.8 million to 3.2 million, the increase occurring above all in the 1890s. But this growth was not accompanied by large-scale industrialisation. Even in 1910, 66 per cent of the population was dependent on agriculture, and only 12 per cent on industry and 5 per cent on commerce and transportation. Only 15 per cent of all Finns lived in towns in 1910 (compared to 8 per cent in 1880). The population increase occurred largely in agriculture. Labour was cheap for both industry and agriculture, productivity was low and technological innovation limited. The most rapidly growing sector of Finnish trade was timber production, which dominated Finnish exports by the turn of the century. The Finnish nationalist movement was therefore an alliance of the emergent urban bourgeoisie with the rich timber producers and the landowning, labour-employing peasantry. Politicisation was carried into the countryside, for if it was to broaden its base in a country so overwhelmingly agrarian in structure, the movement had to gain the support of the rural bourgeoisie. It was helped by unusually high levels of education for a society so economically backward; by 1900, it was estimated that nearly all people over the age of fifteen could both read and write. With this background, the Finnish Women's Association took the unusual step of expanding its activities into rural areas. By 1894, three out of its six branches were reading and lecture groups for peasant women, and the Association's leader waxed lyrical over the growing ability of the female peasantry to think for itself. The involvement of the peasantry was almost unique among contemporary feminist movements; it was part of the realignment of classes that was to result in the bitter civil war of 1918.

The transition to radical feminism in Finland took place in the 1890s, although votes for women was not a major political issue at any time until 1904. The dominant political question even for the more radical feminists was that of national self-determination. Women had possessed the communal vote since 1863 in rural areas and since 1872 in towns, and in 1897 a bill giving women eligibility in communal elections was passed by the Diet but rejected by the Russian government. This of course cemented the nationalist and feminist causes even more firmly together. The feminist movement in Finland did support votes for women in 1884, the year of its foundation, but this was largely due to force of circumstances; the question of female suffrage on a taxpaying qualification was being debated in the Diet in that year, and the feminists felt obliged to send in a petition. After this, the main focus of the feminists' attention was on moral reform and philanthropy, and their political activities centred on the nationalist movement. In 1892 a new group, the Union of Women's Societies (*Kvinnosaksför-bunds Unionen*) emerged, concentrating its attention on the suffrage. It was led by the teacher Lucina Hagman (1853-1946), who had studied in Sweden, Germany and Switzerland. At about the same time, the Swedish-speaking Finns also formed a separate women's society to defend the interests of their own linguistic and racial group. These new developments were part of a general reorientation of Finnish nationalism. Its original aim of attaining equality with the Swedish-speaking elite in Finland had been largely achieved by the 1890s. Now it began the attempt to gain freedom from the Russians. The moderate feminists, led by Baroness Alexandra Gripenberg, were identified with the Old Finns, who were prepared to compromise with the Russians. Hagman and the radicals shared the more assertive nationalism of the Young Finns, a more hard-line party of liberal Finnish nationalists who were rapidly gaining strength in the 1890s. Before the conflicts inherent in this situation, and in the development of a Finnish-Swedish women's society, could develop, all political groups in Finland were united by a new and increasingly severe policy of repression and russification launched by the Russian government towards the end of the century. This policy was, ironically, to transform the prospects for female suffrage, until then generally neglected in favour of nationalist issues, within a very short space of time.[43]

Nationalism also played a role in the development of the feminist movement in the smallest of the Nordic countries, Iceland, which came under the Danish Crown until 1944. The Icelandic Women's Association (*Kvenfélag Islands*) was founded in 1894 to gather women's support for the foundation of an Icelandic University. It then went on to press for equal rights for women in economic and educational matters, collecting 2,200 signatures for a general petition in 1895 — a considerable number considering that the total population was less than 50,000. A Married Women's Property Act was passed in 1899 and girls were admitted to the newly founded High School in 1905. Iceland was a very old-established country, but at the end of the 1890s it was just beginning to change from a land of peasant farmers and fishermen into a more modern society. The emergence of feminism coincided with the modernisation of the fishing industry, the ousting of Norwegians from their dominant position in Icelandic trade, and the formation of Reykjavík as a major urban centre. It was characteristic of minor nationalisms such as this that demands tended to centre on the establishment of native educational institutions. By playing their full part in supporting these demands, women gained the right to benefit from them. Radicalisation of the feminist movement took place after the creation of moral reform (temperance) societies in which women played a leading part. The Icelandic Women's Rights Association (*Kvenréttindafélag Islands*) was founded in 1907 by Bríet Bjarnhédinsdóttir (1856-1940), editor of a women's magazine, who had attended an international women's suffrage congress the previous year. She toured the country and by 1908 had founded five branches with a total of four hundred members. The Association was fortunate in being able to present women's rights as a nationalist issue, not only for reasons similar to those operative in the Finnish case, but also because various women's rights bills (including enfranchisement of widows and spinsters for municipal elections in 1882, and eligibility in these elections in 1888) had been held up by the Danish King's veto until 1902. In the 1900s the nationalists pressed for manhood suffrage, and in the prevailing excitement the feminists gathered no less than 12,000 signatures out of a total population of less than 50,000 people for a female suffrage petition. Full equality for all women in municipal suffrage became law in 1908, but although the Icelandic Parliament, the Althing, voted as part of a general constitutional reform to enfranchise women for all elections in 1913, a crisis in relations with Denmark held up progress until the war. Once again, women's rights and national self-determination became identified with one another through the opposition of the ruling foreign power.[44]

Not only in Iceland, but also in all of the five Nordic countries, in Sweden, Denmark, Norway and Finland as well, feminism was remarkably well-developed and well-supported by the turn of the century. The complexities, the twists and turns of the course taken in the growth of some of these movements — notably, perhaps, those of Denmark and Norway — illustrate the way in which some feminist movements deviated in the details, though not in the fundamentals, of their development from the basic model outlined in Chapter 1 of this book. In all five of these cases, there is a pattern of moderate or economic feminism leading through moral reform to the demand for the suffrage. In addition to this, however, three important influences on the growth and development of feminist movements can be observed in the case of the Nordic countries. The first, which we have already seen operating in the cases of Britain and the United States, is perhaps the most obvious — the widening of the political nation under pressure from liberal reform movements to include new groups of the population. Wherever manhood franchise was extended, whether it was to American blacks, British artisans or Norwegian peasants, the idea of its further extension to women, and the conviction that this was not only possible but desirable, began to take a hold. This kind of influence was operative at the moderate beginnings of feminism, in stimulating demands for equality of an essentially economic and educational nature, just as much as it was later on in the transition to radicalism. It follows from this that there was a second, retarding influence on feminist movements, in the shape of entrenched aristocratic or conservative ruling élites (as in Sweden) or autocratic, non-elected governments (as in Finland) – in practice, of course, the two tended to go together, as indeed they did in a mild way in Sweden. We shall encounter both these major foci of resistance to feminism in other countries later in this chapter. Resistance to *them* was probably strongest where the resisters belonged to a different nationality from the entrenched élites or authoritarian governments.

This third influence on the growth of female emancipation movements, nationalism, could as we have already seen be a major driving force behind feminism itself, not least because of the role played by women in national revivals. This was the case in Norway, Iceland and Finland, but it was even more strikingly so in the area to which we now turn, the Habsburg Monarchy.

The Habsburg Monarchy

The feminist movements which have been the object of our attention so far were all to a greater or lesser degree successful in attaining their objectives. However strong the obstacles to women's rights and female suffrage were in countries such as Great Britain or Sweden, they were certainly not strong enough to prevent feminism from making a successful progress from moderate to radical goals and from gaining a very large measure of support in the legislature for their demands. In America, Australasia, Britain and the Nordic lands, Protestant culture, political moderation, the existence of a wide range of guaranteed civil rights, including freedom of assembly and association and liberty of speech, the growing power of middle-class liberalism and the decisive role played in the political system by legislative assemblies – though this came relatively late in Sweden and Denmark – all these factors favoured the smooth development of large and active female emancipation movements. In the countries to which we now turn, however, many, and in some cases most of these conditions were absent; and though to a limited degree economic and social changes were taking

place similar to those which lay behind the emergence of feminism elsewhere, the movements to which these developments gave rise ran up
against far greater difficulties than their counterparts in Britain, America,
Australasia and the Nordic lands ever had to face.[45]

The first of these countries in which feminism failed to develop
smoothly or to secure the gradual acceptance of its aims, was the
Habsburg Monarchy, a large and heterogeneous conglomeration of
nationalities and kingdoms in the south-eastern part of Central Europe,
ruled by the Habsburg Emperor Franz Josef. The Empire was united by
no principle save the dynastic one. It included Bohemia (roughly
speaking, present-day Czechoslovakia), Hungary and parts of what are
now Poland and Yugoslavia. The various constitutent parts had their
own legislatures, but these had very limited powers, even in Hungary,
which had its own government and had enjoyed a considerable amount
of autonomy since 1867. The ruling bureaucracy and army were based
in Vienna and were dominated by German speakers. Until Prussia
defeated the Habsburg Empire in the war of 1866 and united Germany
under its own leadership, Habsburg Austria, where feminism emerged
earliest in the Habsburg Monarchy, had considered itself part of
Germany. After 1870, however, it had no real say in German affairs.
There was no genuine middle class in Vienna, for the city gained its size
and prominence largely through its status as the administrative centre
of the Empire, so that the 'middle classes' were in reality mostly civil
servants. Nor was there after 1870 any real nationalist movement in
Austria, since the Germans identified with the supranational interests of
the Habsburgs, who were their chief employers and maintained them in
a superior status to that of the other nationalities of the Empire. A
further obstacle in the way of the emergence of organised feminism was
the fact that German-speaking Austria was overwhelmingly Catholic in
religion. Finally, the Austrian constitution after the failure of the 1848
revolution was an authoritarian one, in which the powers of the legislative assembly were very limited indeed.

In circumstances such as these, it is surprising that any feminist
movement emerged in Austria at all. Nevertheless, on 13 November
1866 there appeared the Vienna Women's Employment Association
(*Wiener Frauenerwerbverein*). The date was significant: in November
1866 Austria was in the midst of a national political and economic crisis
following her crushing defeat in the Six Weeks' War with Prussia. Despite its economic aims, therefore, the Association owed its foundation
to circumstances that were essentially political. The years immediately
after the war of 1866 were years of uncertainty in Austria, in which the

liberals saw their chance. The ferment of liberal activity was reflected in the foundation of societies such as the Women's Employment Association. Its parent body was the Association for Economic Progress (*Verein für volkswirtschaftlichen Fortschritt*), run by liberal men. Initially, the Women's Employment Association campaigned for the admission of women to jobs in the postal and telegraph service, and founded a commerce school. In 1870, at the Association's General Assembly, Marianne Hainisch (1839-1936), who later became the leading figure in the Austrian feminist movement, urged members to press for the admission of girls to grammar schools — a very modest and typically moderate feminist proposal. But the Association rejected this suggestion and merely asked for a *Höhere Mädchenschule*, in which the education would fit girls not for the professions (as Hainisch wanted) but for motherhood. This cautious approach was characteristic of moderate feminists in authoritarian states, where too radical a programme might result in their being closed down by the police.

In the 1870s and 1880s branches of the Association were formed by German women in Prague and also in Brünn. But — as the official history of the movement remarks — 'until the end of the 1880s the Austrian and in particular the Vienna women's organisations confined themselves to questions of employment, education and welfare'. In 1869, women had been admitted to teaching posts in primary schools, and in 1870 an Association of Women Teachers and Educators was founded. In 1872 women were admitted to the post and telegraph service. They formed a union in 1876. The 1870s, therefore, saw the gradual realisation of the aims of the moderate feminists, though these aims, as we have seen, were extremely modest. The most remarkable absentee from the Austrian feminists' list of demands was the reform of the Civil Law, the *Allgemeines Bürgerliches Gesetzbuch* of 1811, according to which wives were obliged to obey their husband's directions for managing the household and their children. The 1811 Code does not seem to have been entirely illiberal, for it owed some at least of its provisions to the Enlightenment of the eighteenth century. Although women could not be represented in court or engage in trade without their husband's permission, they were granted considerable legal powers over their own property and its usufruct, and were legal persons entitled to enter into contracts and take up any job (save trade) without asking anyone's permission. In practice, of course, these rights were seldom claimed. Nevertheless, the position of Austrian women in Civil Law, according to which the husband had the duty to give financial support to his wife but not vice versa, was sufficient to convince the feminists that it was unnecessary to campaign against its provisions. This was in contrast to the situation in Germany, where Enlightenment law codes prevailed in many areas until the end of the nineteenth century, and the Civil Code of 1896 that replaced them actually brought about a worsening of women's position in a number of respects. It was for these reasons that feminism in Austria was, more than its counterparts elsewhere, a movement that aimed initially to improve the lot of the *unmarried* middle-class woman.

The problems that faced the Austrian feminists were formidable. The Parliament, the Reichsrat, not only had no real power but was also unable to function properly for long periods due to violent quarrels between the different nationalities represented in it (quarrels that usually expressed themselves in ruthless filibustering and obstruction of business). Ministers were appointed by the Emperor and were not responsible to the legislature. It was difficult therefore for the feminists to achieve their goals by the usual method, familiar in other countries, of allying themselves with parliamentary parties and putting pressure on the government through the legislature. More seriously still, women in Austria were banned from joining or forming political associations by a law of 1867. All attempts by the feminists to have this law repealed came to nothing, so no female suffrage society was ever founded. The law also acted as a deterrent to feminists from touching upon any matters that might be deemed 'political' and so lead to the dissolution of their organisations. It was thus surprising that a limited measure of radicalisation actually did take place within Austrian feminism. Here however the situation was even more unusual. The existing franchise in Austria was exceptional in giving a number of important rights to limited groups of women. In the reaction following the 1848 revolution, property franchises had been established in many parts of the Empire, and these explicitly included women. As in the German Empire, where a similar situation existed, this only enfranchised a small number of women, since many women lost their property on marriage. But while in Germany only some two thousand women were enfranchised in this way, in the Habsburg Empire the numbers were considerably larger. The geographical spread of this form of enfranchisement was much wider. Austrian women had more opportunities than their German sisters to control their own property after marriage, and in some areas women in the professions, including teachers, were also enfranchised, whether or not they held property. Neither in Austria nor in Bohemia could women stand for election, and their votes had to be cast by a male proxy. Still, these rights existed on a large enough scale to be meaningful to the middle-class women of the feminist movement. In the late nineteenth and early twentieth centuries they came increasingly under threat, for the Habsburg régime was gradually being forced in this period to remove property franchises by the growing pressure of Liberals and Social Democrats whose strength was increasing as Vienna industrialised. As the government removed the property qualifications stage by stage in the 1890s and 1900s, they also removed the women's vote. Paradoxically, therefore, the radicalisation of Austrian feminism largely consisted in the rallying of feminists to oppose this reduction in their existing voting rights, rather than (as in, say, Denmark or Norway) in the conscious advance of the feminist movement to demand new and wider forms of legal and political equality.

The first step in this process took place in 1890, when the government removed the right of propertied women to vote in local elections in Vienna. The schoolteacher Auguste Fickert (1855-1910) held a meeting on 3 October 1890 to protest. Fickert's meeting marked the beginning of what the official history of Austrian feminism terms the 'ideological phase' of the feminist movement. In common with radical feminists elsewhere, Fickert also attempted to organise working-class women. Her efforts were frustrated by the Social Democrats, but she went on nevertheless to found the General Austrian Women's Association (*Allgemeiner österreichischer Frauenverein*) in April 1893. This organisation incorporated many of the usual radical feminist aims, including even the vote; it was saved from police repression because of the wide-ranging nature of its programme, in which 'non-political' points predominated. As far as the suffrage was concerned, its aims were restricted to preserving existing rights. Predictably, therefore, they failed to generate much support, though they were backed by the small German Liberal Party. It was not until the Social Democrats managed to persuade the government, frightened by the prospect of the 1905 Revolution spreading from Russia to the Habsburg lands, to grant universal manhood suffrage in 1906-7, that the idea of female suffrage gained any real measure of support, even within the feminist movement. The reform of 1906-7 removed the last significant municipal female voting rights, and the feminists now felt able to broaden their demands. They petitioned for the repeal of the law banning them from forming political associations and demanded universal suffrage for all women. Although the supporters of manhood suffrage were not prepared to risk losing their bill by including women as well, they did support the feminists after universal suffrage for men had safely become law. Even the moderate feminists gave at least passive support to these demands.

But the chaos that reigned in the legislature after 1907, and the continued lack of ministerial responsibility and parliamentary government,
prevented matters from going any further until the First World War.[46]

The defensive struggle against the loss of women's voting rights took
on its most dramatic form in Bohemia, where propertied and professional women had had equal direct active and passive voting rights for
the Landtag since 1861, and an equal proxy vote for municipal elections. The Czech feminists were much better placed than their Austrian
counterparts to resist the removal of these rights. The Social Democrats
were far less powerful in Prague than in Vienna. In 1906 the Austrian
Socialists opposed female suffrage in Austria for fear of jeopardising
the manhood suffrage bill. The liberals were a weak force in Austrian
politics; indeed they had almost disappeared in 1897, as the Catholic
and anti-semitic right and the Social Democratic left pulled support
away from them at both political extremes. In Prague, the feminists
could link their cause to that of the liberal nationalists who dominated
Bohemian politics. The social structure of Bohemia, with its large-scale
heavy industry, powerful Czech middle class and non-existent native
aristocracy, contrasted sharply with that of Austria, with the bourgeoisie of Vienna, created by the Imperial administration, permeated by
quasi-feudal social values and owing its allegiance not to German
nationalism but to the supranational Empire, the small-scale craft
industry and peasant agriculture in the hinterland, and the powerful
aristocracy dominating the court and the government. In Bohemia,
the Czechs, who increasingly controlled the professions, the administration and the skilled working class, and took a growing part in the
ownership and management of heavy industry, were fighting a bitter
struggle against Vienna and the old-established German class of big
landowners, bankers and industrialists. An important part of Czech
nationalism was the existence of a large and influential minority of
Czechs adhering to Protestantism, which, as we have seen, was favourable to the development of feminism. Austria, by contrast, was almost
entirely Catholic in religion.

The first record we have of Czech feminism is of the Women's
Club of Prague (1901) and the Committee for Women's Suffrage (1905), both founded by F. Plamnikova. The strong nationalist orientation of these organisations was clear from the very
beginning. 'The Women of Bohemia', they complained, 'who
have some rights in their own kingdom, are classed by the Austrian Government with criminals and other undesirable citizens.'
In 1912 the Czech suffragists refused to send delegates to a

conference of Austrian, German and Slovene feminists in Vienna because (according to the Austrians) 'they rejected the use of the German language for the proceedings, against international convention'. In 1909, indeed, they even went so far as to demand that Czech be made the fourth official language of the International Woman Suffrage Alliance, alongside English, French and German – a proposal which (not surprisingly) was defeated by a large majority. In taking this extreme line, they were in fact doing no more than the Czech nationalists in general, who regularly obstructed and filibustered the Imperial Austrian Diet in an attempt to get their own way against the other constituent national groups.

In keeping with its policy in other parts of the Empire, the Habsburg Government made strong efforts in these years to reform the Bohemian Diet. Extension of manhood franchise entailed here as well as in Vienna the abolition of female property-qualified voting. The Czech nationalist Liberals and Independents presented counter-proposals to the Diet demanding equal and universal suffrage rights for both sexes. Vienna replied with the demand that women must be disfranchised. The Czech feminists protested that this was an unwarrantable intrusion in Bohemian affairs. They called a mass meeting attended by Czech nationalist leaders and 'directed attention to their achievement along the lines of culture, education and politics, to the schools they had established and the steps they had taken to fit themselves for intelligent voters'. The meeting petitioned the Bohemian Diet, while the Women's Club collected signatures for a general female suffrage petition. By framing its objectives in a purely nationalist spirit (its programme demanded a just representation for Czech nationality, freedom of the nation as well as for the individual, economic improvement for Bohemia, and other national concessions, and made little mention of feminist aims), the Women's Suffrage Committee sought to secure full backing from the nationalists. The suffragists managed to get even the Agrarian Party to support them – by 1910 it had 40,000 women in a total membership of 100,000. Most remarkable of all, they persuaded the parties to put up women candidates in by-elections to the Bohemian Diet. However, in 1911 they complained that 'the selfishness of men always finds suitable reasons for slipping out of promises and programmes, and no woman has yet been elected'. Women candidates were simply being put forward for hopeless seats.

In 1912 matters came to a head with a public declaration by the Habsburg Government of its intention to remove women's active and passive suffrage in Bohemia. This was of course only one element in a struggle which was creating an almost total paralysis of the Czech Diet at this time. Nevertheless, the feminists ensured that it was not neglected. They issued a 'Women's Appeal to the Bohemian Nation' which was published in all newspapers. Although the rights concerned were property-qualified, the feminists attempted to broaden their appeal by insisting that their main aim was the vote for all women; the immediate issue simply took priority at the time. A subcommittee of the Permanent National Committee in Bohemia reported to the Diet on 26 March 1912 on the matter. The three large landowners and the three German representatives on the Committee voted against female suffrage. The three Bohemian representatives presented a minority report in favour. The balance of forces on the Committee presented a neat illustration of the division of opinion over votes for women in Bohemia. With the backing of the liberal nationalists, the feminist movement put up a candidate for a by-election to the Bohemian Diet; remarkably, the woman was elected. But the Habsburg-appointed governor of Bohemia refused to ratify the election; and the paralysis of the Diet, which was eventually dissolved altogether in 1913, ensured that in practical political terms the election was in any case wholly without significance. In Bohemia, as in Austria, the impotence of legislatures confronted with arbitrary governments doomed the feminist challenge to failure.[47]

In Hungary, conditions were if anything even more difficult. The feminists' basic problem lay in the social and political character of Hungarian nationalism, the political force that would logically be their main ally. Hungary almost entirely lacked a genuine native middle class. What little finance and industry there was, was dominated by Jews and Germans. They found themselves in sharp conflict with the numerically very strong lesser aristocracy and gentry, who were incurably feudal and conservative in outlook. Nevertheless, it was this feudal nobility and gentry who provided the main support for Magyar nationalism in Hungary. Up to 1867, their nationalism had been that of the underdog, the main social conflict in Hungary between the native lesser nobility, whose religion was Calvinist, represented by the Liberal Party, and the great Catholic estate-owning aristocracy, who owed their allegiance to the Habsburg Court. After the settlement of 1867, which gave the lesser Magyar nobles control of Hungary, they became a conservative force, not least because they now represented, like the Germans in Austria and Bohemia, a dominant national group, controlling substantial minorities of other nationalities (Romanians, Serbs, Croats, Germans, Slovaks, Poles, Ruthenes and others). The main problem of the Magyars after 1867 was therefore to prevent the disruption of their own kingdom by dissident nationalists. Their will to resist reform was strengthened by the fact that any extension of the manhood suffrage was bound to enfranchise substantial numbers of non-Magyars (the electorate in Hungary numbered one million out of a total population of about seventeen million, and most of the electors were Magyars). The extension of the Hungarian franchise was often used as a threat by the Vienna government to bring the Magyars to heel, though it was never seriously put into effect.

All this made things extremely difficult for the feminists in Hungary. The nationalists were prepared to countenance a moderate form of feminism. Women had been active in the nationalist movement since 1790 and in fact the achievement of Hungarian self-government in 1867 had led immediately to the creation of a moderate feminist movement 'for the improvement of the education of girls'. In 1895 the moderates had gained their major objective, the opening of the universities. Women were already being admitted to the professions at that time. These reforms provided the basis for the emergence of a radical wing of Hungarian feminism. In 1904 the moderates founded a National Council of Women uniting 52 societies (104 by 1913). It contained a strong moral reform element, and campaigned against alcohol, pornography, duelling and 'white slavery'. It educated domestic servants, petitioned for the weekend closing of brandy shops, and established temperance hostels in slum areas. But it continued to be dominated by the nationalist gentry and aristocracy. Its first President was Countess Batthyány, its second, who led it through the years 1910-40, during most of which the reactionary authoritarian régime of Admiral Horthy was in power, was Countess Apponyi. Its report to the 1909 International Council of Women was presented by Countess Andrássy. These women were married to leading politicians in the more conservative wing of the nationalist movement. Because of their political connections, and because of the general complications of the suffrage question in Hungary, they were slow to accept the idea of votes for women. Indeed, in 1909 Countess Andrássy went out of her way to emphasise that there was no interest at all among Hungarian women for female suffrage. Some nationalists supported a limited female suffrage on the grounds that it would increase the Magyar vote, since most propertied women were Magyars, and most non-propertied women were not. In 1912, for example, the Prime Minister, László Lukács, after receiving various feminist deputations (including one for a limited female franchise from the National Council of Women, clear evidence of its Magyar nationalist orientation), announced his intention of introducing a bill to this effect. This set the issue alight; and the controversy frightened Lukács into withdrawing his proposal in favour of other methods of shoring up the Magyar vote. These considerations effectively prevented any endorsement of radical feminism by the Magyar noblewomen.

The only real supporters of full female suffrage in the wider Hungarian political world were the Jewish liberal Democratic Party, led by V. Vászonyi, who presented a feminist petition for women's suffrage to the Hungarian Diet in 1913, and the Romanian nationalists, who brought in a bill for universal adult suffrage in the same year (which would of course benefit them as a national minority). In addition, 150 deputies formed a parliamentary women's suffrage league in 1908; but these also, like the majority of feminists, were aristocratic nationalists who saw in a limited female suffrage a means of perpetuating Magyar domination. As in Austria, so in Hungary, the Social Democrats were opposed to women's suffrage. Their opposition in this case however went further than the usual argument that it would endanger the prospects of enfranchising the men they represented. In Hungary they opposed votes for women with a quite extraordinary vehemence. In part this was because it was too obviously an instrument of aristocratic hegemony, or would be if implemented in the only likely form, a restricted property franchise. In part it reflected a growing extremism and polarisation in Hungary which was to culminate in the Soviet Republic and White Terror of 1919, an extremism which also to some extent affected the suffragists. In part it reflected the bitterness with which the Social Democrats' struggle for the vote was waged; vast and often violent demonstrations were generally countered with extreme police brutality. In 1912, at the height of the manhood suffrage struggle, the Social Democrats called a General Strike and held mass demonstrations in front of the Diet; the police opened fire, killing six and wounding 182. Female suffrage appeared a mere reactionary bourgeois deviation in the light of such struggles. The two political forces which most favoured female suffrage in the rest of Europe led the opposition to it in Hungary. The liberals, led by Gyula Justh, and the Social Democrats, combined to oppose the female suffragists in a desperate attempt to secure the enfranchisement of the male urban masses. The need to appease the Social Democrats led the moderate nationalists in turn to drop their discussion of a limited female suffrage based on property.

When radical feminism emerged in Hungary, it was among Jews, not Magyars. The Union for Women's Rights, founded in 1904 in connection with the formation of the International Woman Suffrage Alliance, was effectively led by Rosika Schwimmer (1877-1948), a close associate of the radical feminists Anita Augspurg and Lida Gustava Heymann in Germany. It mounted a campaign very similar to that of its German counterpart, with pamphlets, meetings and questionings of candidates at elections. Deputies were bombarded with telegrams; political meetings were faced with suffragist speeches from the floor; Social Democratic parades and demonstrations were leafletted; a deputation of forty women addressed the Chamber of Deputies in a prearranged public session. A massive meeting was held on 16 September 1912, attended by an estimated 10,000 people. Sixty branches of the feminist movement were represented. These probably included some local groups belonging to the aristocratic-nationalist wing of the feminist movement. The suffragist leaders and most radical feminists, including Schwimmer, were associated with the tiny Jewish bourgeois liberal Democratic Party. Their campaign reached its height in the disturbances of 1912, immediately after Lukács had withdrawn his promise to include a property franchise for women in his electoral reform bill. Schwimmer arranged a demonstration with placards outside the Diet and went into the public gallery with a group of her colleagues; the police, however, removed the leaflets they had concealed in their muffs. In the subsequent campaign, both Justh's party and the Social Democrats excluded women from their meetings, sometimes by force, and sent hecklers and even organised groups of toughs to disrupt suffragist meetings. The suffragists strengthened their position by inviting the International Woman Suffrage Alliance to hold its Congress in Budapest in 1913; the authorities and the politicians were forced to modify their hostility at least for the duration of the Congress in order not to make too unfavourable an impression on international opinion. But the conservative orientation of Magyar nationalism, the complexities of Hungarian politics and – as in Austria and Bohemia – the limited powers of the legislature and the police restrictions on civil liberties, combined to ensure that they had made little progress by the time that the war broke out in 1914.[48]

The Hungarian case suggests that when we begin to look at the development of feminism in countries where social structures were more heavily influenced by feudalism, and political systems less inclined to constitutionalism, than in Britain, America, Australasia or the Nordic lands, the variations in the development of feminism, in terms of the model outlined at the beginning of this book, appear to be considerably greater than elsewhere. Certainly, the same influences are there. Economic development was turning Vienna, Prague and Budapest into industrial cities in the late nineteenth and early twentieth centuries. A middle class was emerging. Liberal and nationalist ideologies were becoming more widespread. In Prague and Budapest at least, there were sizeable Protestant sectors of the population. But these influences were overlaid by two features of the Habsburg system which combined to complicate and distort the development of feminism: racial and national conflicts on the one hand, and governmental authoritarianism on the other. The result was that feminism in all three major industrialising areas of the Empire was exceptional in some way. In Austria, although the feminist movement clearly progressed in the early 1890s from a purely moderate to a more radical phase, the emergence of a fully radicalised movement was made impossible by the laws banning women from taking part in politics. In Hungary, radical feminism did develop in a vigorous and thoroughly radical way, but it was quite separate from mainstream moderate feminism, neither developing out of it nor having much effect on it. Magyar nationalism, the desire to preserve things as they were in order not to be swamped by hostile 'subject peoples' such as the Romanians, prevented Hungarian feminists from adopting a radical programme; that was left to the Jews who provided Budapest with its middle classes. Nowhere else did the moderate-radical split in feminism follow racial lines as in Hungary. The Bohemian feminist movement was the most peculiar of them all. Here the usual distinction between moderate and radical seems to have been absent altogether. The feminist movement developed late. It was fanatically nationalist, even to the point of putting nationalist aims well above feminist ones on its list of demands. Its aims were moderate, even conservative, for though it favoured an extension of the suffrage and other rights in principle, in practice it devoted itself to fighting to preserve a limited property franchise from being removed by the Austrian authorities. In order to do this it adopted radical tactics, including putting up a candidate in an election. And it secured multi-party backing strong enough to ensure that its candidate actually won − an event unique in Europe at the time, though women were already being elected on single party tickets in Finland. Despite this support, it failed to secure the ratification of its candidate's election. It was exceptional in almost every respect. Like its Hungarian counterpart, it had to strike a bargain with nationalists which in some ways severely limited its freedom of action, though in others it benefited greatly. In the end, all three feminist movements came up against the awkward fact of Habsburg authoritarianism. They lacked a sovereign or responsible legislature to put their demands into effect. As we shall see in the case of the German Empire, this constitutional obstacle could have an extremely damaging effect on feminism.

The German Empire

The power of an authoritarian political system to stunt the growth of reform movements such as feminism is nowhere more clearly illustrated than in the case of Germany. In many ways, Germany seemed in the late nineteenth century to possess a good many of the preconditions necessary for the growth of a strong feminist movement. Although there was a strong Catholic minority, the dominant religious culture of the country was Protestant. Educational standards were generally high. There was a large and well-established middle class, far more advanced and numerous than its counterpart in Austria-Hungary. In the nineteenth century, nationalism was one of the most powerful forces in German politics and society. Yet all this was really only superficially comparable to the preconditions for feminism in areas such as the Nordic countries. German Protestantism was not open or progressive, like that of Denmark after the triumph of the Grundtvigian reform in the middle of the century, nor did it tolerate large-scale independent and reforming sects like that of Britain or America. Since the era of the Reformation, the German Protestant Church had been a state church, its ministers more or less state servants, its doctrines socially conservative, its policies dedicated to upholding the *status quo*. The middle class was certainly large, but it had suffered a setback when in 1848 it had failed to established parliamentary constitutionalism. After 1848, the nationalist movement had become divorced from liberalism. The aim of nationalism in Germany was not to free the country from foreign domination, but to unite the various small political units into which it was divided. When this was accomplished in 1870-71, it was not by the liberal bourgeoisie, but by the authoritarian militarism of Prussia. Most of the middle classes acquiesced in the unification, and were content to live in a German Empire in which political and social power lay in the hands of the military aristocracy, the small élite of heavy industrialists, and the Emperor, the powers of legislative assemblies were minimal, and the liberty of the individual to oppose the government strictly curtailed.

The German feminists shared the attitudes of the liberals. Literary feminism began, as we saw in Chapter 1, with the Enlightenment theorist Theodor Gottlieb von Hippel, and feminist theories of a kind were advanced during the Romantic era. As in other countries, Protestant sectarian revivalism had an influence on the rise of feminism; and in the Revolution of 1848, the radical liberals had also encouraged feminist ideas. Louise Otto-Peters (1819-95) had publicised the demand for female equality in every sphere, including the vote. But in the reaction of the 1850s it was not possible to form an organised movement. When one eventually emerged, it was at the height of nationalist excitement in 1865, the year after the Schleswig-Holstein crisis, when many North German liberals were coming to see in Bismarck's Prussia the force that would lead Germany towards unification within a very short space of years. The General German Women's Association (*Allgemeiner Deutscher Frauenverein*) was led by Otto-Peters, but it contained little of the crusading radicalism of 1848. Its concerns were limited to education, philanthropy and economic questions. Even in these spheres it was extremely careful not to put forward any 'advanced' ideas. In education, for instance, it did not aim at equality for women, but merely requested that girls receive a more efficient training for motherhood, instead of merely getting an inferior version of the education received by boys. Though there were no state grammar schools for girls until the mid-1890s, the General Association did little to bring about their establishment. Nor did it demand the admission of women to the universities save in the case of medical students; it supported the appointment of women physicians to treat women patients who might be too embarrassed to bring gynaecological complaints to male doctors for treatment. As far as economic rights were concerned, the General Association concentrated on petitioning the Imperial Parliament, the Reichstag, for the incorporation of married women's property rights into the Civil Law Code under preparation in the years 1873-96, together with the establishment of legal majority for women (this came in 1884) and the granting of limited rights to women over their children.[49]

Several topics were explicitly rejected by the General Association. It refused, for instance, to respond when the English social reformer Josephine Butler appealed to it to oppose the state regulation of prostitution in Germany. It also rejected the idea of presenting the Reichstag with evidence of the suffering caused to women by their lack of property rights, because to do so would be indelicate. After 1878, when the Social Democratic Party was outlawed (until 1890), it broke off contacts with the labour movement and restricted the range of its philanthropic activities accordingly. In 1876, it rejected the literary feminist Hedwig Dohm's call for the formation of a female suffrage society. In 1888 it even refused to send official representatives to the founding congress of the moderate feminist International Council of Women, explaining that 'in Germany we have to work with great tact and by conservative methods'.[50] To some extent, there were good legal reasons for this caution. In the German Empire, public life was closely supervised by the political police, and the Combination Law of 1851 made it illegal for women to take part in political meetings or join political associations in most parts of Germany, including Prussia. The police frequently enforced this law, above all against left-wing groups. If the feminists incorporated female suffrage into their programme, then they too would be liable to dissolution as a political association. Indeed, so sensitive was the General Association to the possibility of being defined as a political society that it even refrained from petitioning for the repeal of the Combination Laws, thus perhaps contributing to the impression that women were quite content with things as they were.

But the reasons for the General Association's timidity went deeper than this. German feminism actually retreated between 1865 and 1875, as liberalism declined with the defection of large sections of the middle class to conservatism during the process of unification under Prussian leadership. The General Association, which demanded full equality in education, including the admission of girls to boys' grammar schools (considered immoral by the authorities) in 1865, was asking for no more than the proper education of women for motherhood by 1875. A similar retreat can be observed in other spheres as well. In the 1870s and 1880s the General Association oriented itself increasingly towards charity and philanthropy. The reason for this scaling-down of the feminists' objectives can be sought in the decline of German liberalism from the mid-1860s onwards. It was in large measure a consequence of the political weakness of the middle classes in Germany. The landed aristocracy, above all in Prussia, had consolidated their position in the agrarian and administrative reforms of the early nineteenth century, and the middle classes were not sufficiently developed in 1848 to bring the revolution of that year to a successful conclusion.

Industrialisation came late to Germany, but once it got under way its pace was exceptionally quick. The stages of social development were telescoped, as it were, so that the aristocracy was still dominant even when the proletariat was emerging onto the political scene. As a result, German politics were rapidly polarised into right and left wings whose extremism grew with time. The room for liberal compromise, on which feminism depended, became smaller. In the 1890s, however, it seemed for a time that things might be different. Bismarck departed in 1890, and the political scene became more relaxed. In the same year, the number of Germans engaged in agriculture fell below 50 per cent for the first time. Industrial society now really began to have an effect on the nature of German politics. A whole range of voluntary associations and pressure groups sprang up in the 1890s, and political parties began to organise on a formal and professional basis instead of being loose associations of local notables and deputies. A reorientation of liberalism began to take place, in which middle-class groups started to look for solutions to many of the problems of industrial society through social and political reform. These developments, together with the continuing expansion of primary education and the growing opportunities in this and other spheres for the employment of middle-class women, created an almost ideal climate for the radicalisation of the German feminist movement.

The transition to radical feminism in Germany took place in two stages, the first of which can be dated fairly precisely to the years 1894-1902. It was in 1894 that the moderate feminist General German Women's Association attempted to bring under its aegis all the new female philanthropic societies founded in the late 1880s and early 1890s by founding a National Council of Women, which it called the Federation of German Women's Associations (*Bund Deutscher Frauen-vereine*). Until 1902 the new Federation was controlled by the moderates, but inevitably their grip relaxed. By 1901 the Federation had 70,000 members, far outnumbering the Association, which only reached 14,000 in 1914. And in 1900-2 many of the older generation of moderate leaders either retired or died, leaving the way open to a new generation of more radical spirits, chief of whom was Marie Stritt (1856-1928), probably the most important German feminist of the Wilhelmine period. Stritt became President of the Federation in 1899 and did much to steer the movement to the left, and, like her more radical colleagues Minna Cauer (1841-1922), Anita Augspurg (1857-1943) and Lida Gustava Heymann (1868-1943) went through major radicalising experiences in the 1890s. The first was the campaign which the feminists, above all Augspurg and Stritt, mounted against the Civil Law Code passed in 1896 — a Code which failed to improve the legal position of middle-class women in any significant way and even worsened it in some respects. The fact that the feminists' arguments were not even taken seriously by the legislators outraged Augspurg and Stritt and their followers. At the same time, German feminism was developing a moral dimension in the emergence of a movement against the state regulation of prostitution, especially after several of the more radical feminists had met the Abolitionist leader Josephine Butler in the late 1890s. In 1902 the German Abolitionists, led by Cauer, Heymann and Augspurg, succeeded in converting the majority of the Federation's members to their point of view.

By this time, however, the radical feminists had had enough of being ignored or laughed at by the legislature, the Reichstag. In 1902, led by Augspurg and Heymann, they founded a female suffrage society, while in the same year the influence of Stritt helped secure the endorsement of the principle of votes for women by the Federation, in which of course the moderates were still very strong. As in Austria, the feminists faced the problem that women were legally barred from forming political societies — but this did not apply in Bremen, Baden, Württemberg or Hamburg, the second largest city in Germany, where the German Union for Women's Suffrage (*Deutscher Verband für Frauenstimmrecht*) was founded. The Union was dominated in its early years by moral reformers, and the abolition of state-regulated prostitution was one of its major aims. Its formation in 1902, along with the other events of that year, marked the beginning of the second phase of the transition to radicalism in German feminism. This phase, which came to an end in 1908, was marked by three major characteristics. First, the largest organisation of German feminism, the Federation of German Women's Associations, expanded rapidly, while at the same time developing a steadily more radical ideology and programme. Indeed, it continued growing at an astonishing rate right up to the outbreak of the First World War, when it probably had over a quarter of a million members. Many of the member associations were of course only vaguely feminist in orientation. But in 1907 they all subscribed to the Federation's new programme of demands issued in that year, which included the abolition of state-regulated prostitution, equal education and further education for girls, coeducation, equal pay, promotion and prospects, and full and equal suffrage rights.

The second development of this phase, the most radical in the history of German feminism, was perhaps even more startling. A group of Abolitionists led by the Nietzschean feminist Helene Stöcker broke with the moral repressiveness of the movement against state-regulated prostitution and began to advocate the use of contraceptives and the legalisation of abortion, as well as a more wide-ranging programme of equality for unmarried mothers and illegitimate children, as a means of curing the social ills that led women to become prostitutes in the first place. Stöcker and her followers, who included many leading figures in the radical feminist and female suffrage movements, evolved a radical ideology, which they called the 'New Morality', to justify these demands. Elsewhere, of course, other feminists had also advocated sexual freedom, but they had never gained even a foothold in the organised feminist movement. The German situation was practically unique in this respect. By 1908 Stöcker's followers had even succeeded in persuading

the Legal Commission of the Federation of German Women's Associations to endorse the legalisation of abortion; once more, the influence
of Marie Stritt, the Federation's President, was instrumental in securing
this endorsement of radical principles. In some ways, this extraordinary
development reflected the isolated position of the feminists within the
conservative and undemocratic German political system, which pushed
them to more radical views by equating them with the Social Democrats; it was also characteristic of the radical ideas of social experimentation held by many groups of intellectuals on the right as well as the
left. There is a parallel here, as we shall see, with the fate of radical
feminism in Tsarist Russia, which became even more extreme and
daring than its German counterpart, and for very similar reasons.

None of these ideas of course ever secured even a qualified acceptance by the German authorities or legislatures. The same may be said
of the ideas of the female suffrage movement, whose growth and expansion constituted the third major characteristic of the radical years up to
1908. The German suffragists believed in moral reform, democracy and
pacifism — a combination of views that was too advanced even for the
left-wing liberals who provided the main source of support for female
suffrage movements in other countries. The left-liberals refused to endorse the idea of female suffrage despite the fact that the Suffrage
Union worked for them at election time. The individual politicians who
supported the suffragists were themselves often on the left of the left-
liberal movement, and many of them abandoned it when it supported
the government in 1907-8. Many of the candidates for whom the suffragists worked explicitly rejected the idea of female suffrage. The union
of the various left-liberal splinter groups in 1910 brought little change,
since the South German liberals made non-acceptance of female suffrage a condition of their joining. The feminists pushed the united left-
liberal Progressive Party a little closer to acceptance of female suffrage
in 1912, but without committing it to including it on its programme.
Liberalism in Germany was traditionally cautious and conservative, and
at this time it was moving to the right, partly out of fear of the growing
power of the Social Democrats, partly in the hope of extracting concessions from the government by showing support for it. In any case, it
was impossible for the liberals even to introduce a bill into the Reichstag
(only the government could do this). The only serious attempts to get
the Reichstag to discuss female suffrage were undertaken by the Social
Democrats when in 1895 and on a number of subsequent occasions
they attempted to amend government bills so as to include the provision
of votes for women. Even these attempts largely failed since the Conser-

vatives, Catholic Centre Party and National Liberals considered the subject too frivolous for discussion, while the left-liberals were so embarrassed by their internal divisions on the matter, and by a rather guilty feeling that they ought to be supporting it even if they did not, that they did their best to avoid giving the topic a mention.

The Suffrage Union was very small. In 1908 after six years, it still had fewer than 2,500 members. The legalisation of female participation in politics throughout Germany in the same year led to the establishment of suffrage societies in the great political centres of Berlin and Munich, and the movement expanded rapidly after this. In 1913 the Suffrage Union had 9,000 members. By the middle of 1914 the total number of suffrage society members in Germany was about 14,000, much more than in 1908, but still, when it is considered that Denmark, with a female population only a twentieth the size of Germany's, had a suffrage movement nearly twice as large, it was not very impressive. Moreover, by this time, the German suffrage movement was split into a number of different factions whose mutual hostility stood in sharp contrast to the relative friendliness towards one another of the two main Danish suffragist groups. The problem was that German politics at this time was being polarised over the issue of universal manhood suffrage, which the Social Democrats wanted to be substituted for the three-class property franchise which obtained in the dominant German state, Prussia. The government and the landed aristocracy which depended to a considerable extent on this system for their survival in power, refused to alter it to any significant extent. Groups caught between the two extremes, such as the liberals, were divided. The Suffrage Union had begun by committing itself to campaigning for the vote for all women, partly because of its concern to win the support of working-class women, partly as a consequence of the radicalism of its leaders and their desire to oust the aristocracy from their dominant position in the political system, partly because it seemed the only logical thing to do since universal manhood suffrage already obtained for the Imperial Legislature, the Reichstag. The liberalisation of the Combination Laws in 1908, after which women were admitted to political assemblies and associations all over the Empire, brought many more conservative women into the suffrage movement, and the majority of its members also began to move to the right with the middle classes and liberal parties with which they were mostly associated.

The decision of the left-liberals to abandon the opposition which they had hitherto shown to the state and the Wilhelmine régime, and to join with other parties in forming a coalition in the Reichstag in support of the government in 1907-8, the so-called Bülow Block, was really the precipitating factor in the disintegration of the German Union for Women's Suffrage, a process which was one of the main features of the phase after 1908. Augspurg and Heymann, the suffragist leaders, did not go back on their decision, reached in the very different political climate of the years 1898-1902, to oppose the Wilhelmine system of politics. They saw this move on the part of the left-wing liberals as a betrayal, severed their connections with them, and attempted to go over to a policy of independent militancy, borrowing some of their tactics and techniques from the suffragette movement in England (though they firmly rejected violence and illegality). But they failed to carry the majority of members with them. The end result was the rapid disintegration of the whole female suffrage movement in a series of bitter struggles lasting from 1910 to 1914, as dissatisfaction grew among members with the social and political radicalism of its leaders — a radicalism that may have been understandable in 1902, but which no longer seemed appropriate ten years later. By 1914 there were three separate and mutually hostile female suffrage societies in Imperial Germany. Only one, the German Women's Suffrage League (*Deutscher Frauenstimmrechtsbund*), supported universal suffrage, and it had only 2,000 members compared with 3,000 for the right-wing German Alliance for Women's Suffrage (*Deutsche Vereinigung für Frauenstimmrecht*) and 9,000 for the old Suffrage Union, which was moving over to support of property franchises and was abandoned by Augspurg and Heymann in 1913. The female suffrage movement in Germany was in fact caught in an inescapable dilemma, the nature of which only became clear towards the end of the first decade of its existence. Born in an atmosphere of hostility to the Wilhelmine state, it could exist only by working within that state's established political structure. It aimed above all to bring about a fundamental reform of German politics through the granting of votes to women. Yet female suffrage could itself only be achieved through such a reform as the feminists thought it would bring about. Full and equal political rights for women in this context presupposed the existence of full and equal political rights for men. But the Germany of Wilhelm II was not a democratic country. All adult men could vote for the Reichstag, but that assembly's powers were strictly limited. It was often ignored or snubbed by the government. An overwhelming vote of no confidence, such as the Reichstag passed over the 'Zabern Affair' in 1913, could be — and usually was — simply disregarded. Moreover, the Diets (parliaments) of the federal states of which Germany was composed retained very considerable powers, and were generally elected on a very restricted property franchise, particularly in Prussia, the dominant and by far the largest and most populous state of the Empire.

For equal political rights for women to become a reality, therefore, these franchises had to be replaced by universal suffrage. Only in this way could the forces of political and social reform gain enough electoral strength to be able to put measures such as female suffrage into effect. In demanding universal female suffrage, the German suffragists differed from many of their colleagues in other countries, who asked for a limited property franchise. In those countries where a liberal constitutional system already existed, the feminists were concerned to preserve middle-class privileges against the encroachments of the working class; in Germany these privileges had not yet been won, and to begin with at least, the suffragists feared the aristocratic ruling class more than the proletariat. Yet the chances of achieving votes for all were growing slimmer all the time, as the growth of the socialists SPD made not only the ruling élite but also — and this was the significance of the foundation of the Bülow Block — the middle classes — more and more determined to keep the Social Democrats out of the political system through the denial of equal political rights for all. As the first decade of the twentieth century progressed, state after state within the German Empire revised its franchise in a conservative direction by introducing more stringent property qualifications; more ominous still, as the power of the SPD reached a new height in 1912, the ruling clique around Wilhelm II began to turn to the threat of a *coup d'état* to forestall the threat of democratisation. In such a political atmosphere, the optimism with which the female suffrage movement began its career seems cruelly misplaced, the fate that ultimately befell it sadly inevitable. For as the suffragists themselves admitted, in the last four years before the war they were totally absorbed in their own internal struggles, and contributed next to nothing to the real struggle, the struggle for the vote. As for female suffrage itself, it was not even a remote possibility in 1914.[51]

The German feminists were having problems in other areas besides the suffrage by the outbreak of the First World War. Women were admitted to full-time study in German universities over the period 1902-8, and a reform of the educational system in Prussia in the latter year brought a more generous provision of secondary schools for girls, though these schools still lagged far behind those provided for boys both in number and in academic standards. But no progress was made in getting control for married women over their own property or in securing for unmarried women entry into the legal profession or the civil service. Women were admitted to the medical profession after the 1890s, but only in small numbers. The campaign to abolish the state regulation of prostitution, unlike its counterparts in England, America and the Nordic lands, was a total failure, for regulation depended not on any Act of Parliament but rather on a wide interpretation of the powers of the police, whose legal sanction was dubious but whose political backing from German administrations was very strong. In 1912 there emerged a 'German Society for the Prevention of the Emancipation of Women' (*Deutsche Gesellschaft zur Bekämpfung der Frauenemanzipation*), small but with influential pan-German, anti-semitic and militarist support. By this time, however, the feminist movement was itself becoming less interested in the emancipation of women, for after 1908 the moderates quickly took charge once more. This development indeed is important enough to warrant special consideration in a later chapter in this book, on the decline of feminism. As far as the German feminist movement *before* 1908 was concerned, its paradigmatic progress from moderation to radicalism was retarded by the authoritarian political system and feudally over-determined society within which it operated. Moderate feminism in Germany was unusually moderate, radical feminism exceptionally radical. These influences operated with even more devastating effect in the case which we now examine, that of Tsarist Russia.

Tsarist Russia

In Tsarist Russia, feminists faced a state apparatus that was far more authoritarian than either its German or its Habsburg counterpart. The effects on the feminist movement were correspondingly far more inhibiting and retarding. That this was so has not been apparent to all scholars. It has recently been argued that the feminist movement in Russia was 'more successful than any other in Europe'. Women in Russia, it has been claimed, 'possessed more civil rights, constituted a far greater percentage of the student body in middle and higher education, counted 280 doctors in their number, achieved a greater expansion of employment opportunities, and opened four university-level institutions for women'.[52] These assertions are not very convincing. The assessment based on them derives from a fundamental misunderstanding of the nature of Russian politics and society in the mid-nineteenth century. It also rests on a superficial view of the position of women in Russian society. In reality, conditions in Russia were even less favourable for the development of a feminist movement than they were in Germany or the Habsburg Empire. Nineteenth-century Russia was governed autocratically by the Tsar, who derived his legitimacy from his patrimonial claim to own the land and its people. The bureaucracy was responsible to him alone. There were no independent institutions. Every kind of activity was regarded as a kind of state service. Justice was a facet of administration. Russia was a police state in which opposition was treason. According to the Criminal Code of 1845, for example, any attempt to limit the Tsar's authority, or even the failure to denounce someone who intended to do so, was punishable by death.

In the 1850s this system of government, in which the initiative for change could come only from the Tsar and his agents, suffered a serious defeat at the hands of Britain and France in the Crimean War (1854-6). The Tsar Alexander II, who succeeded to the throne at the end of the war, was determined to make his state more militarily efficient and to bind his subjects to it by ties of self-interested loyalty rather than brute unquestioning obedience to superior force. Alexander II's reforms, which ranged from the reorganisation of the army to the abolition of serfdom (1861), included the creation of a larger and better-trained bureaucracy. The prerequisite of this was the expansion of education.

There was no middle class in nineteenth-century Russia in the conventional sense of the word. The country was overwhelmingly rural and peasant in social structure. A small number of minor provincial nobles provided the social basis for the literary and political life that began to emerge in the more liberal atmosphere of Alexander II's reign. Many of these families stayed in the capital St Petersburg (now Leningrad) or in Moscow for part of the year, and it was here, in the only two large cities in Russia, that intellectual, cultural and political life went on. The provincial nobility supplied the personnel for the intelligentsia, created in the 1830s and 1840s by the growth of bureaucracy and the spread of education. In the absence of a mercantile, industrial or professional middle class with a separate identity from the state machinery, it was the intelligentsia who provided the only criticism of state and society.[53] It was from this tiny, isolated group that the earliest Russian feminists came, in the liberal atmosphere of the early years of Alexander II's reign. The initial expression of feminism was, as everywhere, literary. Supported by the government or by their families, the intelligentsia lived in a non-competitive world where their existence was assured, and they indulged in abstract theorising about the nature and purpose of state and society, marriage and the family, rather than addressing themselves directly to practical problems of economic and social reform. This abstract tradition of thought led directly to radical theories which were rejected by the earliest organised feminists, although the relationship between the literary discussion of female emancipation and the organisation of women in the struggle for equal rights was perhaps less tenuous in Russia than it was in other countries.[54]

The feminist movement in Russia was more than usually isolated from the mass of women, since it related almost exclusively to a tiny minority of women in the two large cities and in the provincial nobility, and did not touch on the overwhelming majority of peasant women in the vast Russian hinterland. Even among the merchant class, the seclusion of women was common until the 1870s. Among the intelligentsia, the spread of education was producing by the 1850s a growing feeling that the restrictions to which they were submitted were anomalous. The police state required citizens to acquire an internal passport before travelling, and this was not available to women without the permission of their parents or (after marriage) husbands. Education of a formal kind was only really available in Moscow and St Petersburg. There was no coeducation. In 1856 there were 51,632 women attending all levels of schools in Russia, making up 10.7 per cent of the student population. The quality of their education may be gauged from an official statute of 1845 on state secondary schools or institutions for girls:

> Woman, as a lower creation appointed by nature to be dependent on others, must know that she is not fated to rule but to submit herself to her husband and that only through strict fulfilment of her responsibilities to her family can she assure her happiness and gain love and respect both within the family circle and without.

It is scarcely surprising, then, that the existing system of girls' education, which concentrated largely on the social graces, came under strong attack in the drive to reform that followed Russia's defeat in the Crimean War. The rapid reorganisation and extension of education in the late 1850s included girls' schools; 131 were opened, including 37 grammar schools. It also influenced the private education which the girls of the provincial nobility received, or gave themselves, at home. For these women, an advanced education was necessary to enter the world of the intelligentsia on an equal basis. Out of the intellectual discussion groups set up by such women in St Petersburg and Moscow, the Russian feminist movement emerged.[55]

The leaders of this movement all came from this background. Mariya Trubnikova (1835-97), daughter of one of the aristocratic Decembrist revolutionaries of 1825, derived her feminism from reading Western literature, and had personal contacts with Josephine Butler, whom she met in England in the 1860s. Trubnikova's reading circle recruited the two major feminist leaders, Anna Filosofova (1837-1912) and Nadezhda Stasova (1832-95). All these women came from wealthy backgrounds and devoted themselves from the early 1860s onwards to the foundation of various philanthropic organisations with a feminist slant, including publishing translations of non-Russian books through a women's cooperative, providing cheap lodgings, meals and employment for working-class women, sewing workshops and so on.[56] These were moderately successful − by 1900 the society for cheap lodgings had provided jobs for 40,000 women and in that year alone found lodgings for 600 − but by their nature they could only manage to cater for a very small proportion of the destitute women of the capital.[57] Their major achievement lay in the organisational experience they gave to the feminists who ran them.[58] As far as active pressure for the enlargement of women's rights was concerned, the feminists confined themselves exclusively to educational matters; the lack of a real middle class made the lobbying for economic rights carried out by Scandinavian feminists irrelevant, while the continuing impossibility of legal political activity made any more radical initiative unthinkable.

These circumstances also meant that the kind of steady and seemingly inevitable progress towards greater equality for women which occurred in more liberal countries was out of the question in Russia. At the beginning of the 1860s, women had started appearing at university lectures, but in 1862 they were expelled by order of the government after a series of student riots for which they were − without any evidence − held partly responsible. After this, there was no question of admitting women to universities. As a consequence, women seeking an advanced education went abroad. By 1873, there were 100 Russian women studying at Zürich alone, and there were 34 at Bern the following year. Russian women were also applying to other universities in Europe, even in Germany, where their lack of educational qualifications usually served as an excuse for refusing to admit them. Study abroad was a liberating experience for Russian women. It committed many of them to radical political ideologies which they attempted to put into operation when they returned home. The government therefore banned women from studying abroad and promised to provide facilities at home. The feminists had already sent in a series of petitions asking for the establishment of separate university courses for women, to be held in the university buildings when they were not in use.

Our goal [said the writers of the second and third of these petitions] is to raise the level of women's education generally and, at the same time, to provide the opportunity for some capable persons to achieve the knowledge necessary for taking positions as teachers in the girls' secondary educational institutions. All the salaries and other expenses encountered with the opening of the courses would be paid from student fees.

The feminists were encouraged by a letter of support from John Stuart Mill; but the petitions were signed by a mere 400 out of the 200,000 women aged seventeen and over in St Petersburg. Nevertheless, the extreme caution of these proposals — all that was being asked for was permission to establish *private* education courses — overcame the opposition of the education minister, who had earlier opined that women did not need university education and that the 400 petitioners were sheep, half of whom had records with the secret police for subversion. Further petitions, a considerable number of applications for such courses, and the support of a number of unversity professors, led to a series of concessions on the part of the government which culminated in the establishment of higher education courses and public lectures roughly along the lines proposed (1869). However, the academic level was low, far below that of the universities, the presence of police spies was obtrusive and intimidating, and the education provided was by its very nature patchy and unsystematic. Similar courses were a total failure in Moscow. In 1873 one of the St Petersburg courses (the Vladimirsky) was placed under the special supervision of the secret police. However, the courses were a popular success, attracting many hundreds of women every year, and in 1876 the government finally felt obliged to regularise them, give them official financial support, and improve the standard of education they offered. Clearly this was considered preferable to the radicalising effect of the unofficial study groups which had been founded on the periphery of the original courses by students dissatisfied with the meagre intellectual fare they were offered. In addition, special medical courses were established to train women physicians — something not only demanded by the feminists but also increasingly necessary to the government as its annexation of territories in Central Asia brought under its control Muslim tribes in which women would not consent to medical treatment by a physician who was not of their own sex.[59]

In the 1870s, girls' secondary education continued to spread. From 1864 to 1875 the number of girls at grammar schools increased from 4,335 to 27,470. From 1876 onwards, however, the feminists met with a series of setbacks. Eight hundred women registered for the higher education courses in that year, but some of the lecturers employed by the government were reactionary, to say the least, and the courses were not permitted to give degrees or to cultivate contacts with the universities. Graduates were refused the right to teach in secondary schools. Limits were set on entry by stiff qualifications imposed by the government. Police supervision continued. Courses were also established in Moscow, Kiev and Kazan, but none of them came up to the standard of the St Petersburg courses. All these courses were widely supported by liberals in the new local government (*Zemstvo*) system, which made them doubly suspect to the government. The courses did not lead to women's admission to the professions, for as these emerged in the 1860s and 1870s the government took care to exclude women from them, and in any case admission generally required a university degree. Women could practise as lawyers' clerks, but not lawyers, midwives but not physicians, except in very rare and special instances (despite their possession of adequate qualifications). They could teach in nursery and primary schools but not at any more advanced level. The government continued to see the courses as a seedbed of dissent. Finally, after the assassination of Tsar Alexander II in 1881 by a woman revolutionary, Russia was plunged into a period of renewed repression and reaction in which the dominant figure in educational and cultural policy was the obscurantist conservative Konstantin Pobedonostsev, who opposed higher education for women on principle. The women's medical courses were closed in 1883 and the higher education courses for women were all shut down in the mid-1880s, with the exception of Professor Bestuzhev's course in St Petersburg, which was saved by a personal appeal to the Tsar from some of the more well-connected feminists. Even this victory was won at the cost of accepting a series of restrictions which (among other things) excluded the natural sciences from the curriculum, limited the annual intake to 150, doubled the fees, set a strict quota on the number of Moslem and Jewish students, increased police and government supervision and reduced the role of the feminist Society to Finance the Higher Courses for Women. The result was a renewed wave of Russian women studying abroad.[60]

The feminists were thus effectively little better off in 1894, when the new Tsar, Nicholas II, came to the throne, than they had been thirty years earlier. But Filosofova and her associates were tenacious women. They continued to struggle for a reversal of the decisions of the 1880s. Largely because of the continued expansion of girls' secondary education (84 girls' grammar schools with 25,073 pupils in 1881, 154 with 45,106 in 1895, compared with 215 boys' grammar schools with 65,751 pupils in 1881, 215 with 64,711 in 1895), and the reluctance of Nicholas II to allow women to study abroad, the government increased quotas for the St Petersburg course and established a Medical Institute for Women leading to full medical qualification (1895). The major influence in this decision was a report by the Chief of Police in 1894 which alleged that 42 per cent of the 114 Russian women studying medicine in Swiss universities in 1891-2 were disloyal. He concluded that

> to make it possible for our women, at the most impressionable period of their lives, to receive a medical education within the Fatherland must, in effect, protect them from the pernicious influence of the émigrés and facilitate the development in them of a political attitude more favourable to the government.[61]

In Russia, it was this kind of consideration that dominated official thinking about women's education, rather than any concern for the women themselves or even for Russia's image in the world.

The Russian feminists, therefore, were in an inescapable dilemma. In 1857 the French feminist Jenny d'Héricourt gave Mariya Trubnikova the following shrewd advice:

> Surround yourself with women, form committees, establish a large institution as a model, set up a journal, but *do not* meddle in general politics. Let the exclusively masculine régime vanish by itself. If you start to attack it, it is so powerful in Russia that it will crush you.[62]

The trouble was, the 'exclusively masculine régime' did not 'vanish by itself'; and the experience of other countries suggested that feminists had to 'meddle in general politics' if they were to be successful. In Russia, however, 'general' politics did not exist. Overt opposition or criticism was punished by police repression. Real reform was only possible through revolution; and the more radical feminists rapidly abandoned feminism altogether to concentrate on revolutionary activity. By electing to work within the system, Filosofova and the moderates were condemning themselves to relative ineffectiveness, though the education they helped provide was invaluable in itself. Even so, they were regarded as dangerous radicals. The St Petersburg Police Chief Trepov complained that *any* attempt to develop a corporate spirit among women would inevitably lead to 'nihilism'. In such circumstances the development of a feminist movement in the conventional sense of the word was more or less impossible.

The main problem perhaps was that there were simply no social foundations in Russia which might support an active feminist movement or the political institutions on which feminist movements everywhere depended — political parties, civil rights, active legislatures, free newspapers and the like. In the 1890s, however, these finally began to develop in Russia. The country began to industrialise, encouraged by Sergei Witte, chief minister under the new Tsar, Nicholas II, who succeeded in 1894. The 1890s saw a vast boom in railway construction, and the industrial growth rate was close to 9 per cent, an astonishing figure. All this involved a considerable amount of social upheaval. The population of St Petersburg grew from 877,000 in 1880 to 1,907,000 in 1910, that of Moscow from 612,000 to 1,481,000 in the same period. With the expansion of the cities, the sudden growth of industry, the establishment of rapid communications and the spread of administrative services to cater for the new social problems which emerged, came the coalescence of political parties. These included the Social Revolutionaries (1901), continuing the terrorist and peasant-populist orientation of the old intelligentsia of the 1870s; the Social Democrats (1903), a Marxist party oriented towards the new working classes; and the liberals (1903), representing the local (*zemstvo*) gentry and technicians (teachers, physicians, etc.) and the moderate majority of the administrative and professional intelligentsia. In 1905 the growing social and political ferment came to a head with the defeat of Russia in a war with Japan, which gave the signal for vast peasant uprisings in the overpopulated countryside and massive workers' strikes on the railways and in the main towns. Imperial administration broke down more or less completely for several months and workers' committees attempted to take over the running of Moscow and St Petersburg. In this chaotic situation, free political activity was possible in Russia for the first time.[63]

The changing situation of Russian society had already wrung some minor concessions from the government for the feminists before the turn of the century, including an extension of the rights of women doctors in 1898. In 1904 the Women's Medical Institute was incorporated into the state education system. Women's higher education courses were reopened in several cities including Moscow after the turn of the century. The extent of these advances was shown by the fact that there were some 6,000 women in higher educational institutions in Russia by 1904-5; government restrictions ensured that this represented only half of those who applied. The changed attitude of the government was demonstrated in 1904 by an official message of thanks and congratulation to Anna Filosofova and her colleagues from the Tsar for their twenty-five years of 'fruitful activity' in the Society to Finance the St Petersburg Higher Courses for Women. For their part, the moderate feminists responded by redoubling their efforts to secure official support for their aims. Unfortunately for them, however, the upheavals of 1905 removed the premises on which their quarter-century of cautious and careful work had been based and made their aims and methods wholly irrelevant. The mass of younger middle-class women considered the education offered by the women's courses an inferior one and they flocked to the universities when these opened their doors to women in the atmosphere of institutional autonomy created by the 1905 Revolution.[64]

Just as the courses organised by the moderates Filosofova, Stasova and others had educated many of the women who took part in the revolutionary movement of the 1870s, so they had also formed the starting point for the development of a radical wing of the Russian feminist movement which emerged onto the public scene in the 1905 Revolution. In 1895 the moderates had joined with the younger generation in forming a women's club, forced by government restrictions to call itself the Russian Women's Mutual Benefit Society and to concentrate on philanthropic causes. The Society's leaders had believed that it had helped develop a feminist consciousness among its members, but the younger women in its ranks had resented the moderates' failure to turn it into an active organisation dedicated to fighting for women's rights.[65] Their chance came with the 1905 Revolution. On 17 October the Tsar was forced to proclaim in the 'October Manifesto' civil liberties and the calling of a Parliament (Duma) with legislative functions and a wide electorate. This was the starting point for the development of a radical feminist movement, for it was clear that for the first time a distinction was emerging in Russian political life between the rights of men and those of women. As one of the feminists later remarked,[66]

In Russia until the Manifesto of 17 October, men and women were equal in not having political rights. Perhaps it was thanks to this that within the Russian educated class there was not such a wall between men's and women's worlds as in Europe. Together we dreamed about freedom, about the rights and responsibilities of citizenship; together they were to be achieved. How, suddenly, half way there, could they cut women off from the long list of rights for all?

Rights for women, according to Sergei Witte, had not been discussed in the preparation of the October Manifesto. The feminists were galvanised into action. The moderates in the Mutual Benefit Society, which had reached a membership of 2,000 by the turn of the century, were spurned by the younger feminists, who formed the All-Russian Union of Equal Rights for Women. Even as late as February 1905, Filosofova had been booed at a meeting of the Mutual Benefit Society for proposing the signature of a protest against government repression, a measure evidently considered too daring by most members. In the face of such attitudes, younger activists turned to the Union of Equal Rights, which was led by Mariya Chelkhova, Olga Volkenshtein and Zinaida Mirovich — all writers, journalists and intellectuals. The Union resolved

that under the present régime women are deprived of all political rights; that the struggle for women's rights is inseparably connected with the struggle for the political liberation of Russia; and that since women are more than half of the population, the granting of political liberty only to men would delay both the economic development of the country and the growth of political awareness in the country. [It demanded therefore] National representation, based on Universal Suffrage by ballot without difference of sex, nationality or religion; the inviolability of the individual and the home; liberty of creed, word, press, meeting and association; rehabilitation of everyone undergoing punishment for political or religious reasons; recognition of proprietary and other rights to all nationalities in the Russian Empire; equal political and civil rights for women of all classes without restriction for married women.

The Union's founding congress in May 1905, with delegates from 216 local associations, demanded equal rights in political life and civil law. By 1906 the Union had 64 branches with 10,000 members; by 1907 there were 80 branches and perhaps 12,000 members. It sent the first Duma a petition with 5,000 signatures for a wide range of legal reforms, and carried on propaganda by printed leaflet and word of mouth on a considerable scale. It joined the Union of Unions shortly after its foundation in 1905 and persuaded this organisation of professional associations to support its aims. In November the *zemstvo* officials' congress also endorsed its programme. The Union of Equal Rights had close ties with the Constitutional Democrats (Kadets), the main left-wing liberal party; one of its leading members, Ariadna Tyrkova, was on the party's Central Committee, and another, Anna Milyukova, was married to the party's leader. The Kadets supported women's suffrage and equal rights, as did the parties to their left, and there was considerable support for the Union's ideas in the first Duma, in which the Kadets were the leading party.[67]

Despite its strictly limited powers, however, the Duma was never really accepted by the Tsar. As he recovered the initiative in the course of 1906, the Tsar sponsored the organisation of murder squads known as the Black Hundreds, dissolved the Duma, revised the electoral law, and set about repressing the opposition with the police. One device by which the Tsar hoped to strengthen conservatism in the Duma was the giving of the vote to women, who, if they possessed enough property, could vote by proxy for their husband or son. The number of women involved was very small, and the Kadets and feminists were alienated rather than appeased, all the more so because of the accompanying repression. The Tsar's measures led to an increase of political antagonisms which damaged liberals such as the Kadets. The Union of Equal Rights for Women urged a boycott of the elections for the Second Duma, and strongly opposed the new repressive policies. As a result, it attracted the unfavourable attention of the police and murder squads, and some of its members were threatened with imprisonment or death. By 1908 its membership had fallen to a mere one thousand. Nevertheless, in the same year, Union members joined the government-sponsored and (initially, at least) wholly inactive Russian League for Equal Rights for Women in large enough numbers to take it over completely. In this guise the Russian suffragist movement seems to have continued in existence with about 1,000 members until the outbreak of the First World War, continuing to put pressure on the Duma for reforms. That some progress at least was made — further educational reforms, equal inheritance laws, abolition of internal passports — was however just as much due to the efforts of the moderate feminists in the Women's Progressive Party, founded in 1905, and above all in the Mutual Benefit Society, which had been inevitably radicalised by the emergence of the suffragists on its left, in a manner common to other countries (e.g. Germany) at roughly the same time. Led initially by Anna Filosofova, who was more sympathetic to the radicals than were many of her colleagues, the Mutual Benefit Society espoused the cause of women's rights and sent to the Second Duma a petition with 7,000 signatures asking for the vote. The Second Duma too was dissolved by the Tsar, the electoral laws revised still further, and the Third Duma (1907-12) was dominated by the right. In the Fourth Duma, elected in 1912, the left and the Kadets were well-represented, and some of the moderate right-wing Octobrist Party deputies may have lent their support in that year to a Kadet-sponsored bill enfranchising a wider range of propertied women than already possessed the vote. Though the bill passed, it was rejected by the government, and a similar bill introduced the following year was defeated.[68]

The last public demonstration of the feminists was held in 1908, when a Congress of Russian Women, with over 1,000 delegates, was organised by the Mutual Benefit Society. Police surveillance prevented any discussion of women's rights.[69] In such circumstances, feminist action was clearly once more becoming as difficult as it had been before the 1905 Revolution. In Russia, it had required a breakdown of state authority before feminism could even emerge; and the reassertion of state authority sealed its fate. Even in the brief liberal interlude of 1905-8, the feminists had not really been able to escape from the dilemmas that faced their predecessors of the 1860s. They were still caught between overwhelmingly powerful forces of reaction on the one hand and revolution on the other. The logic of history and their own situation forced the Union of Equal Rights to cooperate closely with men and to include all social groups, even peasants, within their ranks. These policies undoubtedly helped the phenomenal increase of membership which the Union experienced in the first two years of its existence. But they could not disguise the fact that the Union was still led and dominated by members of the intelligentsia, nor that it represented a 'special interest' group whose claims seemed increasingly irrelevant to male politicians when set beside the other great issues of the day. The Russian feminist movement was torn apart by social and political antagonisms even more rapidly than its counterparts in the radical suffragist movements of Central Europe.

To some degree, Russian feminism did follow the usual pattern of development experienced by feminist movements elsewhere, even if the liberalisation of the political system which was a precondition of the radicalisation of feminist movements was achieved by revolution rather than by reform. Russian feminism began as a moderate feminist movement connected with philanthropic societies in the 1860s and underwent a transition to more radical aims and tactics after the Revolution of 1905. In other respects, however, the Russian feminists were unusual. Their concentration on educational rather than on economic objectives during the moderate phase reflected the fact that their background was in the intelligentsia rather than the bourgeoisie (which scarcely existed in Russia at that time). The radicals' origin in the 1905 Revolution and the political ferment of the preceding years gave their programme a flavour that was far more political than moral, as much concerned with general political freedom as with the specific rights of women. Finally, the gap between moderates and radicals was noticeably wide in Russia, above all when we consider the period before the turn of the century, in which meaningful political reform was so manifestly impossible that the more radical spirits among the feminists usually turned to revolutionary conspiracy and rejected organised feminism altogether.[70]

France, Belgium, Holland and Italy

The authoritarian polities and feudal or semi-feudal social formations whose influence retarded feminism or prevented it from succeeding, all lay in Central and Eastern Europe. In many countries in Western Europe which had a more liberal political constitution and a more advanced society, the feminists fared little better than they did in Russia, Germany or the Habsburg Empire. The obstacle in countries such as France, Italy and Belgium was not political or social so much as religious; for it is here that the feminists came up against the most persistent and intractable of their enemies, the Roman Catholic Church. Here, therefore, feminist movements took on a distinctly anti-clerical character and allied themselves with the forces that aimed to reduce the Church's influence in society. How this tactic then interacted with the various cross-currents of national politics and social change, and how successful it was likely to be, can best be observed perhaps in the case of France, whose feminist movement has been especially closely studied by historians.[71]

Organised feminism in France did not emerge until the foundation of the Third Republic in 1870 in the wake of France's defeat by Prussia in the war of that year and the consequent collapse of Louis Napoleon's authoritarian Second Empire. As we saw in Chapter 1, feminist protests had not been lacking at the time of the French Revolution of 1789-94; they were repeated during the short-lived Second Republic of 1848-51. But these protests were ephemeral. They failed to find a permanent, institutionalised form. Conditions for the emergence of organised feminism in France before 1870 were peculiarly unfavourable. The Revolution of 1789 failed to extend its benefits to women; 'the fourteenth of July', wrote a French feminist in 1882, 'is not a national celebration, it is the apotheosis of masculinity.'[72] The closure of the revolutionary women's clubs in 1793 was followed by the legal guarantee of female inferiority in the Civil Law Code prepared by the Revolution and eventually promulgated by Napoleon I under the title of the *Code Napoléon*. The Code reflected Napoleon's authoritarianism and contempt for women ('what we ask of education', he once said, 'is not that girls should think, but that they should believe').[73] The husband had full legal powers over his wife, her property and her children, powers which even extended, through his relatives, beyond the grave. The wife was legally obliged to obey her husband, and could not engage in legal transactions without his approval (i.e. she was a legal minor). If the wife committed adultery, she could be imprisoned for two years and divorced, and if she was caught in the act and killed by her husband, he could not be charged with murder. A husband, however, could commit adultery with impunity. Only if he introduced a permanent mistress into the household could he be sued for divorce by his wife, and she had no legal protection if she committed an act of violence against him even in these circumstances. Such conduct did not render the husband liable to imprisonment either; the most he had to fear was a fine of 2,000 francs. Based on these premises, the case law of the early and mid-nineteenth century brought more circumscriptions of women's rights.[74] Further legal restrictions forbade women to attend political meetings or to wear trousers and made unchaperoned females liable to arrest by the Morals Police as prostitutes.[75]

The *Code Napoléon* was backed up by the influence of the Catholic Church, which from the time of Napoleon I onwards was closely allied to the French state. The Church opposed divorce. It insisted that 'women belong to the family, and not to political society, and nature has made them for domestic cares, and not for public functions'.[76] The confessional was frequently used to reinforce the doctrine of female submission. The Falloux Law of 1850, which established primary schools for girls, gave the Church an effective monopoly of female education. Unqualified nuns could teach, unqualified lay women could not. Lay women teachers faced considerable local hostility in rural areas and were frequently driven out by a combination of slander and innuendo from villagers and competition from nuns. Lay secondary education for girls was more or less non-existent before the end of the Second Empire. The Church opposed the secularisation of education.[77] At the same time, while political consciousness was spreading throughout the country with the advent of universal manhood suffrage in 1848, it did not extend to women; the politicisation of the masses, which was the main achievement of the 1848 Revolution, was emphatically the politicisation of the male masses. Republicanism spread to the provinces in the 1850s, helped by the newly built railways which heralded the breakdown of provincial isolationism and the creation of a unified nation.[78] But it did not spread to the female sex. These developments occurred at the same time as a major increase in the tempo of French industrialisation in the 1850s and 1860s. Between 1850 and 1870 new industrial towns such as St Etienne mushroomed to an enormous size; the population of towns with over 20,000 inhabitants increased from 25.5 per cent of the French population in 1851 to 34.8 per cent in 1881, and that of Paris from 1,053,000 in 1850 to 2,269,000 in 1880.[79] All this initiated a secularisation of the mentality of large masses of Frenchmen. Its counterpart was what one historian has called 'the progressive feminisation of the permanent cadres of Catholicism'.[80] Small wonder, therefore, that Bishop Dupanloup regarded the secularisation of female education as part of 'a profound and vast enterprise of impiety directed against the faith of young French women'.[81]

In these circumstances, feminism in France was almost bound to be directed against the Catholic Church and those political régimes and parties — monarchist and Bonapartist — which stood closes to it. Consequently it was allied to the forces of republicanism and anti-clericalism which triumphed in 1870. Feminism in France, like its counterparts in other countries — notably Russia — was born of a revolution, and could only take on an organised existence with the removal of an authoritarian régime and its replacement by a liberal one. The earliest French feminists therefore thought of themselves as revolutionaries. It was their declared aim to extend the benefits of the great revolution of 1789 to the women of France. They also took up some of the ideas of the utopian socialists and received a good measure of support from their disciples.[82] The earliest feminist leaders all began their career in the republican movement.[83] The spread of anti-clericalism, free-masonry, philanthropy and liberal reformist movements in the period of industrial growth and mild liberalisation at the end of the Second Empire laid the groundwork for the emergence of organised feminism; and it has been calculated that more literary works of a feminist orientation were published under the Second Empire than in any other comparable period in the nineteenth century, culminating in the issue of a French translation of Mill's *The Subjection of Women* in 1869.[84] It was against this background that the first French feminist organisation was established under the 'Liberal Empire' of the last years of Napoleon III: the Society for the Demand for Women's Rights (*Société pour la Revendication des Droits de la Femme*), founded in 1866. Despite the fact that it included radical republicans such as Paule Mink, Louise Michel and Elie Reclus, this group was moderate in character, aiming only to improve women's education and to prevent prostitution through higher pay for working women. It did not last long.[85] Its radical members took part in the Paris Commune, the last of the great Parisian revolutions, crushed in an orgy of blood and violence by the new republican government in May 1871.[86]

The Society was gravely damaged by the Commune; its radical members were arrested and imprisoned or forced into exile, and its bourgeois majority eventually merged it in 1881 with a newer feminist organisation tied firmly to the moderate republican cause, the Society for the Improvement of Women's Lot (*Société pour l'Amélioration du Sort de la Femme*), founded in April 1870 by Léon Richer and Maria Deraismes, who between them were to dominate French feminism for 20 years.[87] The legacy of fear left to bourgeois republicanism by the Commune, with its myth of the 'woman incendiaries' (*Pétroleuses*) who were supposed to have set Paris on fire, forced the feminists to proceed cautiously in the 1870s, and indeed until 1877 there was a further deterrent to activism in the fact that French royalists still remained powerful enough to prevent the establishment of the Republic on a sound and permanent basis. But caution was far from foreign to the natures of the two feminist leaders. Léon Richer (1824-1911), the movement's propagandist and founder-editor of its magazine, *Le Droit des Femmes* (1869), was a journalist, a freemason and an anti-clerical who concentrated on demanding the reform of the *Code Napoléon*. Maria Deraismes (1828-94), the first woman freemason (1882), a literary feminist in the 1860s, a wealthy *grande bourgeoise* and the movement's major speaker and organiser, launched her main attack in the direction of the Church, which she characterised as obscurantist and reactionary. Neither of the two leaders initially wanted the vote for women, believing correctly that this, if granted, would lead to the triumph of political Catholicism and the defeat of the Republic. Their tactic was gradualist, laying slow siege to the 'masculinist system' which they saw as dominating French society. Consequently, despite their attachment to the principles of the French Revolution and their background in traditions such as freemasonry and anti-clericalism, they were fundamentally moderate and cautious, and frowned upon outbreaks of revolutionary violence such as the Paris Commune.

Richer and Deraismes were 'Opportunists'; they not only shared the combination of political caution and rhetorical boldness which characterised this party of conservative republicanism, but they also came from the same Protestant anti-clerical background. They were connected with many of the leading Opportunist politicians. Like them, they saw the Republic as a means of bringing new social groups and classes –

in this case, women — emancipation and equality, provided, of course, that these classes owned property and supported the Republic. Richer and Deraismes petitioned the Chamber of Deputies for economic independence for women, for the legalisation of divorce and for the expansion of girls' secondary and higher education. Despite the modesty of these aims and the caution of the methods used to further them, however, the Society was banned by a monarchist government in 1875. In 1877, with the victory of the republicans at the polls, it regrouped and began operating cladestinely. In 1878 it became legal once more. Richer held an international feminist congress in Paris to mark the occasion; but most of the delegates were French *men*. These vicissitudes owed little to the organisation's campaign for women's rights. It shared the suppression of 1875 and the reappearance of 1877-8 with a number of other anti-clerical republican groups which fell foul of the monarchist government of these years. Once these troubles were past and the Republic was securely established, many of the goals which Richer and Deraismes had set themselves in 1870 were soon reached. In 1879, girls' teacher training colleges were founded in all the French departments, and 1880 saw the admission of women to lectures at the Sorbonne and the establishment of a uniform and general system of girls' secondary education. In 1881, women were allowed to open post office savings accounts in their own names. In 1884, finally, divorce was legalised for the first time since 1816.

This progress cannot be regarded as testimony of the feminists' success. Most of the educational reforms were due to the régime's hostility to the Catholic Church, and not to pressure from the feminists. And the pace of reform was clearly very slow, the limitations of the gains of the early 1880s all too apparent. It was not until 1938 that married women became independent legal persons and even then this important legal reform clashed with so many other existing laws that it was in practice unworkable. Divorce by consent was not allowed under the law of 1884, and it was only in 1904 that the guilty party and the co-respondent with whom the adultery had been committed were allowed to marry legally. In education, women teachers were professionalised by the reforms of 1879-80, but the universities opened to female students only gradually in the course of the 1880s. Entry into the professions was possible, but difficult. In 1882, there were seven female physicians practising in France; in 1903 there were ninety-five. This was a large increase, and represented a considerable achievement, but in absolute terms it was still small. There were only twelve women barristers in 1914 (ninety-six in 1928). Even as late as 1930, the universities had only six female professors. There was also a quota on women in the civil service. In formal legal terms women certainly had more freedom of action in these respects in France in 1914 than, say, in Germany, Russia or the Habsburg Empire. But in practice, this legal freedom often meant little. The problem was that legislative social reforms came only very gradually in France, where the pattern of political life, in which parliamentary government was accompanied by chronic ministerial instability, prevented insecure and short-lived governments from endangering their fragile unity through controversial legislation. While the ministers quarrelled, the civil service governed, and the permanent officials of justice and administration invariably took a conservative line on social questions. Seen from the perspective of the early Third Republic, of course, all this was far from clear; but it had become evident by the end of the 1870s that the road trodden by Richer and Deraismes was going to be a very long one indeed. The policy of gentle pressure for piecemeal reform was not bringing rapid progress. Nor was it bringing the moderate feminists many followers. In 1876 Richer disclosed that at the time of its suppression the Society had only 150 or 160 members and that its meetings averaged an attendance of only 10 or 12. Richer's magazine was often in financial trouble and was forced to close down in 1891. Even so, it lasted far longer than other feminist periodicals, most of which were purely ephemeral. The feminists enjoyed the patronage of one or two prominent Frenchmen, notably the novelist Victor Hugo, but they failed altogether to break through the barriers of republicanism and anti-clericalism and become a popular movement.

Richer attempted to alter the situation in 1882 by launching a second moderate feminist group, even more conservative than the first. Deraismes had lent her support to female suffrage earlier in the year, and Richer believed that this 'radicalism' was alienating potential supporters. His new group was the French League for Women's Rights (*Ligue Française pour le Droit des Femmes*). Its programme, which included the revision of the Civil Code, the abolition of regulated prostitution, free access to the professions and improved education, but which did not mention the vote, reinforced Richer's emphasis on the step-by-step approach which he evidently feared Deraismes might be abandoning. The League had recruited 194 members by the end of 1883. This was a miserable figure for an organisation which Richer apparently intended to be a mass movement. Moreover, ninety-six of the members were men, and these played the major role in its activities. Worse still, the only branch outside Paris, in Nantes, defected in 1885 after repeatedly censuring the parent society over financial matters. Many of the men left, so that in 1892 the League had ninety-five members, sixty-two of them women. Only forty of those who had joined in 1882-3 were still members. Since the League, after its failure to secure a mass basis, relied on the tactics of using its (male) political contacts to put pressure on the legislature for reform, this was unfortunate, even if it did represent a welcome increase in the proportion of women within the organisation. Nevertheless, Richer persisted in the tactics of gradualism, accusing his rivals of compromising the cause by their rashness, and claiming that 'one point alone divides us: how to proceed'. Radical methods, he claimed, endangered the republic as well as the emancipation of women, and the vote must await the liberation of French women from the tutelage of the Church. Paradoxically, he thought that civil equality would lead inevitably to the vote, and so presumably to the destruction of the Republic, but he avoided the need to oppose civil rights as well by championing the cause of lay education, which would produce a 'new woman' loyal to reason and republicanism. In 1889 Richer arranged a second women's rights congress to coincide with the hundredth anniversary of the French Revolution. But discussion of female suffrage was ruled out of order, which was a further cause of friction between Richer and Deraismes; the latter thought its emphasis on philanthropy excessive, and the embarrassment of two simultaneous rival congresses was only narrowly avoided. At the congress, the rival societies of Richer and Deraismes competed for the support of delegates. The congress largely endorsed Richer's moderate programme. But its significance lay elsewhere. In contrast to the previous congress in 1878, the majority of the French delegates were female, and Richer's retirement in 1891 completed the feminisation of French feminism. Maria Deraimes died in 1894, and many of the other early feminists disappeared from the scene in the late 1880s. The 1889 congress therefore marked the end of the first phase of French feminism, a phase in which the anti-clerical nature of the movement had, in the view of the younger generation of feminists, constituted a major reason for its lack of success.[88]

Moral feminism in France really dated from Josephine Butler's visit to Paris in 1874. She aroused some support for her international federation against state-regulated prostitution among the Protestant *haute bourgeoisie*, people such as the Monod family, who came to play a major role in French feminism after the turn of the century. The French system of regulation, which, like the German, depended on police initiative rather than on Act of Parliament, was unshaken by their onslaught: the only success scored by Butler's movement on the

European continent was in fact in Calvinist Switzerland, where regulation was abolished in 1907. Since moral reform was the province of Protestant philanthropists in France, it is not surprising that it had no immediate connection with the rise of radical feminism, which was founded by Hubertine Auclert (1848-1914). Auclert came from a less wealthy background than the moderate leaders, but shared their anticlericalism and their commitment to the feminist cause. Auclert founded a feminist society with the blessing of the moderate leader Léon Richer in 1876, when his group was banned, but in 1878, when she was prevented by the moderates from discussing female suffrage at the international congress of that year, she launched out on her own. Auclert was a radical, impatient figure who altogether lacked the moderates' commitment to policies of 'Opportunism'. Her group, renamed the Women's Suffrage Society (*Société le Suffrage des Femmes*) in 1883, aimed to secure for women full equality before the law, equal access to the professions, equal education, equal pay for equal work, divorce and the vote. Auclert thought that the moderates were too narrowly class-bound and wanted to recruit proletarian women to a movement that would transcend social barriers. This was a view characteristic of radical feminists everywhere. Richer and Desraimes, she argued, wanted to take the 'masculinist fortress' by siege — the indirect method typical of moderate feminism. Auclert proposed instead to take it by storm, in the usual radical feminist manner. Auclert's wide-ranging programme really centered, as the title of her society from 1883 onwards implied, on the vote. The tactics she used were remarkably advanced, much more so than those of radicals in other countries, and owed much to the nature of the French political tradition.

In Germany, for example, the mere holding of a public protest meeting was itself a radical tactic, while in France the long revolutionary tradition made public assemblies acceptable to the moderates even before the radicals emerged. Accordingly, the methods favoured by Auclert in her assult on the bastions of male privilege were more extreme than those employed by radical feminists elsewhere. They included street demonstrations in 1885 and an unofficial 'shadow election', held to coincide with the general election of the same year, in which fifteen women stood for office and gained a good deal of notoriety for the movement. Auclert not only lobbied socialist congresses to support her aims and petitioned the Chamber of Deputies on behalf of women's rights, she also attempted to register herself to vote (on the basis that *les français* applied to women as well as men) and, when refused, declared her intention of withholding payment of taxes: 'I do not vote, I do not pay.' She was joined by twenty followers, but in the end, after various appeals, all of them paid up (Auclert after bailiffs tried to seize her furniture). She also founded a magazine, *La Citoyenne*, which lasted from 1881 to 1891, and, like her taxation protest, used sensational methods to draw public attention to women's demands for political rights. The arguments she advanced in the magazine were the common suffragist ones of the day. Women were equal to men in every respect, more women died in childbirth than men on the battlefield, and (as Joan of Arc had shown) they could fight as well, though of course they were opposed to war and chauvinism and would have prevented the French invasions of Tunisia and Indochina had they had the vote. Alternatively, she argued after the 'war-in-sight' crisis of 1887, equality for women would unite the nation and prepare it for the coming struggle with the Hun. These contradictory arguments reflected the need to refute the contradictory reasons used by male supremacists for not giving women the vote more than they revealed any inherent illogicality on Auclert's part.

Auclert's main difficulty, however, lay not in combating militaristic arguments against women's suffrage, but in convincing republicans that women would not vote for Catholicism and monarchism (the two went together in late nineteenth-century France). Despite her insistence that women would be quickly educated into rational and scientific attitudes by the possession of full political rights, she never succeeded in persuading the republicans to run the risk of finding out whether she was right. Very few deputies, perhaps a dozen or fifteen, endorsed female suffrage in the 1880s, and the municipal suffrage was only supported by a handful of departments and municipalities, the first being the Council of the Department of the Seine in 1907, followed by some twenty-four councils at all levels down to *arrondissement* by 1914 — a tiny number. The leading republican of the 1870s and early 1880s, Léon Gambetta, was so unenthusiastic about women's rights that as Auclert remarked, the one service he performed for the feminist cause was in his death in 1883, when it was revealed by autopsy that he possessed a brain no larger than a woman's, despite the fact that he was generally agreed to be highly intelligent. Nor were socialists much more helpful. Deprived of the prospect of rapid success, Auclert's society indulged instead in harmful internal strife. Serious quarrels rent the suffrage movement in 1881, when Auclert's expulsion of two dissident members led to a series of defamation suits, and Auclert engaged in a constant war of words with the moderates Richer and Deraismes, who tended to oppose an immediate campaign for votes for women on anti-clerical grounds. These quarrels were all the more damaging since the suffrage society never seems to have had more than a hundred or so members. Finally, when Auclert went to live with her husband in Algeria in 1888, she quarrelled at a distance with her deputy, Maria Martin, who closed down *La Citoyenne* in 1891 and refounded it as *Le Journal des femmes*, which lasted until Martin's death in 1911. Martin also helped found a new group, Women's Solidarity (*Solidarité des femmes*), and Auclert found herself with only a literary role to play on her return in 1892. Manoeuvred out of the suffrage movement, Auclert did little except write in the 1890s, and after the turn of the century she became steadily more isolated and extreme. She died in 1914, a lonely and embittered woman.[89]

The female suffrage movement in the meantime had reformed in 1909, in the shape of the French Union for Women's Suffrage (*Union française pour le Suffrage des Femmes*), led by Jeanne Schmahl and Jane Misme, with 300 members. Schmahl was eventually succeeded by Marguérite de Witt-Schlumberger. All these leaders were Protestants and republicans, mainly associated with the Radical party. This as much as anything was the cause of their failure; they were never able to broaden their support beyond a relatively narrow circle of women. Their most dramatic gesture was made in 1910, when a mock election for women received more than half a million female votes. Even this was inspired not by the suffragists but by an enterprising newspaper seeking publicity. Moreover, the Union found it difficult to overcome the fragmentation which bedevilled French feminism. On the eve of the First World War there was not only the Union for Women's Suffrage in existence, but also Auclert's tiny Women's Suffrage Society and 'Women's Solidarity', originally founded by Maria Martin. All of these had more or less identical aims. Then there were the old-established League of Women's Rights and the League for the Amelioration of Women's Status, both of which were affiliated to the Union for Women's Suffrage, though their main interests lay elsewhere. The Union for Women's Suffrage established branches in Bordeaux, Clermont-Ferrand, Rouen, St-Etienne, Boulogne, Nîmes and St Quentin. By 1913 it was claiming a membership of 10,000. Much of its numerical strength however derived from the fact that unlike, say, the Swedish Suffragist movement, it was not so much a society with individual members as a coalition of a number of societies, including not only the two oldest moderate feminist groups, but also temperance associations and trade unions of women clerks and female post and telegraph workers. The branches of the Union itself were mainly composed of female students or, by its own admission, in more than one town, of little more than isolated individuals. Seen in this light, its performance before the First World War looks far from impressive. The national support for the French suffragists came mainly from a handful of Protestant or republican intellectuals, left-liberal idealists such as Élie Halévy and Baron d'Estournelles de Constant. The mass of Radical (republican) politicians were opposed to giving women the vote on the grounds that this would strengthen clericalism and endanger the Republic. There was probably something in this, though 'the Republic in danger' was always a convenient excuse for postponing controversial reforms. The Radical domination of the Senate stopped the passage of a women's suffrage bill voted by the Chamber of Deputies after the war, and Frenchwomen had to wait for the end of the Republic in 1945 before they got the vote. By a curious irony, therefore, anti-clericalism was not only the major force behind the rise of feminism in France, it was also the major obstacle to its success.[90]

The generation of feminists who succeeded Richer and Deraismes realised this, and tried to dissociate feminism from anti-clericalism. Their only chance of success would have been to persuade the Catholics and clericals to back them. Despite the emergence of a Catholic female suffrage movement, this was out of the question. In any case, the leaders of French feminism after the turn of the century were Protestants not Catholics. They swung the movement over to a more moderate line, and the remaining radicals frequently gravitated towards socialism in disgust with the lack of support accorded them by France's equivalent of the liberal party. French government under the Third Republic was certainly socially conservative; under a confusing succession of short-lived ministries, the bureaucracy continued to govern the country without trying to change it. The main obstacle was not the system of government but the Catholic Church. This point may be simply illustrated by looking outside France to two other countries nearby, Belgium and Holland. Both countries were parliamentary, constitutional, dominated by the middle class. Belgium had the larger population, its cities were bigger, its industry incomparably more developed, its social structure considerably more advanced. Yet it was the Netherlands that boasted the strong feminist movement, not Belgium. The Association for Women's Suffrage (*Vereeniging voor Vrouwenkiesrecht*), founded in 1894 and led by Aletta Jacobs (1851-1929), the first fully qualified female physician in Holland, had sixty-two branches with 6,500 members in 1909, 100 branches with over 10,000 members in

1911, and 108 branches with 14,000 members in 1913. In addition there was a separate Dutch Association for Women's Suffrage founded in 1907 with 4,800 members in sixty-two branches by 1913 — the split had taken place over universal versus equal suffrage demands in a petition to be submitted in connection with a proposed revision of the constitution. Both organisations were very active. They mounted a number of poster and pamphlet campaigns, lobbied political parties, questioned candidates at elections, staged processions on a special Women's Suffrage Day in 1910, and even sent round women's suffrage boats to harangue the inhabitants of Amsterdam from the canals.

While the Dutch feminists were forging ahead, the Belgian feminists remained effectively in the moderate stage, concentrating mainly on the reform of the Napoleonic Code (by 1908 they had only got as far as obtaining the right to act as witnesses in law). Certainly the Dutch feminists were frustrated by the accession of the conservatives to power with a large majority in 1909, and they were just as concerned as their Belgian counterparts to reform the Napoleonic Code. But in 1913 female suffrage was a major public issue in the Netherlands, while the Belgian suffragist leader was forced to admit that 'the situation in Belgium . . . is different from that in any other country. Women's Suffrage is not a burning question . . .'. In Belgium, the fear that women would swell the clerical vote caused even the socialists to drop female suffrage from their programme in 1902. The manhood suffrage bill then in progress depended on the liberals for its successful passage through the Belgian Parliament, and the liberals were adamant in their refusal to tack on a female suffrage measure, so the socialists had an additional reason for not pressing their claim. As one of the suffragist leaders remarked, the liberals were 'hopelessly hostile to our claims, as they fear the religious fanaticism of the Belgian women'. The Belgian Socialist leader, Emil Vandervelde, was quite explicit in his references to the female Catholic vote. He was also strongly anti-feminist in other respects. As we shall see in the next chapter, the general cultural influence of Catholicism in countries such as France, Italy and Belgium extended even to the socialist movement; the champions of women's rights in the Socialist International invariably came from Protestant backgrounds. As far as the women's suffrage organisation itself was concerned, the Belgians could safely afford to ignore it: in 1910 the Feminist Union for the vote (*Union Féministe pour le Suffrage*, founded in 1907) only had three groups, with forty members in Brussels, twenty-seven in Ghent and fifty in Antwerp, making a grand total of 117 altogether.[91]

The power of Catholicism can be observed even more strikingly in the case of Italy, where nationalism and liberal constitutionalism had triumphed in the unification of the country in the 1860s. No organised feminist movement emerged until the industrial revolution began to take hold of Northern Italy, to which the feminist movement was confined, in the 1890s. Moderate feminism began with the economically-oriented Society for Women's Work in 1898 and a similar group, the Association for Women (*Associazione per la Donna*), founded in the same year, which aimed to secularise women's education. A National Council of Women was founded in 1903. A female suffrage movement emerged relatively quickly, influenced by the liberalisation of politics in the 'Giolitti era' — which culminated in the advent of universal manhood suffrage in 1912. The National Committee for Women's Suffrage (*Comitato Nazionale per il Voto alla Donna*), founded in 1905, united a number of recently founded local committees, mainly in the North. The suffragists managed to get considerable support from the right wing of the socialist party and a few liberal intellectuals, but the knowledge that the mass of women would vote Catholic prevented the majority of Italian politicians from supporting female suffrage. Moreover, the Catholic Church itself — as in other countries, such as Germany — created its own women's movement which rapidly secured far more widespread support than the feminists could ever hope to attract. Little or no progress was made towards improving women's position in other spheres either. By the outbreak of the First World War, the rise of a mass Catholic political party boded ill for the feminists' future prospects. The suffrage movement itself remained pitifully small. In 1907 it could only muster 600 signatures for a petition to the Italian Parliament.[92] At the same period the feminists in Protestant Iceland, which had a total population the size of an Italian provincial town, presented a similar petition to its Parliament with twenty times this number of signatures.

This survey of feminist movements in the nineteenth century has been necessarily incomplete. There were also active and organised feminist movements in Argentina, Bulgaria, Greece, Portugal, Romania and Habsburg-ruled Polish Galicia. If there is a paucity of recent research and readily available printed source material for feminism in the countries with which this chapter has already dealt, however, then for these other feminist movements there is almost none at all, certainly not enough to be able to generalise about them with any degree of confidence. There were also feminist movements in Canada and Switzerland;

their history is too uneventful to bear recounting at any length, though it is briefly touched on later in this book. The only other feminist movements existing on an organised basis before 1914 were those of Serbia and South Africa; they too are dealt with in a later chapter. The feminist movements not covered in this chapter will probably fall into one or other of the major categories with which it has dealt. Indeed, to chart the main variants of the feminist movement in relation to the general pattern of feminist development outlined in Chapter 1, and also in relation to the main types of social formation within which this development took place, has been the chief purpose of the present chapter, rather than to provide an exhaustive compendium of feminist history wherever it occurred.

This chapter has not followed the entire course of the feminists' development; it has stopped at the radical stage. Before we can go on to examine the later phases in the development of feminist movements it is necessary to turn to the rise of the major rival to bourgeois feminism in the nineteenth and early twentieth centuries, the socialist women's movement, which aimed to mobilise the women of the working class. The emergence of the socialist women's movement was in turn to have a profound effect on the later development of bourgeois feminism itself.

Notes

1. Roger Thompson, *Women in Stuart England and America: A Comparative Study* (London, 1974).
2. Eleanor Flexner, *Century of Struggle: The Women's Rights Movement in the United States* (Cambridge, Mass., 1966), pp. 8-9, 25.
3. Alice S. Rossi, 'Social Roots of the Woman's Movement', in Alice S. Rossi (ed.), *The Feminist Papers. From Adams to de Beauvoir* (New York, 1974), pp. 250-1; Thompson, op. cit., pp. 262-3.
4. Barbara Welter, 'The Cult of True Womanhood: 1820-1860', *American Quarterly*, Vol. 18 (1966), pp. 151-74.
5. Rossi, op. cit., p. 252.
6. See also Carroll S. Rosenberg, 'Beauty, the Beast and the Militant Woman: A Study in Sex Roles and Social Stress in Jacksonian America', *American Quarterly*, Vol. 23 (1971), pp. 562-84; William G. Rothstein, *American Physicians in the Nineteenth Century: From Sects to Science* (Baltimore, 1972); Gerda Lerner, 'The Lady and the Mill Girl: Changes in the Status of Women in the Age of Jackson', *Mid-Continent American Studies Journal*, Vol. 10 (Spring, 1969), pp. 5-15; Janet W. James, 'Changing Ideas About Women in the United States 1776-1825' (PhD, Radcliffe, 1954); Elizabeth B. Warbasse, 'The Changing Legal Rights of Married Women 1800-1861' (PhD, Radcliffe, 1960).
7. Flexner, op. cit., pp. 13-15.
8. Rossi, op. cit., pp. 3-39, 241-50.

9. Ibid., pp. 251-65; Keith Melder, 'The Beginnings of the Women's Rights Movement in the United States, 1800-1840' (PhD, Yale, 1964); Glenda Riley, 'From Chattel to Challenger; The Changing Image of the American Woman 1828-1848' (PhD, Ohio State, 1967).

10. Glenda Riley, 'The Subtle Subversion: Changes in the Traditionalist Image of the American Woman', *The Historian*, XLII (Feb. 1970), pp. 210-27.

11. Andrew Sinclair, *The Better Half. The Emancipation of the American Woman* (London, 1966), pp. 56-7; Flexner, op. cit., p. 70.

12. Flexner, op. cit., p. 73.

13. Printed in William L. O'Neill, *The Woman Movement: Feminism in the United States and England* (London, 1969), pp. 108-11.

14. See the critical examination of the mythology surrounding the Seneca Falls Declaration in Ross Evans Paulson, *Women's Suffrage and Prohibition: A Comparative Study of Equality and Social Control* (Brighton, 1973), pp. 32-43.

15. Ibid., pp. 36-7.

16. Flexner, op. cit., p. 65.

17. Ibid., p. 82; Sinclair, op. cit., pp. 65-6, emphasises the low priority of the vote for ante-bellum feminists.

18. Flexner, op. cit., pp. 78-101. See also William L. O'Neill, *Everyone Was Brave: The Rise and Fall of Feminism in America* (Chicago, 1969), pp. 13-14. O'Neill regards the educationalists as anti-feminist, and it is true that the women's rights leaders appear to have taken little interest in their views. Cf. Flexner, op. cit., pp. 23-40. Sinclair, op. cit., lays great stress on the urban origins of feminism.

19. In this assessment they were correct; it did not recur until the end of the First World War.

20. Similar reasons were behind the denial of the vote to women by liberal reformers in some other countries. This should not be regarded as a cynical betrayal; the dilemma was a real one.

21. Eleanor Flexner, *Century of Struggle. The Women's Rights Movement in the United States* (Cambridge, Mass., 1966), pp. 142-55; B. Quarles, 'Frederick Douglass and the Women's Rights Movement', *Journal of Negro History*, Vol. XXV/1 (1940), pp. 35-44; William L. O'Neill, *Everyone Was Brave: The Rise and Fall of Feminism in America* (Chicago, 1969), pp. 15-20; Andrew Sinclair, *The Better Half: The Emancipation of the American Woman* (London, 1966), pp. 185-9; Blanche G. Hersh, ' "The Slavery of Sex": Feminist-Abolitionists in 19th Century America', (PhD, Illinois, 1975).

22. Sinclair, op. cit., pp. 190-200. Flexner, op. cit., pp. 148-55; O'Neill, op. cit., pp. 15-24; Aileen S. Kraditor, *The Ideas of the Woman Suffrage Movement 1890-1920* (London, 1905), pp. 46-7.

23. O'Neill, op. cit., pp. 26-7. It is perhaps also worth noting that Woodhull supported state-regulated prostitution. See also Flexner, op. cit., pp. 152-5; Sinclair, op. cit., p. 192 ff.

24. Flexner, op. cit., p. 154. Ibid., pp. 113-30, 156-92, 215-21; William L. O'Neill, *The Woman Movement: Feminism in the United States and England* (London, 1969), pp. 43-59, 72; Sinclair, op. cit., pp. 99-105, 293-4; Esther Pohl Lovejoy, *Women Doctors of the World* (New York, 1957), pp. 8-129; Ann Douglas Wood, ' "The Fashionable Diseases": Women's Complaints and their Treatment in 19th-Century America', in Mary Hartman and Lois Banner (eds.), *Clio's Consciousness Raised: New Perspectives on the History of Women* (New York, 1974), pp. 1-22.

25. David Pivar, *Purity Crusade: Sexual Morality and Social Control 1868-1900* (London, 1973); Ross Evans Paulson, *Women's Suffrage and Prohibition: A*

Comparative Study of Equality and Social Control (Brighton, 1973), pp. 13-16; Janet Zollinger Giele, 'Social Change in the Feminine Role: A Comparison of Woman Suffrage and Woman's Temperance 1870-1920' (PhD, Radcliffe, 1961), pp. 76-92; Sinclair, op. cit., pp. 222-8; Flexner, op. cit., p. 183.

26. Flexner, op. cit., pp. 216-25, 248-9; Kraditor, op. cit., pp. 7-8; Sinclair, op. cit., pp. 294-7; Ralph W. Spencer, 'Dr Anna Howard Shaw: The Evangelical Feminist' (PhD, Boston, 1972), pp. 279-443. Spencer makes a brave attempt at defending Shaw's performance, but he is still forced to admit that she was a failure as an administrator (pp. 419-25) and that she was hypercritical of other feminists and all too ready to take personal offence (pp. 426-43).

27. Cf. Kraditor, op. cit., pp. 60-1.

28. See below, pp. 203-9.

29. For a fuller discussion of these connections, see below, pp. 211-15 (also for an account of the winning of female suffrage in the American West).

30. Paulson, op. cit., pp. 122-31; S. Encel, N. Mackenzie, M. Tebbutt, *Women and Society: An Australian Study* (Melbourne, 1974), Chapter 3.

31. Encel, *et al.*, op. cit., Chapter 14 *passim*; Anthea Hyslop, 'Temperance, Christianity and Feminism: The Woman's Christian Temperance Union of Victoria, 1887-97', *Historical Studies: Australia and New Zealand*, 1976, pp. 27-49; D. Scott, 'Woman Suffrage: the Movement in Australia', *Journal of the Royal Australian Historical Society*, Vol. 53, No. 4 (Dec. 1967), pp. 299-320.

32. Patricia Grimshaw, *Women's Suffrage in New Zealand* (Wellington, 1972), pp. 27-82.

33. O.R. McGregor, 'The Social Position of Women in England 1850-1914: A Bibliography', *British Journal of Sociology* VI (1955), pp. 48-60; O'Neill, *The Woman Movement*, p. 22; Constance Rover, *Women's Suffrage and Party Politics in Britain 1866-1914* (London, 1967), pp. 4-5; Eric Trudgill, *Madonnas and Magdalens: The Origins and Development of Victorian Sexual Attitudes* (London, 1976), pp. 65-78; S. Checkland, *The Rise of Industrial Society in England 1815-1885* (London, 1964), pp. 320-1; Patricia Branca, *Silent Sisterhood. Middle-Class Women in the Victorian Home* (London, 1975) (applies mainly to lower middle class women).

34. Ann Oakley, 'Wisewoman and Medicine Man', in Juliet Mitchell and Ann Oakley (eds.), *The Rights and Wrongs of Women* (London, 1976), pp. 17-58.

35. For the general background, see John Vincent, *The Formation of the Liberal Party 1857-1868* (London, 1966); Asa Briggs, *The Age of Improvement* (London, 1959).

36. Rover, op. cit., pp. 211-23 for a complete list of female suffrage bills and voting on them.

37. Ibid., pp. 53-71; W.L. O'Neill, *The Woman Movement*, pp. 29-32, 71-2; Theodore Stanton (ed.), *The Woman Question in Europe* (New York, 1884); Lovejoy, op. cit., p. 152; May Wright Sewell (ed.), *The World's Congress of Representative Women 15-22 May 1893* (Chicago, 1894), pp. 415-21; P.F. Clarke, *Lancashire and the New Liberalism* (Cambridge, 1971); Michael Barker, *Gladstone and Radicalism: The Reconstruction of Liberal Policy in Britain 1885-94* (London, 1975). For Josephine Butler and the movement to combat the state regulation of prostitution, the best source is G.W. and L.A. Johnson (eds.), *Josephine Butler. An Autobiographical Memoir* (Bristol, 1909). See also Constance Rover, *Love, Morals and the Feminists* (London, 1970). Indispensable for the 'moral climate': Trudgill, op. cit., pp. 186-203, 234-47.

38. Gunnar Qvist, *Fredrika Bremer och kvinnans emancipation* (Gothenburg, 1969), p. 380; Gunnar Qvist, *Kvinnofrågan i Sverige 1809-46: Studier rörande kvinnans näringsfrihet inom de borgerliga yrkena* (Gothenburg, 1960).
39. Details of Swedish feminism in Sewell (ed.), op. cit., pp. 527-33; IWSAC 1911, p. 129; IWSAC 1909, p. 121; WSP, pp. 75-6; Gunhild Kyle, *Svensk flickskola under 1800-talet* (Gothenburg, 1973); Gunnar Qvist, 'Kvinnan, hemmet och yrkeslivet', *Den svenska historien* 8 (1968), pp. 284-8. There are fragmentary English accounts of early Swedish feminism in Theodore Stanton (ed.), *The Woman Question in Europe* (New York, 1884) and B.J. Hovde, *The Scandinavian Countries 1720-1865: The Rise of the Middle Classes* (Cornell, 1943), Vol. II. The most recent account, with biographies of leading Swedish feminists, is in Inge Dahlsgård (ed.), *Kvindebevaegelsens hvem-hvad-hvor* (Copenhagen, 1975). For general background, see Ingvar Andersson, *A History of Sweden* (London, 1955), pp. 400-7; Steven Koblik (ed.), *Sweden's Development from Poverty to Affluence 1750-1970* (Minneapolis, 1975), esp. pp. 89-228; and William M. Lafferty, *Economic Development and the Response of Labor in Scandinavia* (Oslo, 1971), pp. 129-43.
40. Dahlsgård, op. cit., pp. 190-200, 380-2, 400-1, 417; Gyrithe Lemche, *Dansk Kvindesamfunds Historie gennem 40 Aar. Med Tillaeg 1912-1918* (Copenhagen, 1939), pp. 26-8, 33-88, 118-21, 230-4, 244; Paulson, op. cit., p. 118; Erwin K. Welsh, 'Feminism in Denmark 1850-1875' (PhD, Indiana, 1974), pp. 151-9, 208, 217, 256-62; WSP, pp. 79-82; IWSAC 1909, p. 131; IWSAC 1911, p. 92; Lafferty, op. cit., pp. 153-9.
41. Brief but illuminating discussion of nationalism in E.J. Hobsbawm, *The Age of Revolution 1789-1848* (New York, 1962), p. 166.
42. WSML, pp. 43-4; WSP, pp. 65-6; ICWT 1899, Vol. I, p. 132, Vol. III, p. 19; ICWT 1909, p. 214; Dahlsgård, op. cit., pp. 316-21, 377-8, 416; Paulson, op cit., pp. 74-7, 94, 95 n.24, 106-8, 110-11, 117, 120, 154n.48, 169n.2, 170-2; Lafferty, op. cit., pp. 116-28; T.K. Derry, *A Short History of Norway* (2nd ed., London, 1968), p. 189; T.K. Derry, *A History of Modern Norway 1814-1972* (Oxford, 1973), pp. 60-205.
43. Sewell (ed.), op. cit., p. 523; Hugh Seton-Watson, *The Decline of Imperial Russia* (London, 1952), pp. 39-40; C.M. Cipolla (ed.), *The Fontana Economic History of Europe*, Vol. 4(2) (London, 1973) pp. 375-485 (general essay on Nordic economies by L. Jörberg); Dahlsgård, op. cit., pp. 253-4, 401; WSP, pp. 54-8.
44. Anna Sigurdardóttir, 'History of Women in Iceland' (Icelandic Women's History Archive, Reykjavík, 1975); Laufey Valdimarsdóttir, *A Brief History of the Women Suffrage Movement in Iceland* (London, 1929); IWSAC 1911, pp. 111-12; J. Nordal, V. Kristinsson (eds.), *Iceland 874-1974* (Reykjavík 1975), pp. 25, 48-52.
45. This is not to imply, of course, that the opposition faced by feminists in these countries was trivial or half-hearted, or that there was anything inevitable about the way in which these feminist movements developed; on the contrary, as we have seen, feminists in America, Denmark and other countries faced many setbacks and suffered many disappointments. But the difficulties faced by feminists in Russia, Germany, the Habsburg Monarchy and France were even greater.
46. Martha Braun *et al.* (eds.), *Frauenbewegung, Frauenbildung und Frauenarbeit in Österreich* (Vienna, 1930), pp. 13-83; and for the general political background, C.A. Macartney, *The Habsburg Empire 1790-1918* (London, 1968), pp. 603-86, 749-809.
47. IWSAC 1909, pp. 42, 87; IWSAC 1911, pp. 81-4; IWSAC 1913, pp. 107-14;

Marie-Hélène Lefaucheux, *Women in a Changing World: The dynamic story of the International Council of Women since 1888* (London, 1966), p. 277; Macartney, op. cit., pp. 603-86.

48. WSML, pp. 102-3; ICWT 1909, pp. 378-80; IWSAC 1911, pp. 107-8; Macartney, op. cit., pp. 687-809.

49. Margrit Twellmann, *Die deutsche Frauenbewegung im Spiegel repräsentativer Frauenzeitschriften. Ihre Anfänge und erste Entwicklung (1843-1888)* (Meisenheim am Glan, 1972), Vol. I; Jutta Schroers Sanford, 'The Origins of German Feminism: German Women 1789-1870' (PhD, Ohio State, 1976); Catherine M. Prelinger, 'Religious Dissent, Women's Rights and the Hamburger Hochschule für das weibliche Geschlecht in mid-nineteenth-century Germany', *Church History* 45/1 (March, 1976), pp. 42-55.

50. Quoted in Irmgard Remme, 'Die Internationalen Beziehungen der deutschen Frauenbewegung vom Ausgang des 19. Jahrhunderts bis 1933' (PhD, West Berlin, 1955), p. 17. For the events reported in this paragraph, see Twellmann, op. cit., Vol. I, pp. 139-77, 196, Vol. II, pp. 526ff.

51. Richard J. Evans, *The Feminist Movement in Germany 1894-1933* (London, 1976), *passim*. See also Amy Hackett, 'The Politics of Feminism in Wilhelmine Germany 1890-1918' (PhD, Columbia, 1976) and Amy Hackett, 'Feminism and Liberalism in Wilhelmine Germany 1890-1918' in B.A. Carroll (ed.), *Liberating Women's History: Theoretical and Critical Essays* (Urbana, 1976), pp. 127-36.

52. Cynthia H. Whittaker, 'The Women's Movement during the Reign of Alexander II: A Case Study in Russian Liberalism', *Journal of Modern History* 48 (2), June 1976 (microfilm demand publication).

53. Richard Pipes, *Russia under the Old Régime* (London, 1975).

54. Richard Stites, 'M.L. Mikhailov and the Emergence of the Woman Question In Russia', *Canadian-American Slavic Studies* 3/2 (Summer, 1969), pp. 178-99.

55. Ruth Dudgeon, 'Women and Higher Education in Russia 1855-1905' (PhD, George Washington University, 1975), pp. 1-13. Despite its title, this is by far the best and most informative account of Russian feminism before the First World War. See also Cathy Porter, *Fathers and Daughters. Russian Women in Revolution* (London, 1976), p. 62.

56. Porter, op. cit., pp. 85-103; Dudgeon, op. cit., pp. 38-43; Barbara Engel, 'From Feminism to Populism. A Study of the Changing Attitudes of the Russian Intelligentsia 1855-1881' (PhD, Columbia, 1974), pp. 66-8.

57. Dudgeon, op. cit., p. 43.

58. Richard Stites, 'Women's Liberation Movements in Russia 1900-1930', *Canadian-American Slavic Studies* 7/4 (1973), p. 461.

59. Dudgeon, op. cit., pp. 74, 125, 77n. 26, 78-81, 84-109; Porter, op. cit., pp. 105-15.

60. Dudgeon, op. cit., pp. 156-92.

61. Ibid., p. 252.

62. Engel, op. cit., p. 69.

63. Lionel Kochan, *Russia in Revolution 1890-1918* (London, 1966), pp. 1-19, 57-60; C.M. Cipolla (ed.), *The Fontana Economic History of Europe*, Vol. 4 (2) (London, 1973), p. 750.

64. Dudgeon, op. cit., pp. 252-300.

65. ICWT 1899, Vol. VII, pp. 89-90.

66. Dudgeon, op. cit., pp. 355-6.

67. ICWT 1899, Vol. VII, p. 129; Dudgeon, op. cit., pp. 357-8 and p. 357 n.31; Stites, 'Women's Liberation Movements', p. 465; IWSAC 1911, p. 123. Union resolution quote in WSML, p. 140.

68. WSML, pp. 143-4; IWSAC 1909, pp. 116-18; IWSAC 1911, p. 124; Dudgeon, op. cit., pp. 355-64; Stites, 'Women's Liberation Movements' p. 465; Hugh Seton-Watson, *The Decline of Imperial Russia* (London, 1955), p. 269.
69. Detailed account of this Congress in IWSAC 1909, pp. 64-5.
70. See below, pp. 177-83. Rochelle L. Goldberg, 'The Russian Women's Movement 1859-1917' (PhD, Rochester, 1976) is mainly useful for its detailed account of the Congress of Russian Women held in 1908 (discussed briefly on p. 123 above).
71. Apart from the studies cited below, and in notes 6-11 to Ch. 1 above, see also James McMillan, 'The Effects of the First World War on the Condition of Women in France' (D.Phil, Oxford, 1976), which contains material on French feminism.
72. Patrick K. Bidelman, 'The Feminist Movement in France: the Formative Years 1858-1889' (PhD, Michigan, 1975), p. 2.
73. Gordon Wright, *France in Modern Times* (Chicago, 1960), p. 90.
74. Theodore Zeldin, *France 1848-1945, Vol. I: Ambition, Love and Politics* (Oxford, 1973), pp. 343-4.
75. Bidelman, op. cit., p. 30.
76. Louis de Borrald, quoted ibid., p. 14.
77. Theodore Zeldin (ed.), *Conflicts in French Society: Anticlericalism, Education and Morals in the 19th Century* (London, 1970), pp. 51-93, 201-13.
78. Zeldin, *France*, pp. 477 ff. In 1848 France had 1,800 km. of railways; in 1870, 17,500 km; Carlo Cipolla (ed.), *The Fontana Economic History of Europe*, Vol. 4 (1), (London, 1974), p. 46.
79. Ibid., Vol. 4 (2), p. 750; Georges Dupeux, *French Society 1789-1970* (London, 1976), pp. 10-11.
80. Claude Langlois, 'Les Effectifs des Congrégations Féminines au XIXe Siècle', *Revue d'Histoire de l'Eglise de France*, Vol. 60, No. 164 (1974), pp. 37-64.
81. Bidelman, op. cit., p. 42.
82. For a discussion of the utopian socialists, see below, pp. 153-6.
83. Bidelman, op. cit., pp. 89-91.
84. Ibid., p. 122.
85. A detailed account is given in Bidelman, op. cit.
86. A large number of women were active in the Commune. See Edith Thomas, *The Women Incendiaries* (London, 1967).
87. The sequence of these various societies seems to have been as follows: 1866 – *Société pour la Revendication des Droits de la Femme*. April 1870 – *Association pour le Droit des Femmes*. June 1870 – *Association pour l'Avenir des Femmes*. 1873 – *Société pour l'Amélioration du Sort de la Femme*. 1881 – *Société pour l'Amélioration du Sort de la Femme et la Revendication de ses Droits*. 1882 – *Ligue Française pour le Droit des Femmes* (see Bidelman, op. cit).
88. Bidelman, op. cit., pp. 134-71, 276, 292, 373 *et passim*; Zeldin, op. cit., pp. 343-62. 605-39.
89. Bidelman, op. cit., pp. 184-271. See also below, pp. 193-4.
90. IWSAC 1909, pp. 96-100; IWSAC 1911, pp. 97-8; IWSAC 1913, pp. 123-4; Suzanne Grinberg, *Historique du Mouvement Suffragiste depuis 1848* (Paris, 1926).
91. WSML, pp. 71-8; WSP, pp. 118-21, 127-8; IWSAC 1909, pp. 85-6, 111-3; IWSAC 1911, pp. 80, 115-17; IWSAC 1913, pp. 104-7.
92. See Pieroni Bortolotti Franca, 'Femminismo e socialismo dal 1900 al primo dopoguerra', *Critica Storia* VIII (1969) pp. 23-62; Società Umanitaria, *L'Emancipazione Femminile in Italia. Un secolo di Discussioni 1861-1961*

(Florence, 1961); Comitato pro Voto Donne, *Diciassette Anni di Lavoro e di Lotta per la Causa Suffragista* (Turin, 1923). See above, pp. 89-90.

3 SOCIALISTS AND REVOLUTIONARIES

ᵠ Feminists and the Working Class

Nineteenth-century feminism was and remained an essentially middle-class movement. Its ideology reflected the social aspirations of the bourgeoisie as well as expressing the emancipatory urge of the female sex. Its benefits were theoretically intended to extend to the whole of womankind, indeed ultimately to the entire human race. In practice, as we saw in the case of John Stuart Mill's classic formulation of the feminist creed, they applied only to the women of the middle classes.[1] Despite this, middle-class women were not alone in fighting for female emancipation; nor was liberalism the only political ideology to incorporate liberation of the female sex. As the industrial revolution spread across Europe and America in the course of the nineteenth century, bringing with it the rapid growth of industrial towns and cities, so the women of the new urban working classes began to add their voices to those of their social superiors in the call for women's rights. Middle-class feminists, of course, were very much aware of the social problems caused by the onset of industrialisation; of poverty, disease and privation in the new slums, of appalling working conditions and meagre wages in the new factories. Indeed, a major impulse behind the emergence of feminism and the mobilisation of middle-class women for the feminist cause lay in the growth of social welfare organisations designed precisely to deal with problems such as these.[2] Many early and above all most radical feminists regarded the economic and social problems of the working classes, and in particular of working-class women, as a serious obstacle to the attainment of their ultimate goal of a society based on equality of opportunity for all. Radical feminists often criticised the moderates for confining their attention to the women of the middle classes. The radicals believed that *all* women should be united in the struggle for their rights, and that the benefits of feminist reforms should not be limited to a relatively small and wealthy minority of the female population.

The feminists' opportunity lay in the fact that male trade unions were frequently hostile to female labour and believed that women's work undercut men's wages. As a consequence, the unions were indifferent to the need of women workers for unionisation in defence of their interests. They certainly did not want to recruit women themselves. Trade unions in the nineteenth century functioned as men's clubs, where the presence of women was deemed inappropriate; the men's wives, too, would certainly have suspected these institutions had women been allowed to attend. Early trade unions in particular were also based on skilled crafts, where women workers were few and far between; female labour was concentrated in unskilled jobs, in domestic work and in casual employment. Working women were also very difficult to unionise. Most of them saw employment either as a brief interlude before marriage, or as a purely temporary expedient designed to help the family out of economic difficulties. Education, socialisation, lack of job prospects, poor wages and terms of employment and the nature of their work combined to give working women a lack of interest in commitment to a union. Only where conditions were particularly bad, as in the glovemaking trade in Chicago, or the textile industry in Crimmitschau in Germany, did they organise and come out on strike, and even this rarely led to the creation of a permanent organisation.[3]

[The solution to all these problems, thought the feminists, lay in women's trade unions. These developed in Britain and the United States in the 1870s.] They were invariably founded by middle-class feminists. The leading figure in the British movement was Emma Paterson, a women's suffrage activist, who joined with other middle-class reformers such as Charles Kingsley, Arnold Toynbee and Harriet Martineau in forming a Women's Protective and Provident League in 1874. When the League attempted to affiliate with the Trades Union Congress, permission was initially refused; the unionists disliked the prospect of admitting 'middle-class ladies'. But in 1876 the League succeeded. After Paterson's death, the League was led by Lady Dilke, wife of a left-wing liberal politician. The League faced several crippling difficulties. Most women's trade unions affiliated to it were ephemeral; many of them, like the Matchmakers' Society, owed their existence to strikes. The most successful of them joined the men's trade unions. In 1886 there were 2,500 women in women's unions, while the female membership of the mixed-sex cotton workers' union stood at 30,000. In 1889, the Women's Trade Union League became a Federation of all trade unions admitting women. This was partly a tactic designed to overcome male opposition to the unionisation of women, expressed in statements such as that made by Henry Broadhurst, the secretary of the British Trades Union Congress, who declared:

They [the men] had the future of their country and children to consider, and it was their duty as men and husbands to use their efforts to bring about a condition of things, where their wives should be in their proper sphere at home, instead of being dragged into competition against the great and strong men of the world.

This was not the feeling of the majority. But while the women's unions remained separate and under middle-class feminist leadership, they made little impact. It was only after the turn of the century, under the energetic leadership of Mary Macarthur, who helped the integration of the women's trade unions into the trade union movement and co-operated closely with the Labour Party, that they met with any measure of success. By 1905 they had 70,000 members, recruited from trades where there were no other opportunities for them to unionise. The opposition of male unionists had been overcome only when it was clear that the women's unions were fighting with them, not against them.[4] The price for this was the abandonment of ties with middle-class feminism.

In America, the national Women's Trade Union League, founded in 1903 and uniting many previously existing women's trade unions, was also led by middle-class women. Its leaders soon found that it was necessary to involve themselves in strikes if they were to gain any support. When a strike began — as in the Triangle Shirtwaist Company in 1910, for example — the WTUL moved in, and brought the resources of its wealthy supporters and the commitment of its organisers and administrators into action. The result was that the WTUL gained a good deal of support, while at the same time minimising the element of class hatred aroused by such conflicts. Nevertheless, like its British counterpart, the American WTUL also soon found itself swallowed up by the labour movement, when it became involved in the struggle being waged between the moderate skilled workers' union movement, the American Federation of Labor, and the revolutionary anarcho-syndicalist Industrial Workers of the World. Reformists to the core, the women backed the AFL, and agreed not to support strikes, such as the textile workers' dispute in Lawrence, Massachusetts, which were run by the IWW. The AFL then began providing the WTUL with funds to organise textile workers in opposition to the IWW. Most feminists went along with this development, but inevitably it meant that they lost control over the WTUL to the male leadership of the American Federation of Labor, which was really more concerned to use the women to defeat rival organisations than to organise them in defence of their interests.[5]

Class cooperation between bourgeois feminists and the women of the proletariat was, then, limited in scale and duration. There were many reasons for this failure of the feminist movement to cross the class barrier. Bourgeois feminists often showed little understanding of the real problems of working-class women. They frequently opposed all restrictions on women's employment as an unwarrantable limitation on their freedom of action. Alexandra Gripenberg, the leading Finnish moderate feminist, spoke for many of her fellow feminists in other countries when she declared at the International Council of Women in 1899 (the word order is hers):

> Restrictions are in opposition to one of the chief principles of our times, the right to self-determination for the individual, which principle most certainly involves the right for the grown-up man and woman to choose their own work and its conditions. No good can come from this principle being abandoned, even if it be in the name of humanity. But these restrictions are also the destroying wind which already in its bud kills women's hope for equal rights. We cannot ask for privileges for women on the ground of their sex and at the same time want them to be recognised as men's equals before the law.[6]

In 1909, the Swedish women's organisation (*Svenska Kvinnornas Nationalförbund*) also reported that it had 'strongly opposed', though without success, a bill to prohibit women in certain industrial employments to work by night, as a restriction on women's liberty and right to work.[7] The feminists' lack of knowledge of the realities of working-class life, and their superficial and legalistic approach to women's rights evidently blinded them to the fact that economic and social circumstances could often push poor women into jobs that were extremely dangerous, and that proper safeguards were often necessary to protect their health at work. They were limited by their background, by their individualism, and by their liberal ideology and associations.

In the 1870s, the British women's trade unions, led by Emma Paterson, opposed the limitation of women's working hours. In 1874, hours were in fact reduced from sixty to fifty-seven hours a week. Paterson claimed that successful lobbying prevented further legislation in 1878.[8] There were further reasons for such hostility. Often, the motives of those who promoted such legislation can fairly be described as anti-feminist. The unions supported it as a means of limiting, perhaps even as a beginning to the process of eliminating altogether, the competition of women in the labour force. Governments and political parties concentrated above all on limiting the working hours of women so as to allow them to continue to keep home. Speeches in favour of such legislation were frequently accompanied by loud praise of the family and denunciations of the feminists who (it was alleged) wanted to break it up.[9] Morally conscious feminists also feared that employers would sooner dismiss women than introduce costly safety measures demanded by the law. Working women, deprived of part of their earnings by the limitation of their maximum hours of work, might take to prostitution in order to make ends meet.

Everywhere paid less than men for equal work, everywhere discriminated against [as the Swedish women's suffrage association (*Landsforeningen för Kvinnans Politiska Rösträtt*) said in 1911 of working women] they are utterly at the mercy of forces over which they have no control. Law-making bodies, understanding neither women nor the meaning of this woman's invasion of modern industry, are attempting to regulate the wages, the hours, the conditions under which they shall work. Already serious wrong has been done many women because of this ill-advised legislation. Overwhelmed by the odds against them in this struggle for existence, thousands are driven to the streets. There they swell that horrid, unspeakably unclean peril of civilisation, prostitution — augmented by the White Slave Traffic and by the machinations of male parasites who live upon the earnings of women of vice.[10]

This was perhaps an unusually forceful statement of this particular point of view, but it did express the feelings of a wide range of feminist opinion.

Those feminists who were concerned about the plight of working-class women to a sufficient degree to do something about it were generally in a minority. By and large, it was the radical wing of feminism that actively tried to recruit the women of the proletariat; 'moderate' feminists were unwilling to countenance the radicalisation of tactics necessary to make such recruitment successful. In France, indeed, the most radical of the feminists operated within the confines of the labour movement itself.[11] This was going too far to the left for most feminists, who remained solidly bourgeois in outlook. There was much concern among the larger women's organisations about the 'servant problem', but this was seen mainly from the employer's point of view. A British representative at the International Council of Women in 1899 remarked: 'The difficulty about domestic servants appears to be twofold. (1) There are not enough servants. (2) The servants that there are are not good enough.'[12] That the 'difficulty' lay in the unattractive nature of the job did not enter the speaker's mind.

A similar condescension also appeared even in the attitudes of those more radical feminists who sympathised with the aspirations of working-class women and wished to help them towards emancipation. In Germany, for example, the radical feminists engaged in frequent and bitter disputes with the moderates during the 1890s and early 1900s over whether the women of the Social Democratic Party should be admitted to the bourgeois women's movement. This was a purely academic question, for after 1896 the Social Democratic women had no intention of even cooperating with the bourgeois feminists, let alone joining them. The radical feminists created their own organisations for working women and also gave financial support to women's strikes such as the great textile strike at Crimmitschau in 1906. But their intention in doing so was either to win over working women from their allegiance to socialism, or to win over the socialists themselves from their belief in revolution and commit them instead to a policy of moderate reformism. They were attempting to extend feminism across the class divide. They criticised socialist women such as Clara Zetkin for preaching 'class hatred'. What they wanted instead was class cooperation. The aim, according to Minna Cauer, the leading German radical feminist, was to 'improve' and 'educate' working women. They were to be helped to emancipate themselves as individuals. The feminists were not interested in emancipating them as a class. Emancipation *from* the working class, rather than emancipation *of* the working class, was what they offered. They set up organisations to train working women for skilled jobs, to educate them, to help them raise themselves as individuals into the middle class. They were suspicious of the organisations which working women themselves created to improve their situation as a social group.[13] In America, many feminists went along with the Progressives in seeing labour organisations as corrupt and tyrannical 'machines'. The Young Women's Christian Association, for example, which had close ties with the more socially conscious wing of the feminist movement, endorsed the eight-hour day but also remarked that

There seems to be no reason why the Industrial Centers of the Association should not take the place of trades unionism and more than fill it . . . The girls are brought together in a closer spiritual contact than any union could give them . . . They believe in collective bargaining, but in the Association they are not likely to be led astray by class emotionalism from their own best interests.[14]

Philanthropic women's organisations of all political shades agreed with
the policy of setting up 'refuges' and 'Industrial Centres' to protect
working-class girls from the evils of big city life. In the case of a conservative association such as the Girls' Friendly Society in England, this
could be tied explicitly to social maternalist purposes and a fundamentally maternalist image of society in which it was the duty of the
upper classes to 'protect' the 'lower orders'.[15] In the case of a radical
feminist movement such as the German *Frauenwohl*, it could be linked
with an attempt to commit working girls to the feminist cause.[16] In
either case it was based on a desire for class cooperation and a rejection
of class conflict. This was natural and wholly desirable from the point
of view of feminists who believed that sexual divisions were more
important than social ones. But they were hindered by their background, even more, perhaps, in the end, by circumstances, by the political and social structures within which they lived, from making the
compromises with proletarian women that were necessary for success.

The feminists wanted ultimately to re-create working women in their
own image. They came to working women conscious of their social
superiority, as 'educated' women 'better placed in life' than the women
of the 'lower orders', as Minna Cauer put it.[17] It was small wonder that
working-class women in many countries increasingly resented the condescension with which they were treated by middle-class feminists. A
working-class woman representing the American Women's Trade Union
League at a NAWSA suffrage meeting in 1913 wrote:

> I feel as if I have butted in wher I was not wanted. Miss Hay gave me
> a badge was very nice to me but you know they had a school teacher
> represent the Industrial workers if you ever herd her it was like
> trying to fill a barrel with water that had no bottom not a word of
> labor spoken at this convention so far. You would have to be a real
> politician now to be a Suffrage. this convention is a verry quite
> serious affair after the hole thing was over some people came to me
> and said I had a right to speak for labour but the kept away until it
> was over . . . I am not goying to wait for sunday meeting, I am
> goying home satturday.[18]

Working-class women had some justification in feeling they were being
used. It was a common theme in feminist propaganda to point to the
vast numbers of women in employment as a justification for giving

women equal rights. Women had an economic interest in the country, it was said; therefore they needed the vote to give it effective representation. Alternatively, it was argued that women were contributing to the country's wealth by working, and therefore deserved the vote and other rights in recognition of this fact. It remained true, however, that many feminists were quite content with a restricted franchise which excluded working-class women from the vote altogether, and that few feminists thought at all about how working-class women might use the vote once they obtained it.[19]

Perhaps the most successful and at the same time the most illuminating instance of a feminist movement's attempt to mobilise working-class women occurred in New Zealand in the 1890s. Conditions in New Zealand were particularly favourable to class cooperation. Industry was on a small scale, class lines were vague, social mobility high, the general tenor of political life ultra-liberal, women's rights already equal to men's in many respects. The women's trade unions were strong, and there was no real socialist movement to speak of; the women's trade unions were generally under middle-class leadership. The New Zealand Woman's Christian Temperance Union which led the campaign for the vote, declared that 'women's franchise will do more for the working class than any combination of unions will ever manage'. Thousands of working women were persuaded to sign petitions for the vote; there was a strong positive correlation between the number of signatures obtained in an area and the strength of the local women's trade union. Yet the 1890 NZWCTU convention voted for a property franchise. After the vote was won, little was done for the needs of working women other than to continue the charitable activities in which the NZWCTU had already been engaged. The truth was that in New Zealand the suffrage issue was centred on a struggle between town and country, and that the feminists, who represented the urban middle classes, were simply using the working women in order to increase their numerical superiority in the face of strong opposition from the conservative-ruled hinterland, which accused them of being unrepresentative of the country as a whole. Once the working women had served their purpose by producing impressive quantities of signatures on suffrage petitions, they were discarded.[20]

In most countries, even this measure of cooperation, one-sided as it was, proved impossible to obtain. The WTUL, both in America and in England, never won mass support until it discarded its feminist leadership and admitted integrated unions. In Germany, the feminists encouraged unionisation only in the small liberal 'Hirsch-Duncker' unions;

the bulk of the labour movement was closely allied to the Social Democrats, rejected the feminists' overtures, and regarded feminist interest in
the unionisation of female workers as hostile competition in the interest
of the bourgeoisie, an attempt to weaken the solidarity of the working
class.[21] In other European countries, the situation was broadly similar,
though in France it was complicated by the tendency of radical feminists to gravitate towards the socialist movement. Even in France, however, the majority of feminists were quite incapable of understanding
the real aspirations of working-class activists. A debate which took
place during a feminist congress in Paris in 1900 sums up the whole
impossibility of a feminist movement across class barriers. Several
working-class delegates were present, and the feminists devoted a good
deal of time to the problems of working-class women. The Congress
passed motions in favour of factory legislation and the eight-hour day.
But deep class differences emerged in the course of a debate on domestic service, as the feminists agreed that to allow servants a day off or to
regulate the employment of young girls would inevitably lead to an
increase in prostitution. The feminists' concern with working-class
morality proved deeply offensive to those working-class and socialist
women who were present. One middle-class delegate urged the working
classes to marry young, and when told by a socialist that their wages
did not allow them to do this, replied that

> the young men of 20 or 25 who are not married get the habit of
> spending money, they live at the café, drink absinthe and apéritifs,
> and then have women; but these women, they have to pay them,
> and the money they spend on that, they would spend much more
> usefully in the interests of their wives and children.

This aroused a storm of protest from the socialists at the congress.
Their views were disregarded. The fact that there had been some controversy did not escape the attention of the presiding officer of the
Congress, Maria Pognon, who was President of the French League for
the Rights of Women. In her closing address, Pognon returned to the
disputes that had taken place during the Congress:

> It grieves us terribly to discover . . . that working women believe
> themselves to be the enemies of bourgeois women. Bourgeois women,
> for our part, are not the enemies of working women, they are their
> friends [repeated applause]. I know that there is a certain party that
> preaches class struggle; well then, I disapprove strongly of this party,

I do not accept class struggle, I accept class union! [Bravos] [22]

The trouble was, bourgeois feminists would only accept class union on their own terms. Working-class women recognised this. They rejected their overtures, and turned to socialism instead.

From Fourier to Bebel

Disillusionment with middle-class feminism turned the active women of the proletariat increasingly back on their own resources. Disappointment with the inadequacies and limitations of liberal feminist ideology also led them towards socialism. Here there was a long ideological tradition to hand with which they could justify the demand for the emancipation of working-class women, a tradition which posed a coherent and viable alternative to the liberal individualist theory of women's rights. The earliest socialist thinkers, the French 'Utopians', took over some of the liberals' views and pushed them to their logical conclusion. Like the liberals, they thought that society should provide equal opportunities for all, and enable every individual to develop her or his potentialities to the full. Unlike the liberals, however, they believed that humans were not isolated individual entities, but social beings in the profoundest sense of the word. The natural state of society was not one of competition but one of harmony and mutual cooperation. The perfect society would be achieved not by removing state intervention but by increasing it, in the interests of all members of society, not just a few. The socialists perceived the limitations of the legalistic approach of liberalism to social reform, and saw through the moralising formulas of 'self-discipline', 'self-control' and 'self-improvement'. Society, they believed, should be run in the interests of the majority — of those who worked and toiled to keep themselves alive. [23]

These beliefs, which, like liberal ideology, derived from the rationalism of the Enlightenment, clearly applied, if taken to their logical conclusion, to women as well as to men; all the more so, in fact, since socialist thought made a point of dealing with the widest possible category of people, and criticised liberalism for restricting the application of its ideas to a minority. The earliest socialist thinkers explicitly included women in their theories. Henri de Saint-Simon and his followers, for example, criticised marriage and advocated communal living, and argued that the emancipation of women was an integral part of the emancipation of the 'useful class', of the workers, engineers and scientists who kept society going. Robert Owen and his disciples, too, believed in communal living and urged a single standard of morality for men and women, with divorce on demand and easily available contra-ception.[24] But by far the most important of these early socialist writers on the emancipation of women was the eccentric but original French thinker, Charles Fourier. Fourier's image of the future society, a mosaic of small, self-governing libertarian and egalitarian communities, was to influence all subsequent pictures of life under socialism. He devoted much of his writing to denouncing the oppression of women.

As a general proposition, social advances and changes of periods are brought about by virtue of the progress of women towards liberty, and the decadences of the social order are brought about by virtue of the decrease of the liberty of women . . . the extension of privileges to women is the general principle of all social progress.

Fourier considered that women were compelled to marry by economic pressures, so that most marriages were loveless. Hence the battery of savage laws designed to maintain reluctant women in 'conjugal slavery'. He criticised women for their failure to rebel against these institutions. 'Slavery', he concluded, 'is never more contemptible than when by a blind submission it convinces the oppressor that his victim is born for slavery.'[25] The origins of women's submission to oppression lay in the fact that 'her whole education had accustomed her to smothering her natural characteristics'. 'In the civilised order it is necessary to stupefy women from their childhood', he wrote; 'It is women who suffer most from civilisation.' In the future socialist society depicted by Fourier, women would be entirely free to choose whatever kind of work they desired and to carry it out as long as they wished.[26] They would be rewarded according to the 'capital, labour and talent' they brought to it. They would be free to marry and divorce as they chose. Children would be cared for communally.

Fourier's theories formed the basis of the socialist approach to women's emancipation. When later socialists in Germany, France and elsewhere, wanted to discuss the problem of women's liberation, above all when they wanted to hold out to women the prospect of an ideal existence in the socialist society of the future, it was to Fourier they turned, not to Marx.[27] But Fourier's ideas were limited in a number of respects. In the first place, he offered no guidance on how the future socialist society was to be created. He simply assumed it would come about by the rational conviction of mankind of its superior merits. Partly for this reason, Fourier had little immediate impact on the working classes, though it was by their plight that he was in the first place moved.[28] Some attempts were made to set up communities according to the guidelines Fourier laid down, above all in America; few of them succeeded for any length of time.[29] It was not easy for working men and women to see the relevance of his ideas. Like most previous writers on women, he confined himself to vague though vigorously expressed ideas on marriage and education. He had nothing to say that was of direct concern to the working-class housewife or the factory girl. He lacked any concept of class struggle. Finally, his ideas were a mixture of the perceptive and the eccentric. He believed, for example, that the planets were bisexual entities constantly engaged in active copulation. He had an obsession with numbers; he enumerated thirty-six kinds of bankruptcy for instance, and a large part of his writing on marriage and the family was devoted to listing seventy-two species of cuckoldry and appending a detailed description of each one. Much of his writing propounded what was at the time an extreme theory of sexual liberation: so extreme was it indeed, attacking almost every kind of sexual repression (which he regarded as a major cause of social and political evils), and advocating almost every kind of sexual activity, including lesbianism, pederasty and flagellation (on the pre-condition of the mutual consent of the partners), that many of Fourier's key ideas remained unpublished until 1967, and many others were ig-nored by subsequent socialist thinkers.[30]

The thinker who had the most immediate and powerful influence on the working classes as far as their attitudes to the emancipation of women were concerned — attitudes as opposed to theory — was not Fourier but Pierre-Joseph Proudhon. While Fourier wrote his major works in the first two decades of the nineteenth century, Proudhon was writing in the 1840s and 1850s, at a time when industrialisation was progressing and the labour movement in France was well under way.[31] Proudhon's thought, like Fourier's, was confused and contradictory, but although, like Fourier, he was self-taught, Proudhon had a gift for the telling phrase and the memorable slogan. On the question of women's emancipation, however, the two thinkers differed profoundly. Proudhon's ideas of socialism were considerably more down-to-earth than Fourier's, although they shared a common vagueness about how they were to be put into effect.[32] Like Fourier, Proudhon believed society should be founded on work, not on property; but the nucleus of Proudhon's social utopia was to be the peasant-artisan family, rather than the free and independent individual.[33] While Fourier peppered his work with outrageous sexual fantasies, Proudhon adhered to puritani-cally rigid standards of sexual restraint. 'If modesty and love were to be taken away from youth, and lust put in their place, young people would very soon lose all sense of morality.' If women were to be made equal with men in public life, concluded Proudhon, men would find them 'odious and ugly', and the end result would be 'the end of the institution of marriage, the death of love and the ruin of the human race'.[34]

Proudhon's views were those of the typical French petty-bourgeois of his day, conservative in many ways, radical in others.[35] His belief that wealth and property should be subjected to social restraints imposed for the good of the community as a whole place him firmly in the socialist camp, but his total hostility to the state, which included even an abhorrence of taking part in elections, also made him the father of French anarchism.[36] His views on state, society and revolution were strongly attacked by Karl Marx; and the history of the First International, the earliest truly international movement of working-class activists and revolutionaries, is to a great extent the history of a clash between the followers of their respective doctrines. Marx and his collaborator Engels had little to say about the emancipation of women, however.[37] For them it was a marginal question; Marx himself barely alluded to it except to repeat, in a slightly modified form, Fourier's critique of marriage in an early unpublished manuscript and in the *Communist Manifesto*.[38] There is also a brief passage on women in *Capital*, much quoted because it is all there is. Later Marxist writers amused themselves with adapting Victorian anthropology (the work of Morgan and Bachofen) to speculations about the role of women in prehistoric and ancient social formations. These works were never intended to have any practical relevance, and their immediate political influence — even that of the most celebrated of them, Engels' *Origin of the Family, Private Property and the State* — was minimal. The influence of Marx and Engels operated rather at a far more general and indirect level, for in shaping socialists' perception of society, it also incidentally helped form their perception of women's place in it.[39]

The seminal book in the formation of socialist attitudes towards women was August Bebel's *Woman and Socialism*. Bebel, an artisan who led the German Social Democratic party from its beginnings in the 1870s until his death in 1913, has usually been described as a 'disciple' of Marx and Engels, and his book is often seen as having 'developed' their ideas in relation to women's emancipation.[40] The first edition of Bebel's book, however, appeared in 1879, before the publication of Engels' *Origin of the Family* (1884), and well before Bebel had even read the basic works of the Marxist canon.[41] It bore few marks of

Marxist influence. Substantial revisions were made in the second edition (1883) and again in the ninth (1891), partly to incorporate the conclusions reached by Engels, partly to include new empirical material. The major influence in the book remained that of Fourier. In later editions, the book was divided into four parts, of which the last, a 150-page depiction of the future socialist society, was almost wholly Fourierist in inspiration, outlining a system, based on work, in which everyone, including women, would freely choose the mode of their existence, the tasks they performed during the day, and the social and sexual relationships they entered into. Women would perform tasks suited to their abilities, and Bebel made it quite clear that he considered these different from men's. Women, he thought, were naturally suited for mothering and bringing up children; indeed, by arguing in the first edition of his book that the need to protect them during childbirth and childrearing gave men their power and supremacy over the female sex, he posited a natural physical origin for sexual inequality that seemed incapable of redress. Women were naturally impulsive and emotional and physically unsuited to heavy manual labour, which destroyed their 'femininity'. Although all occupations, including government, administration, the arts and the professions, would be open to women in the future socialist society, therefore, Bebel left his readers with the impression that most women would opt most of the time for their traditional role of mothering, in which, he assured them at some length, they would have the full support of state and society.

There is some evidence to show that this was the part of the book which readers found most attractive and enticing. But the core of *Woman and Socialism* lay in its second and third parts, which followed on a brief summary of the history of women and the family from the primeval matriarchy to the industrial revolution in Part I. The second part of the book, and at over 220 pages much the longest, was a detailed analysis, inspired by Fourier but resting on extensive empirical investigations, of the oppression of women under capitalism. The penetration of the cash nexus into all aspects of social relations, Bebel thought, had rendered bourgeois marriage loveless and proletarian marriage miserable, it had led to a gigantic growth in the evil of prostitution, with all its fearsome consequences for the women and girls of the working class who were increasingly forced to turn to it to keep themselves alive, and it had destroyed the joy of work and was sucking in vast masses of proletarian women to the grinding boredom, miserable pay and appalling conditions of factory employment. Bebel believed there were two solutions to this situation. One was to fight for equal rights, for women's suffrage, for women's participation in the professions, for equality in Civil and Criminal Law, for equal education, and for adequate legal safeguards against exploitation and poor working conditions. But this, he believed, was a mere palliative. The ultimate solution lay in the socialist revolution, to which he devoted the third part of his book. In fifty clearly-written pages, Bebel outlined his views on the progress of industrial society and the inevitability of its collapse. In later editions of his book, this contained explicitly Marxist elements, though the bulk of Bebel's analysis was still devoted largely to a moral denunciation of the evils of the capitalist system.[42]

Bebel was only a Marxist in the most limited sense of the word. He rejected the idea of violent revolution and trusted in the parliamentary system to bring the proletariat to victory.[43] Of the 557 pages of the 61st edition of *Woman and Socialism*, only three are devoted to the revolution itself, and they are vague in the extreme, more or less dismissing the matter of how the revolution is to be achieved and carried through as a hypothetical question incapable of solution. There is a great deal of evidence to show that most ordinary German socialists learned their Marxism from part III of Bebel's book, and that the great majority of them failed to go on to broaden or deepen their theoretical knowledge.[44] Quite apart from other factors that may have been involved, therefore, it is scarcely surprising that the German Social Democratic Party was immobilist in its tactics, criticising the existing system but doing little to bring about its downfall. But Bebel's book did go well beyond Fourier's work in its concentration on the realities of proletarian existence and its discussion of reformist measures needed to alleviate the worst inequalities and hardships to which the working-class woman was subjected. Most important of all, it encouraged a positive attitude towards women's participation in the labour market. If legislation could be introduced to curb the worst abuses, said Bebel, then women's work outside the home could be immensely beneficial, supplementing the income of the proletarian family and politicising the proletarian woman, who too often showed no understanding for the political or trade union activities of the working-class male.[45]

These views on the positive potentialities of women's work, which owed something to Saint-Simon's general optimism about the effects of industrialisation, were in direct opposition to those of Proudhon and his followers, who argued strongly in the First International that the way to stop the ravages of capitalist industry on the female sex was to ban women's work altogether and send women back to the home. As industry progressed, it became clear that the Proudhonian view was unrealistic, and a majority of socialists everywhere came round to the belief that (in theory at least) the thing to do was to mobilise women in trade unions and political associations and fight for equal pay for both sexes. This, with the insistence on legislation to protect working women and ban their employment in certain 'dangerous' industries, and with the demand for equal rights for women in law, politics and education, was to be the basis for the socialist approach to the problem of women in society during the period of the Second International, which was founded in 1889 almost two decades after the demise of the first and lasted until the outbreak of the First World War twenty-five years later.[46]

Women and Socialism in Germany

Just as Bebel's work formed the theoretical basis for the Social Democratic approach to female emancipation in every country where socialism existed, so the lead in the mobilisation of women to support the socialist cause, and the development of Social Democratic praxis in the emancipation of women, was taken by Bebel's Social Democratic Party of Germany (*Sozialdemokratische Partei Deutschlands*, SPD). In the 1860s and 1870s, the bourgeois women's movement in Germany made several attempts to organise working women, but the organisations so established were soon found inadequate by their members, who were frustrated by their philanthropic, individualist and non-political nature. In 1878, the SPD was banned by the government, and until 1890 membership in it was illegal. This frightened the bourgeois feminists off. By the time they could consider an alliance with groups of working-class women again, in the mid to late 1890s, it was already too late. In the 1880s and early 1890s, associations of working women had sprung up all over Germany, but above all in the great cities of Hamburg and Berlin. Most of their members were married to active Social Democrats. These groups attempted to unite at the end of the 1880s in the Central Association of the Women and Girls of Germany (*Zentralverein der Frauen und Mädchen Deutschlands*), centred on Hamburg, where political activities were allowed to women (as long, that is, as they were not carried out in connection with the SPD). Because of police hostility, however, the Central Association was never able to extend itself far beyond the Prussian suburbs of Hamburg. Its leaders were working-class women with little education, and quarrels and splits — above all, over the administration of the finances — were frequent. Moreover, the Association developed to some extent in isolation from the main SPD. Its ideology, though not very coherent, was at least as much feminist as socialist. The trade unions opposed it because it attempted to recruit working women, and they were sufficiently anxious about the feminist threat that it passed a decree in 1892 that all member unions of the main 'Free' Trade Union Movement, which was close to the SPD, should admit women. This took away much of the Central Association's support. The leading SPD woman, Clara Zetkin (1854-1933), editor of the SPD women's magazine, *Die Gleichheit* (Equality), distrusted the Central Association's feminist elements, and offered it no help. Finally, deprived of members by the unions, cold-shouldered by the party, and attacked in 1895-6 by a new wave of repression from the police, the Central Association collapsed in ruins and ceased to exist.[47]

The foundations for a really successful socialist women's movement in Germany were laid by Clara Zetkin in a remarkable speech delivered to the SPD's congress in 1896.[48] After some hesitation in the early 1890s, Zetkin had accepted the impossibility of merging women's groups into the general party organisation. In most parts of Germany, women were barred from joining political parties, and to allow women to join the party would simply have resulted in the dissolution of the party organisation by the police. At the same time, men in the party were unwilling to see positions of power and responsibility entrusted to women, so that those women who tried to devote themselves actively to the party soon found their efforts frustrated. Zetkin's solution was ingenious. She took Bebel's theory of women's emancipation, and used it to stress that working women's struggle to emancipate themselves was an integral part of the proletariat's struggle for emancipation. Then she emphasised the irreconcilable gulf between bourgeois and proletarian women, and declared that the women of the SPD would never have any truck with bourgeois feminism. Finally, Zetkin linked these ideas with a concrete plan of action. Building on the experience of the early 1890s in Berlin, she proposed an elaborate structure of local agents coordinated by a national team of 'agitators' based on Berlin.[49] Communication and commitment would be maintained by *Die Gleichheit*, the magazine edited by Zetkin herself. The plan was enthusiastically received by the party, and an additional element was added in 1900 by the creation of a biennial conference held by the SPD women's movement in conjunction with the party congress.[50]

By insisting on the unbridgeable nature of the class gap between feminists and socialists, Zetkin allayed the party's fears of separatist or feminist tendencies in its women, and secured its backing for the rapid build-up of an elaborate and basically autonomous structure for its women's movement. Zetkin further gained the trust and confidence of the SPD by ruthlessly crushing all feminist tendencies within the women's organisation. The chief representative of the feminist viewpoint, Lily Braun (1865-1916), was hounded out of the socialist women's movement. Zetkin's task was made easier by the fact that feminism in the Social Democratic party was closely associated with revisionism, a doctrine of outspoken reformism based on a rejection of some of the key tenets of Marxism. Revisionism was formally rejected by the party, and this enabled Zetkin to defeat its female supports, who also advocated cooperation with bourgeois feminism, with comparative ease.[51] Zetkin tied the SPD women's movement firmly to the party majority and the orthodox party line. Its policy was steered by her from her dominant position within the SPD women's organisation in Berlin, and presented formally to the movement and the party in the pages of her magazine *Die Gleichheit*.[52] From 1905, assisted by the general expansion of the party as a whole, and helped by a relaxation in the attitude of the police, the movement began a period of expansion which only ended with the outbreak of the First World War in 1914.

Clara Zetkin was unquestionably the leading woman socialist in Europe, indeed in the world, after the turn of the century.[53] Of her possible rivals, Rosa Luxemburg (1871-1919), who surpassed her in intellect, took no interest in female emancipation, which she referred to as 'old ladies' nonsense'.[54] Zetkin came from a background of middle-class radicalism, and had been educated in the 1870s by Auguste Schmidt (1833-1902), the leader of the bourgeois feminist movement in Germany until the turn of the century. She had become a socialist after meeting a group of Russian revolutionaries in Leipzig, her home town, and during the 1880s she lived with one of them, Ossip Zetkin, in Paris, taking his name, though not marrying him because she wanted to retain her German citizenship. She was not a very original thinker, but she had undoubted political gifts, which she allied with an uncompromising emotional commitment to radicalism. She soon became a Marxist, and her lifelong involvement in the cause of revolution in Russia further radicalised her after the failure of the Russian revolution in 1905. As she moved over to the extreme left of the SPD, so she lost favour with the increasingly reformist party leadership. In addition, the trade unions were beginning to take exception to the SPD women's movement's overt opposition to reformism. The expansion of the movement itself, with its rapidly proliferating organisational structure, made it progressively more difficult for Zetkin to manage its affairs from behind the scenes as she had done at the turn of the century.[55] In 1908, when

women's membership in political parties became legal all over Germany
for the first time, the party leadership took the opportunity of incor-
porating the women's movement more closely into the party and replacing Zetkin with the less radical Luise Zietz at its head. Zetkin continued to edit *Die Gleichheit*, but even here she was forced to include
an ever-increasing amount of non-political matter ('for mothers and
children') in its contents.[56]

Luise Zietz (1865-1922), who replaced Zetkin as leader of the SPD
women's movement, was of working-class origin. She was not an intellectual like Zetkin, and lacked her talent for theoretical synthesis. First
and foremost Zietz was a recruiter. Incessantly on tour, whipping up
support and signing on new members all over the country, she represented the new-style bureaucratic leadership which was replacing the
old-style charisma of women like Zetkin throughout the SPD.[57] Under
Zietz's guidance, the SPD women's movement reached a membership of
nearly 175,000 by 1914. In addition to this, its agitators also took an
active part in the unionisation of women workers, resulting in a total of
nearly 216,000 women trade unionists immediately before the outbreak of the First World War. Zetkin's magazine *Die Gleichheit* also
increased rapidly in circulation, reaching 124,000 subscribers in 1914.[58]
All this made the German Social Democratic Women's Movement by
far the most impressive socialist women's organisation anywhere in the
world. It was the first mass women's emancipation movement organised
by the working classes. It mounted impressive demonstrations and
marches for women's suffrage all over Germany from 1911 onwards;
and it also held countless mass meetings on a wide variety of topics
throughout the year.

The SPD and its women's movement pioneered many advanced policies on female equality. In 1895 the party introduced a motion in favour
of female suffrage into the German Reichstag for the first, but certainly
not for the last time. In 1896 the Social Democrats were almost alone
in offering consistent opposition to the male supremacist Civil Code in
the Reichstag. They consistently demanded a greater measure of
protection for women workers. The SPD women also argued that it was
their duty to take up the neglected heritage of German liberalism,
abandoned by a frightened and reactionary bourgeoisie, and as a consequence urged the equality of women in education and the professions.
They supported equal pay for equal work, and *crèches* for working
mothers. Clara Zetkin urged her readers in *Die Gleichheit* to bring up
their children so that boys would do housework and girls would not
confine their interests and ambitions to so-called 'female' roles. The

party criticised Germany's penal abortion laws and favoured the avail-
ability of contraceptives. It ran educational courses for women which
dealt with intellectual as well as practical questions. Individual women,
such as Rosa Luxemburg and also, though to a lesser extent, Clara
Zetkin herself, played a leading role in the party's affairs. The leader
of the party, August Bebel, was, as we have seen, a convinced supporter of women's rights and the author of an important book on the
emancipation of women.[59]

Nevertheless, the SPD's record on women's rights was not wholly
positive. It did not always translate its ideals into practice. In local
legislatures it sometimes dropped the demand for female suffrage and
merely asked for the vote for adult men.[60] It was sufficiently influenced by bourgeois concepts of sexual 'modesty' to discourage open
discussion of abortion and contraception and declare these things a
matter for the individual conscience – some Social Democrats, indeed,
including Clara Zetkin and Rosa Luxemburg, actually opposed them,
the reason in their case being that the proletariat needed all the people
it could get to make the revolution, and that a high working class birth-
rate would swell the revolutionary masses.[61] Its educational courses for
women were eventually run down precisely because they were thought
'too intellectual'. On equal pay, events were to prove that the party
was merely paying lip service to the idea. In calling for a revision of
sex-role-divisions, Zetkin was in a tiny minority. By demanding greater
protection for women workers, the SPD's main concern was to protect
motherhood and the family. Above all, the attitudes revealed by male
SPD leaders to the women within their own ranks were a whole world
away from the grand theories of emancipation and equality contained
in the party's literature. Social Democratic Women's Congresses were
full of complaints by the women about male party functionaries who
deliberately used bad language to shame them into withdrawing from
the party's decision-making bodies.[62] Male Social Democrats frequently
used sexist humour to ridicule female opponents in debate.[63] Even
August Bebel himself made disparaging remarks about Zetkin and
Luxemburg when they disagreed – they were, he said, irrational, impulsive and confused, 'just like women'. Of his own wife Julie, on the
other hand, he remarked condescendingly that she had been an ideal
'helpmate' and 'supporter of his ideals' throughout their married life.[64]
Within the party, the women's section, run by women and catering for
women, was thought too trivial to be of real importance; hence its
continuing autonomy, even (though in a more limited way) after 1908.
The only SPD magazine allowed to purvey revolutionary views after

1912 was Zetkin's *Die Gleichheit*;[65] the reason was probably that the
party leadership, assuming that these views would be incomprehensible
to the women, and believing that it would not matter much even if
they were not, thought this a reasonable price to pay for the magazine's
continued usefulness in keeping the SPD women's movement free from
the bug of bourgeois feminism. Despite all this, the SPD women as a
whole never considered leaving the party and joining the feminists.

How are we to account for the fact that the SPD invested a large
amount of its money and a good deal of its reputation in building up a
massive women's organisation and in repeatedly insisting on the party's
commitment to female equality, when at the same time it denied
women equality within its own ranks and clearly regarded them as
second-class citizens? The answer is surely to be sought in the first
instance in the place of the Social Democratic movement in the German
political system. Although it was the fastest growing, and by 1912 the
largest party in the Reichstag, the SPD was largely powerless to implement its own policies. Not only was the Reichstag itself unable to exert
a positive influence on the government, which was appointed by the
Kaiser and responsible only to him, but in the country at large the
SPD's members were constantly harassed by police, employers and
governments, stigmatised as traitors out to undermine and destroy the
fabric of German society, sacked from their jobs, arrested and imprisoned on the flimsiest of pretexts, and subjected to a vast barrage
of counter-propaganda aimed at converting them to support the *status
quo* and the parties of the right.[66] The SPD's response was to immu-
nise itself against these influences by withdrawing from society as far
as it could and creating its own 'state within a state', with its own
elaborate organisation, its own press, its own library, its own sports
clubs, its own musical and cultural societies, and so on. Thus protected,
it would concentrate on building up its own internal strength in preparation for the revolution which it awaited with unshakeable but entirely
passive confidence. In the process of creating its own subculture, the
SPD became very worried about the lack of political commitment
among its members' womenfolk. There is abundant evidence to show
that the unions and the party were increasingly prone to anxiety about
the tendency of unpoliticised working-class women to dissuade their
husbands from participating in strikes and political activities, to continue adhering to the Catholic faith, and to bring up their children in a
traditional manner, transmitting to them their own indifference and
lack of comprehension in matters of Social Democratic politics and
ideology. The SPD's campaign to recruit women was largely directed

towards cementing the ideological solidarity of the Social Democratic family, ensuring, as Clara Zetkin put it, that it would be 'supportive and receptive' to the political ideals of its male head, and fostering in it 'understanding for his strivings'.[67]

The SPD women's movement was, correspondingly, largely a movement of married women, many of whom were housewives for most of the time.[68] It was not a movement of women workers. The unions, it is true, did place bulk orders for *Die Gleichheit*, but these were not distributed to women workers, but to male trade unionists for their wives and children to read.[69] The SPD's appeal was consciously directed towards housewives, and there is evidence to show that campaigns based on complaints about high food prices had most success in recruiting women to the party.[70] The SPD would never have been so successful in winning over women to its cause had its appeal not fulfilled a real need in working-class society. Industrialisation, the removal of work from home, and the increasing employment of married women outside the house, were placing new strains on the cohesion of the working-class family. The ideological unity offered by the SPD through the political mobilisation of women was one way of coping with these difficulties. But it meant that in the end the women's role remained a secondary one within the party. The women's movement dealt largely with 'women's questions'. Its role within the party thus corresponded in the last analysis to the role of its members in the proletarian home.

The Socialist Women's International

Working-class parties in nineteenth-century Europe, above all those influenced by the ideas of Marxism, believed strongly in cooperation between the proletariat of different countries. In the 1860s, there had been an attempt, in which Marx himself had played a leading part, to form an international socialist movement, known to historians as the 'First International'. In 1889 a second attempt was made. This 'Second International' lasted until 1914. It was dominated by the German Social Democrats, the SPD, by far the largest and best-organised of the socialist parties of the day. As the SPD women's movement expanded in the mid-1900s, so its leading figure at that stage, Clara Zetkin, who had close ties with other socialist movements through her Russian connections and her residence in Paris in the 1880s, naturally thought of creating a Socialist Women's International. It came into being in 1907, when Zetkin organised an International Socialist Women's Conference in conjunction with the Congress of the Second International held that year in Stuttgart, where she had her home.[71] Among the various member countries, England sent 19 delegates, Germany 16, Austria 7, Hungary 3, France 3, Bohemia 2 and Norway, Belgium, the USA, the Netherlands, Finland, Switzerland, Italy, Sweden and Russia sent one delegate each. This did not provide an entirely accurate reflection of the extent to which the socialist movements of various countries had succeeded in establishing women's organisations of their own. The three French delegates really represented nobody but themselves, for example, while the single Finnish representative could speak for several thousand socialist women in her native land. Apart from this, the balance of numbers at the conference also failed to give an adequate impression of the overwhelming dominance of the Germans. This was more precisely expressed in the administrative arrangements which resulted from the Conference and in the voting on the programme for the movement. The resolutions passed were the work of Zetkin. They reflected the tactical rigidity of the Germans and expressed Zetkin's desire to demonstrate that the gap between socialist and bourgeois women was everywhere unbridgeable. Two principles were affirmed by the Conference. First, that all Social Democratic parties must be firmly committed to votes for men *and* women, and not be allowed to accept the introduction of manhood suffrage, and secondly, that there must be no cooperation with bourgeois feminists.[72]

The principal opposition to the suffrage motion came from the Austrian delegates, representing the women's section of the Social Democratic Party of the German-speaking part of the Habsburg Empire. This was one of the largest and best-organised socialist women's movements outside the German Empire, and it had gained its strength from many of the same factors that underlay the rise of the German movement. As in Germany, so in Austria, women were legally barred from taking part in political meetings and joining political organisations. There was a large and well-organised Social Democratic Party whose theory derived directly from that of its German counterpart. Bebel's *Woman and Socialism* was as influential in Austria as it was in Germany. The party's Hainfeld programme (1888-9), like the Erfurt programme of the SPD, contained a demand for women's suffrage. But the Austrian party's attitude towards women's emancipation was as ambivalent as the German's. Its leader, Victor Adler, both opposed the creation of a separate women's movement and advised the women not to risk violating the Law of Association by engaging in politics. He did reaffirm his belief in female suffrage in 1903, and ten years previously the party had held two large women's assemblies and demanded the vote for the female sex. But Adler was above all a gradualist, and he insisted that the party's first aim must be the vote for men. In Austria, unlike in Germany, this was a real possibility, and Adler did not wish to jeopardise its achievement by advancing the more radical demand for votes for women. Accordingly, the Social Democrats mounted massive demonstrations for *manhood* suffrage; at the beginning of 1907 this was granted, under pressure, by the Crown, which was in a far weaker position than its German counterpart, and therefore offered concessions in a bid to preserve the unity of the Empire.

The Austrian Socialist Women's Movement benefited considerably from the granting of universal manhood suffrage. Like its German counterpart, it had already published its own magazine, the *Arbeiterinnen-Zeitung* (founded 1892), with a circulation of 10,500 in 1907, and in Adelheid Popp it enjoyed a leader of considerable stature. But in 1896 Popp had failed by one vote to get the backing of the Party Congress for an official women's organisation, and despite resolutions passed by women's congresses in 1898 and 1903, trade union opposition had prevented the formation of local women's clubs. In 1907, manhood suffrage prompted a reorganisation of the party. The Czech Social Democrats broke away and created their own organisation, and the women now began to follow suit at a local level, thus presenting the party with a *fait accompli*. Fearful of losing the women altogether, the party agreed to a compromise, helped by a more lenient attitude on the part of the police and by the undoubted fact that female suffrage was 'next on the list' of its programmatic aims, now that universal manhood suffrage had been secured. An official women's organisation was established, linked to the party but with rather more independence than its German counterpart. Women's conferences were to be held every other year. A massive recruiting campaign was launched. Doubtless the Austrian women felt some satisfaction that their agreement to let the party campaign for manhood suffrage first and go on to female suffrage later had been worthwhile. Accordingly, when they came to the Stuttgart Conference in August 1907 all seven Austrian delegates voted against the German motion. After 1907, the Austrian Social Democratic women's movement went from strength to strength. In 1907 it numbered some 4,000 women. By 1911 it had grown to 17,823. In 1913 it contained 28,058 women in 312 different local branches. By June 1914 the circulation of the *Arbeiterinnen-Zeitung* stood at 29,000. It developed a wide range of policies, including equal pay, civil marriage, equality in Civil Law, factory legislation, legal divorce and the public provision of *crèches* for working mothers. Massive demonstrations were held on inflation, housing, unemployment and the federalisation of the monarchy. Above all, like its German counterpart, it came to concentrate on the suffrage, which it increasingly saw as the key to all other reforms, although it was to be proved disastrously wrong. The Austrian Social Democratic Women's Movement remained much the strongest force campaigning for women's rights within Austria itself. It constituted the only really large and well-organised socialist women's movement outside the German Empire.

However, it was by no means the only socialist women's movement organised on the German model. Perhaps the most interesting of the other organisations of this type were to be found in Scandinavia. Like their Austrian counterpart, however, they did not conform in every respect to the German pattern; nor were the attitudes of their parent socialist parties the same either. The largest socialist women's movement after those of Germany and Austria was probably that of Finland. By 1904 the Finnish Social Democratic Party had some 3,895 women members, or 23 per cent of the total membership. Female membership was concentrated in towns and in centres of rural industry such as the Kymi valley with its pulp and paper mills. The exploitation of timber was the country's main industry and, once child labour was eliminated (1883), women provided between 60 and 70 per cent of the force. Female employment rates in this sector remained constant until the First World War, and women workers may well have provided the bulk of members. The 1905 revolution in the Russian Empire had powerful repercussions in Finland, where it began with a nationalistic General Strike and led to the granting of a liberal constitution, including female suffrage, in 1906. During the revolution the Finnish Social Democrats became a mass party, with 9,575 women members in 1905 and no fewer than 18,896 in 1906 (22 per cent of the total). This expansion reflected the political awakening of the countryside, where women were accorded a degree of 'primitive equality' with the men, and took a major part in farm work. The party's women's journal, *Palvelijatar* ('the serving-woman'), was meant for female farmhands. With the growth of Tsarist repression after 1907, the socialist movement declined, and by 1913 there were only 12,280 woman members (23 per cent.) Still, this was a significant number even on a European scale; and, in addition, there were also a number of women who played an important role in the socialist movement as a whole.

The situation in Sweden was rather different. Because of the domination of the Swedish Social Democratic movement by workers in heavy industry, women formed only a very small group within the party. The first Social Democratic Women's Club, in Stockholm, founded in 1892, had fifty-eight members; another similar club formed in Malmö in 1888 counted forty-two women. The women took part in Social Democratic marches and demonstrations as a group. In 1897 a woman joined the party's executive committee, and in 1900 a women's magazine, *Morgonbris*, was founded by the Social Democrats. Despite all this activity, the movement was weak and received little support from the party. The Swedish Social Democrats were formally committed to female suffrage, but they did not discuss the subject at their congress until 1905, and then they voted against a female suffrage campaign by ninety-six votes to sixty-six. An attempt by the women to call a special conference to debate this decision was rejected. The women's movement, which seems to have been about 1,000 strong, allowed its individual members to work with bourgeois feminists, but still rejected any kind of cooperation at a formal level. The Swedish women socialists also supported Clara Zetkin's line at the Stuttgart Congress in 1907. They organised marches and demonstrations on International Proletarian Women's Day in 1912 and 1913 – another of Zetkin's creations, and one of the most successful. By this time, because of the advances made in manhood suffrage, the party was giving them more support. But the dominant tone in *Morgonbris* and in the speeches of Swedish Social Democratic women in 1914 seems to have been one of resignation and despair; one of them opined that Sweden would probably be the last country in Europe to give women the vote. The problem, ultimately, was that the unions continued to put a brake on the party in questions of women's rights. The growth of heavy industry in the late nineteenth and early twentieth centuries had had the effect of reducing female employment in industry to much lower levels than obtained in Finland. Women scarcely played any role in Swedish trade unionism until the First World War, their membership of the main trade union movement (*Landsorganisationen*) rising above 2,000 only in 1907-8. From 1911 to 1916 women formed about 5.5 per cent of trade union membership. The Swedish trade unions played an important role in the Social Democratic Party; their membership was larger, and a syndicalist secession in 1909 which cut the trade union movement from 186,000 to 80,000 (1907-10) also halved the membership of the Social Democrats (112,000 in 1905 to 55,000 in 1910), thus indicating the close connection between the two movements. The trade union movement in Sweden was indifferent to the demands of its female members. Most of these were in the tobacco, bookbinding, clothing and food industries; the textile workers left in 1912. They opposed women taking on overtime work, and by charging women only half the normal membership dues further reduced their status within the movement. Although the similarities in social and occupational structure between the Swedish and German labour movements, both political and trade union, were striking, the crucial difference as far as the recruitment of women was concerned was that the Swedish Social Democrats were not persecuted by the state and so felt no need to construct a 'total subculture'; they thus lacked the incentive which impelled the German Social Democrats to devote so much effort to the recruitment of their wives and daughters to the cause.[73]

Social Democratic women's movements, like their bourgeois counter-parts, usually went through a number of phases in their development. Often they started through resistance to or disillusionment with the attempts of middle-class feminists to recruit working women to their cause, and proceeded to develop their own organisation separate from bourgeois feminism. The early hostility of the labour movement was over-come, usually, at the price of a loss of independence. Not every socialist women's movement followed this pattern, however, as we shall now see.

America, France and Britain

Three socialist women's movements were all in their own way so different from the German paradigm that they deserve separate treat-ment. The first of them was the American. Up to the 1890s, American socialism was dominated by German immigrants who adhered closely to Marxist precepts, rejected cooperation with bourgeois feminism and opposed any special women's rights agitation as divisive. Female partici-pation was low. But in the 1890s the socialist movement diversified, Americanised and widened its horizons from the narrow trade union view which had so discouraged the recruitment of women in the 1860s and the 1870s to a wider appreciation of social change and social reform. Its practical work became increasingly educational in character. In 1901 the foundation of the Socialist Party of America, which belonged to the Second International, opened up new opportunities for socialist and working-class women. Socialist women's clubs sprang up everywhere. Some of the party's leading agitators, like Lena Lewis, were women. Yet these groups were only on the periphery of the party. As they threatened to form an autonomous, and possibly very radical organisation, the party at last took notice. Spurred on by the 1907 Stuttgart Congress of the International, it formed a Women's Commit-tee in 1908. A women's organisation was formed, held congresses and undertook agitation run by the women themselves (despite some efforts by party men to control affairs themselves).[74]

Outwardly, then, the American socialist women's movement became rather like its German counterpart once it got under way in 1908. Bebel's *Woman and Socialism* was the basis for its reading circles and educational groups. They rejected the idea of cooperating with bourgeois feminists in the usual way. This rejection was not accepted in many areas, and it became a major focus of controversy within the movement in 1909-10. The Women's Committee cooperated with the suffragists in 1909, but the party leadership opposed this, fearful lest their women's branch should be swallowed up by the suffragists altogether. The New York socialist women agreed with this view, disillusioned with the feminists after what one of them described as the 'humiliating' experience of cooperating with them in the Triangle Shirtwaist strike of the same year. Others, including the Chicago socialist women, disagreed. Ella Bloor, who was a member of both the Socialist Party and the suffrage movement, argued, during the women's socialist congress of 1910 at which the issue was debated, that the American socialist women's movement had 'less reason to conduct a separate campaign . . . than . . . our comrades in Europe, where the suffrage movement is to some extent conducted on class lines'.[75] This was not entirely accurate; though by this time suffragists in Germany at least were abandoning the idea of universal suffrage, there were also indications that their American counterparts were doing the same thing. But at least the American suffragists never committed themselves formally to a property franchise.

More to the point, while in Germany the socialist women's organisation was at least ten times as big as the female suffrage movement, in America the proportions were the reverse. For various reasons, it seems impossible to put a precise figure on the strength of the American socialist women's movement, but it is unlikely to have been much greater than 15,000 at its height in 1912, and was probably less.[76] The bourgeois suffrage movement was already 75,000 strong in 1910, and its campaigns were far more impressive than any the socialists could mount. Moreover, it also mobilised many other organisations, some of which, such as the Woman's Christian Temperance Union, were a good deal larger than itself, in support of these campaigns. It was hard, therefore, for the socialist women to resist the suffragists' appeal to them to join in the suffrage crusade. In 1911 they participated in a general suffrage campaign in California, and claimed credit for its success, thus legitimating cooperative ventures in further state suffrage campaigns. At the same time, in other areas, separate socialist suffrage campaigns were mounted. In effect, as the compromise finally reached in the 1910 congress indicated, local associations were left to their own devices on this question.

These internal divisions of the American women's socialist movement on the question of cooperation with bourgeois feminists were characteristic of the disorganised and confused nature of the American Socialist Party as a whole. The party could never decide whether to support the women fully or not; one wing endorsed the principle of manhood suffrage, another rejected suffrage of any kind as politically irrelevant. The tensions of which disagreements such as these were the symptoms broke the Socialist Party apart after 1912. Its membership, both male and female, declined. The women lacked an autonomous union movement to back them up; unionism was anti-socialist and craft-oriented, and, as we saw earlier in this chapter, allowed women very little room for manoeuvre. The Women's Trade Union League was first controlled by the feminists, then by the anti-socialist unions. Nor was the Socialist Party ever able to develop an autonomous subculture, cut off from the rest of society, such as gave the German Social Democrats the impulse to place high priority on the political mobilisation of their womenfolk. In these circumstances, the socialist women's movement was a somewhat artificial creation in America. It attempted to revive its declining fortunes by campaigning for birth control, but the post-war 'Red Scare' finally put it out of existence in 1920.[77]

Further opposition to the Germans at the 1907 Stuttgart Conference came from the English and French representatives, though in the end the opponents of the commitment to universal suffrage could only muster a total of eleven votes to the majority's forty-seven. The English objected on two counts. First, they resented the Germans' insistence that there could be no toleration of demands for a limited property franchise. They argued that it could form a useful stepping stone to the enfranchisement of all women. Secondly, the English also objected to the corollary of the Germans' denunciation of a limited franchise, that there could be no cooperation between bourgeois and proletarian women. In this they were backed by the French, led by Madeleine Pelletier, who later complained that the German women had 'rejected what they call bourgeois feminism with an ostentation totally lacking in dignity'. The difference of opinion reflected the fact that neither the English nor the French socialist movement had succeeded in creating the total 'society within a society' that the German and Austrian socialist parties achieved. The relative fluidity of class boundaries, the lack of any laws barring women from participation in politics, the strength of liberalism and parliamentary institutions, all these combined in England and France to allow a certain cooperation between leftist bourgeois feminists and the socialist movement. In addition to this, the labour movement in both France and England was fragmented and internally divided, so that there could be no equivalent of the great monolithic socialist women's movements of Germany and Austria. And in France in particular, the almost total absence of mass support for socialist women's organisations combined with complete indifference to women's rights on the part of the major socialist organisations to allow ample scope for individual middle-class feminists such as Pelletier who hoped to use the labour movement in the struggle for the vote.[78]

The list of such women included Astié de Valsayre, an eccentric middle-class Saint-Simonian who fought a duel with an Englishwoman on the site of the battle of Waterloo in 1866 and spent much of the 1890s attempting to commit the 'Possibilist' party in the socialist movement to women's rights; Aline Valette, a teacher, involved in 'rescue' work among prostitutes, and author of a successful 'Guide for Housewives' who tried to secure the endorsement of women's rights by the 'Guesdist' (Marxist) wing of the movement during the same period; and also the feminist Madeleine Pelletier, who led the fight for women's rights within the united socialist movement until 1913. Their efforts met with little success. Despite the fact that the French socialists were formally committed to women's rights from the mid-1880s onwards, and were periodically persuaded to reaffirm this commitment, they never took any practical steps to put it into effect. When they gave in to pressure from the women to back female candidates at elections, they invariably put them up in constituencies notorious for being hoeplessly reactionary. The solitary exception was in 1906, when Elisabeth Renaud, a middle-class woman strongly committed to socialism, stood in a constituency on the outskirts of Vienne in the Isère and received 2,869 votes, over a quarter of those polled. The circumstances were quite exceptional, however, and owed much to the close connection in the Isère between a women teachers' pressure group and the socialist movement. In other elections in which women candidates stood, the votes they received were derisory. The labour movement continued to be hostile or indifferent. In 1888 the trade unions declared women's factory work a 'monstrosity', and in 1898 they repeated that men should be able to earn enough to support their womenfolk. Guesde himself rejected all suggestions that his party should actively recruit women. In 1890-3 the total number of women in the party was twenty; in 1894-9 it was fifty-three. The numerous attempts to found a socialist women's movement seldom united more than one or two dozen people before collapsing.[79]

The French showed some interest in German ideas on women's emancipation. Bebel's book was the source of most French women socialists' ideas. Clara Zetkin was the model for socialist women such as Louise Saumoneau, who insisted, like Zetkin, that the class struggle was more important than the sex war, and rejected all cooperation with bourgeois feminism. Saumoneau, who was of working-class origin, dominated yet another tiny women's group, the *Groupe des Femmes Socialistes*, founded in 1913. After expelling the feminists from the movement, Saumoneau began an energetic recruiting campaign closely linked to the socialist party organisation. But the war intervened before it could bear any fruit. In 1914, when the socialists had over 90,000 members, the female membership of the party stood at less than 1,000 and there was only one female delegate at the Party Congress. In keeping with the German experience, half the women in the party were wives or daughters of members. Women had no special section of their own in the party, and played no role in the local committees, which were mainly devoted to a discussion of electoral tactics. All but three of the party's deputies in the Chamber favoured votes for women. But female suffrage was regarded as something that could safely be put off until after the revolution. The French socialists were frequently embarrassed by the paucity of women socialists in their country at a time when there were hundreds of thousands of them in Central Europe. But they never translated their embarrassment into action. The history of the socialist women's movement in France is a history of isolated individuals. Some of these, such as Flora Tristan, Louise Michel, or Louise Saumoneau, managed to leave a mark on their times. But none of them ever succeeded in creating a mass movement.[80]

In France, the socialist movement was relatively weak. In 1914, it had 90,725 members and polled 1,400,000 votes; the SPD in Germany had over a million members and in 1912 had polled four and a quarter million votes. But the difference was not so great, particularly when we consider that the population of Germany was between 1½ and 2 times greater than that of France. The rate of female employment in the two countries was not dissimilar. The crucial difference lay in the nature of industry, which was small-scale in France, large-scale in Germany. Small-scale industry meant a large number of artisans, who depended on unpaid female help (that of their families) to keep their businesses going. These were the backbone of the French socialist movement. They saw no reason to involve their womenfolk in politics — unlike the German socialists, who were, after the turn of the century, increasingly drawn from the employees of mammoth industrial concerns. The attitude of the rank and file of the French socialist movement to women thus remained obstinately Proudhonian in character. It was typified by the lifelong opposition of Auguste Keufer, leader of the printers' union and the most prominent and successful of the moderate trade unionists,[81] to the admission of women to his organisation, which in 1913 even expelled one member, M. Couriau, for allowing his wife to work as an independently qualified printer.[82]

These factors were quite different from those at work in the case of England, where industrialisation was far more advanced, but where class collaboration had submerged the nascent labour movement in the liberal party in the middle of the nineteenth century. The emergence of a socialist movement in the 1890s and early 1900s occurred much later than in Germany, where the failure of liberalism in the 1860s had led to an early polarisation of politics along class lines — a process that only began in Britain at the end of the century. Socialism in Britain was therefore a fringe phenomenon, only gradually gravitating towards the centre of the political stage. Like all marginal political movements, it was split into a number of factions in its early days. Ironically, it was the Marxist faction of the movement, the Social Democratic Federation, that proved most hostile to women's rights. Its leader, H.M. Hyndman, was strongly anti-feminist, and another prominent figure, E. Belfort Bax, was a member of the Men's Anti-Suffrage League, a writer of anti-feminist tracts and indeed something of a misanthrope in general. The Social Democratic Federation, perhaps because it was in reality thoroughly confused and eclectic in its politics, containing a spectrum of political opinion broad enough to include both anarchism and anti-semitism, none the less had a strong feminist wing. By 1910 there were ten branches of its women's section. They coexisted uneasily on the far left with syndicalist women's groups, anarchist women (especially in London's East End) and Sylvia Pankhurst's East London Federation of Suffragettes, a splinter group of the bourgeois feminist suffragettes which cooperated closely with the mainstream labour movement. In a sense, Sylvia Pankhurst was remaining true to the suffragettes' origins in the Lancashire labour movement. The Pankhursts posed the nascent Labour Party with something of a problem. Their aim was principally to commit the party to female suffrage; they were feminists first and socialists second, even before they broke off their ties with the party in 1906. Their support of a limited suffrage divided the party, and when

they began militancy, which Ramsay MacDonald condemned in 1914 as
reactionary, they gave those in the party who were less than enthusiastic about female suffrage their chance. The Labour Party, even more
gradualist and certainly far less Marxist than its Austrian counterpart,
was quite prepared to accept manhood suffrage and refused to commit
itself formally to votes for women. Nevertheless, because of the tradition of class collaboration in mid to late nineteenth-century British
politics, it was far more willing to cooperate with middle-class organisations than were socialist parties elsewhere. It worked closely with the
Women's Freedom League, a militant but anti-Pankhurst splinter group
of the suffragette movement, with the women of the intellectual Fabian
Society, and with the Women's Trade Union League. In 1906 it established a women's section, which sent representatives to the 1907 Congress in Stuttgart. This was a loose federation of a number of groups
with a largely middle-class leadership. Like the Labour Party itself, it
was cautious and gradualist. By 1910 it had 5,000 members, making it
one of the larger groups in the Socialist Women's International. Despite
the fact that Bebel's *Woman and Socialism* was by all accounts the most
widely read work of socialist theory on the emancipation of women in
England as well as in other countries, the Women's Labour League was
neither combative nor theoretically inclined. It remained to a great extent middle-class in composition, and its commitment to gradual reform
was never in doubt. The close ties of the Labour Party with the constitutional suffragists, an increasing number of whom were becoming
members of the party out of despair with the Liberals' continued opposition to their cause, meant in practice that it was at least as much feminist as socialist, and probably a good deal more so. This was a curious
situation — a temporary expedient brought about by abnormal and
extraordinary political circumstances — and once the vote was gained,
most of the suffragists probably left the Labour Party, though a minority
may well have stayed.[83]

The heterogeneity of the various national branches of the Socialist
Women's International, and the fundamental differences of opinion
between them on crucial issues such as female suffrage and cooperation
with bourgeois parties, meant that it was difficult to regard the International as a united or organised body, just as it was with the international feminist organisations. The Socialist Women's International
was effectively the creation of one woman, Clara Zetkin. She was its
founder and International Secretary, and her magazine, *Die Gleichheit*,
published only in German, was its official organ. Its headquarters were
in Stuttgart, where Zetkin lived; in fact, they were in her private home.

There was no formal bureaucracy and as an international body the Socialist Women's International had no real existence, not even to the extent that one was enjoyed by its parent body the Second International. The socialist women met only when the Second International met. In between times, Zetkin corresponded with personal friends in other countries, but there does not seem to have been much contact between the different movements at an official level. Though the Germans, led by Zetkin, dominated it even more than they dominated the Second International, their dominance was more theoretical than practical. The writings of Bebel and Zetkin were the basis for socialist theory on women's emancipation in every country, but socialist practice was another matter. Zetkin could get resolutions passed at Congresses, but she had no means of enforcing them, and in fact they were generally disregarded by those socialist women's movements, such as the American, the Belgian and the English, which disagreed with them. Moreover, Zetkin lost her power base in 1908 when she was replaced as leader of the German Social Democratic Women's Movement by Luise Zietz, who entirely lacked her international background and had virtually no interest in international affairs. By 1914 Zetkin was really one of a small and rather powerless radical minority within the SPD, and was no longer able to exert any real influence on the Socialist Women's International. She opposed the First World War, was expelled from the SPD, lost her editorship of *Die Gleichheit*, and eventually gravitated towards the Communist Party; she was however excluded from a real position of power within the Communist Women's International because her conception of Communism was in some ways closer to Rosa Luxemburg's than it was to Lenin's. After 1917, the international revolutionary women's movement was dominated by the Russians rather than by the Germans; and quite apart from the prestige of having participated in a successful revolution, the Russian women also had the advantage of a tradition of female involvement in revolutionary movements that went all the way back to the 1860s. It is to this tradition, therefore, and to its considerable ambiguities and complexities, that we now turn our attention.[84]

From Radical Feminism to Revolution

We saw in a previous chapter that until the Revolution of 1905 Russian feminism was unusually moderate and conservative in outlook and methods. Radical feminism was unable to emerge until the 1905 Revolution because of the extremely repressive attitudes of the authoritarian Tsarist régime. Reformists were either cowed into submission, like the moderate feminists, or driven to revolutionary activities. This is essentially what happened with Russia's missing radical feminists. The Russian feminist movement of the 1860s was subjected to repeated frustration at the hands of the authorities. Such small gains as were made were not infrequently lost as a new wave of repression swept the country. Each setback brought a fresh group of disillusioned young feminists into the ranks of the revolutionary movement, and redoubled the determination of the moderate feminists, led by Anna Filosofova, Nadezhda Stasova and Mariya Trubnikova, to proceed with even greater caution and circumspection than before. Two sources were especially important in providing female recruits for the revolutionary movement. It was characteristic of the Russian experience that both represented the achievements of the feminist movement while at the same time deriving much of their revolutionary potential from the strict limits set by the government on the movement's progress. The first lay outside Russia altogether, in Switzerland. While the Russian government had conceded to the feminists the demand for better secondary education, thus enabling women to qualify for university entrance, it had refused to allow them entry into the universities, so obliging them to study abroad. The favoured university for Russian women in the 1860s and 1870s was Zürich, where there were few non-academic obstacles to their obtaining the medical or other qualifications which they desired. A sizeable group of Russian girls was studying there by the 1870s; indeed, they were so noticeable that they attracted considerable hostility from the local inhabitants. They were thus thrown back on the community of Russian political exiles in the city for their social contacts. Politicised by contact with men such as the anarchist Bakunin and the populist Lavrov, they began to form a political discussion group and to take an active part in the energetic publishing concerns of the revolutionaries. These events soon attracted the attention of the Tsarist secret police, which set up a special section in 1872 'to deal with the ever-increasing flood of women leaving for Zürich, and the deplorable events taking place in their midst'. In 1873 these investigations led to a government decree officially depriving all Russian women attending university courses abroad after 1 January 1874 of their right to obtain either education or employment in Russia. The effect of this decree was decisive; it turned a substantial number of the women into undying enemies of the Tsarist régime. When they eventually returned to Russia, some of them via the Sorbonne, from which the Russian consul in Paris secured their expulsion in 1874, they immediately plunged into the thick of the revolutionary struggle.[85]

Meanwhile in 1869 the Russian government had conceded the establishment of the Alarchinsky courses, preparatory courses for university entrance roughly equivalent to the higher levels of boys' secondary education. Their participations came from merchant, clerical and petty-bourgeois backgrounds, unlike the women of the provincial nobility who had formed the backbone of the feminist movement in the 1860s. Their intellectual enthusiams led them to form reading circles; as their knowledge widened, they came into contact with the revolutionaries, whose concerns were similar to their own. The gravitation of radical feminists towards the revolutionary movement was helped by the movement's strong support for the idea of female emancipation. Consisting entirely of intellectuals, above all of the new waves of students of non-noble origins admitted to the universities after the liberal reforms of the 1850s, the movement devoted itself to bold theorising about the future society, unencumbered by the need to compromise with political reality or take account of the anti-feminist prejudices of a working-class following. The proclamation of 'Young Russia' in 1862, for example, called for the 'complete emancipation of women [and] the abolition of marriage as a phenomenon both highly immoral and unthinkable where there is complete equality of the sexes'.[86] It called for the communal rearing of young children. Almost identical views were put forward by the most influential of the revolutionary writers of the time, Nikolai Chernyshevsky, who declared: 'Hitherto a wife has simply been her husband's servant . . . All relations between man and woman, husband and wife, have therefore always been repulsive.'[87] These ideas were far from original. The concentration of the Russian radicals was still focused on the question of marriage, which had always been the central concern of individual theorists on women's emancipation through the ages, and their ideas on the subject were taken almost verbatim from Fourier. What was original about the Russians was the literalness with which they took these theories. Unlike other writers on the topic, they proceeded immediately to put their ideas into practice.

There was thus a convergence of revolutionary radicalism and left-wing feminism in Russia in the early 1860s. Young women who wished to gain legal independence were helped by the revolutionaries through the device of the 'fictitious marriage', a marriage ostensibly like any other, but in reality carried out in order to transfer the legal power of the girl's parents to her new legal husband, who would then voluntarily relinquish it, shake hands and go on his way. In addition to this, many young women disillusioned with conventional feminism found their way into communes, experiments in group living which again owed much to the inspiration of Fourier. Fourier's fantasising about sexuality was of course largely unknown to the Russians at this period, and there was much theorising in the revolutionary movement about the virtues of chastity. The Russian intelligentsia, suddenly liberated from decades of oppression and swamped with masses of new members from backgrounds that were (relatively speaking) socially deprived, immediately proceeded to demand the reconstruction of the totality of society, which naturally included the redefinition of institutions such as marriage and the family. To a great extent, the movement was one of the young in rebellion against their parents, both personally and in terms of the pervasive paternalism of Russian society as a whole. This gave young male revolutionaries a natural sympathy with the aspirations of their sisters. The degree of oppression under which such men suffered, and the extent to which their rights were circumscribed by state and society, was so great in Russia that they automatically identified with the struggles of the female sex to free itself from a subjection that was scarcely more severe than their own.

In the mid-1860s, as the government clamped down on dissent once more after the Polish revolt (1863) and the attempted assassination of the Tsar (1866), the emphasis of the revolutionary groups and communes shifted away from social experimentation and concentrated more on direct action to achieve the overthrow of the government, first by propaganda and the awakening of the masses, then, finally, when this failed, by violence, by the assassination of the Tsar. The movement became more committed to revolutionary action, suffered harsher repression from the police and became more clandestine and conspiratorial in character, and in the process, issues such as the rights of women were gradually relegated to a secondary position, then dismissed altogether as belonging to the presumed benefits of the revolution that was expected to follow the Tsar's assassination.[88] The last revolutionary proclamation addressed to women alone appeared in 1871. After that, women were subsumed in the audience for the general call to revolution. There is some evidence that women were being used by revolutionaries in the 1870s without regard to their own particular problems. Their dedication was presumed upon to persuade them to become mistresses to rich men in order to help raise funds for the revolution, or, less dramatically, they were used to carry out menial and secretarial tasks without being given a real share in the revolutionary work.[89] This was ironic, since the motive behind the participation of many of these women in the movement was precisely the same need to prove their own worth and independence that in other countries could be fulfilled by legitimate reformist activities.[90] This situation changed once more, however, during the last phase of the struggle against Tsar Alexander II. The proportion of women in the revolutionary movement had been steadily rising. Some 5 per cent in the 1860s, mainly noble in origin, it reached 15 per cent in the 1870s and in the last phase, 1879-81, it was 30 per cent.[91] The group concerned in these last three years, the People's Will, was aimed solely at the assassination of the Tsar. This gave the men little chance to use their superior education to acquire a position of dominance; and the monkish, conspiratorial egalitarianism of the members, each of whom was judged solely by his or her dedication to the cause, ruled out any thought of apportioning labour according to sex. It was in fact a woman, Sofia Perovskaya, who finally carried out the group's death sentence on the Tsar in 1881. Arrested after the deed, she became the first Russian woman to suffer execution for a political crime.[92]

Most histories of the Russian revolutionary movement come to a stop at this point. But the movement in fact carried on its terrorist activities through the 1880s and 1890s and into the twentieth century. In the period 1850-90 twenty-one out of the forty-three people sentenced to hard labour for life (a sentence generally reserved for terrorist crimes) were women.[93] The Socialist Revolutionaries, the heirs to the revolutionary movement of the 1860s and 1870s, continued a policy of terrorism and assassination, in the belief that the resulting disorganisation of the state apparatus could bring about a reconstruction of society on the basis of the peasant commune. Women continued to take a prominent part in this movement; the best known of them was probably Maria Spiridonova, who shot a general in 1906, and became the leader of the left Socialist Revolutionaries in 1917, taking the party into a disastrous insurrection against the Bolsheviks in the summer of 1918. Spiridonova and her numerous female comrades, who formed a large proportion of the inmates of special women's prisons in the early 1900s, were of bourgeois and noble origin, continuing the tradition of an earlier age.[94] The experiences and mythical force of the terrorist groups of the late 1870s, above all the People's Will, had stamped themselves indelibly on the Socialist Revolutionaries, and ensured that women would continue to play a major role in terrorist activities.

Towards the end of the nineteenth century, a second wing of the revolutionary movement emerged in the shape of the Social Democrats, a Marxist-oriented party. Its emergence reflected the beginnings of an Industrial Revolution in Russia, above all in the major cities of Moscow and St Petersburg, in the 1890s and early 1900s. Like the

Socialist Revolutionaries, the Social Democrats also believed in female equality, but very much on the pattern of the German Social Democrats, from whom they derived their ideas on the subject. The party's 1903 programme called for the regulation of women's work and the protection of working mothers.[95] The propaganda of the movement was heavily influenced by the writings of Bebel and Zetkin. The major women's leader in the Russian Social Democratic movement, Alexandra Kollontai, the renegade daughter of a Russian general, wrote *The Social Bases of the Woman Question*, published in 1908, which repeated at enormous length Zetkin's insistence on the need to separate socialist women's movements from bourgeois feminists. From 1905 onwards Kollontai devoted much of her activities to denouncing the Russian feminists at their meetings, culminating in her disruption of the First General Congress of Russian Women, held in St Petersburg in 1908, accompanied by catcalls from the feminists and followed by an attempt by the police to arrest her.[96] Especially after 1905, the Social Democratic women were much more lower class than their Socialist Revolutionary counterparts — half the known female activists in the party were from a worker or peasant background, a quarter were Jewish, and only a quarter noble or merchant in origin. The Social Democrats were not a terrorist organisation, and prestige was acquired through theoretical writings, which gave the men, with their superior education, a distinct advantage. Nineteen women attended the party congress in 1907, but none in 1912, and women played only a minor and subordinate role.[97] In 1913, the radical minority faction in the party, the Bolsheviks, led by Lenin, paid more attention to the recruitment of women; they had encountered strong female resistance in a campaign waged in 1912. They tried to establish a Social Democratic women's movement on the German model, and held a meeting to celebrate International Proletarian Women's Day in 1913. Although a network of working women's clubs was gradually developed, it was impossible in the circumstances to create a large mass movement of proletarian women along the lines of the German movement.[98] All in all, despite the presence in the Bolshevik hierarchy of a number of women (though not Kollontai, who remained, though somewhat uneasily, a Menshevik until 1915), it was clear the the role of women in Bolshevism was much less prominent than it was in the terrorist movement, though it was still far greater than in the German SPD. The predominantly uneducated, lower-class nature of the party's female support, combined with the high prestige of intellectual attainment among the Bolsheviks, made it difficult for women to get to the top in the movement. Like other revolutionaries, too, the Bolsheviks sometimes tended to regard the emancipation of women as something that would have to wait until after the revolution; the revolution would bring it anyway, and for women to demand it before the revolution came was held to be divisive and to distract attention from the all-important task of overthrowing the Tsarist régime.

What socialist and revolutionary women's movements achieved, and how they evolved during and after the First World War, are questions that must await the Conclusion of this book for discussion. It is necessary at this point to turn back to the history of middle-class feminism in its radical phase, where we left it at the end of Chapter 2, and examine the nature of the impact which the rise of the socialist women's movement had upon its further development. That impact, as we shall now see, was profound.

Notes

1. See above, pp. 30-1.
2. See above, pp. 59, 64, 78, 95, 104, 131.
3. For trade union attitudes to women workers, see in particular Madeleine Guilbert, *Les Femmes et l'Organisation Syndicale avant 1914: présentation et commentaires de documents pour une étude du syndicalisme féminin* (Paris, 1966); Gladys Boone, *The Women's Trade Union Leagues in Great Britain and the United States of America* (New York, 1942); US Bureau of Labor, *Report on the Conditions of Woman and Child Wage Earners in the United States* (1910), Vol. X.
4. Boone, op. cit., pp. 20-35.
5. Lois Banner, *Women in Modern America: A Brief History* (New York, 1974), pp. 58-75; William L. O'Neill, *Everyone Was Brave*, pp. 155-61; Allen F. Davis, 'The Women's Trade Union League: Origins and Organisation', *Industrial and Labor Relations Review*, Jan. 1964, pp. 1-17.
6. Countess of Aberdeen (ed.), *International Council of Women: Report of Transactions of the Second Quinquennial Meeting, held in London, July 1899* (London, 1900), Vol. 7, p. 48.
7. Countess of Aberdeen (ed.), *International Council of Women: Report of Transactions of the Fourth Quinquennial Meeting, held in Toronto, Canada, June 1909* (London, 1910), p. 322.
8. Boone, op. cit., p. 22.
9. Discussion with German examples in my *Sozialdemokratie und Frauenemanzipation in Deutschen Kaiserreich 1871-1918* (Verlag J.H.W. Dietz Nachf., Hanover, 1979).
10. *International Woman Suffrage Alliance: Report of Sixth Congress, Stockholm, 12-17 June 1911* (Stockholm, 1911), pp. 69-70. Similar sentiments were voiced by the leading French moderate feminist Maria Deraismes in 1889. Cf. Patrick K. Bidelman, 'The Feminist Movement in France: The Formative Years 1858-1889' (PhD, Michigan, 1975), p. 306.
11. See p. 173 above.

12. *International Council of Women . . . 1899* Vol. 7, pp. 86-7. Cf. Theresa McBride, *The Domestic Revolution* (London, 1975), for an analysis of domestic service in England and France.
13. See Chapter 4 of my *Sozialdemokratie und Frauenemanzipation*.
14. J. Stanley Lemons, *The Woman Citizen. Social Feminism in the 1920s* (Urbana, Illinois, 1973), p. 138.
15. Brian Harrison, 'For Church, Queen and Family: the Girls' Friendly Society 1874-1910', *Past and Present* 61, Nov. 1973.
16. Lida Gustava Heymann, in Zusammenarbeit mit Dr. jur. Anita Augspurg, *Erlebtes-Erschautes. Deutsche Frauen kämpfen für Freiheit, Recht und Frieden: 1850-1940* (ed. Margrit Twellmann, Meisenheim am Glan, 1972), pp. 87-97.
17. Else Lüders, *Minna Cauer. Leben und Werk. Dargestellt an Hand ihrer Tagebücher und nachgelassenen Schriften* (Gotha, 1925), p. 95.
18. Quoted in Aileen S. Kraditor, *The Ideas of the Woman Suffrage Movement 1890-1920* (London, 1965), p. 160.
19. Richard J. Evans, *The Feminist Movement in Germany 1894-1933* (London, 1976); Kraditor, op. cit.; Constance Rover, *Women's Suffrage and Party Politics in Britain 1866-1914* (London, 1967); Patricia Grimshaw, *Women's Suffrage in New Zealand* (Wellington, 1972), pp. 80 ff.
20. Grimshaw, op. cit., pp. 32-3, 47-9, 114-20.
21. See Clara Zetkin, *Zur Geschichte der proletarischen Frauenbewegung Deutschlands* (Frankfurt am Main, 1969), pp. 57-9.
22. Charles Sowerwine, 'Women and Socialism in France 1871-1921: Socialist Women's Groups from Léonie Rouzade to Louise Saumoneau' (PhD, Wisconsin, 1973), pp. 142-56.
23. E.J. Hobsbawm, *The Age of Revolution 1789-1848* (New York 1962), pp. 285-90; George Lichtheim, *A Short History of Socialism* (London, 1970), pp. 3-47.
24. Brief accounts in Sheila Rowbotham, *Hidden from History: 300 Years of Women's Oppression and the Fight Against It* (London, 1973), Chapter 8, and the same author's, *Women, Resistance and Revolution* (Harmondworth, 1974), Chapter 2.
25. Charles Fourier, *Design for Utopia. Selected Writings of Charles Fourier,* ed. Charles Gide (New York, 1971), pp. 77, 80.
26. J. Beecher, R. Bienvenu (eds.), *The Utopian Vision of Charles Fourier. Selected Texts on Work, Love and Passionate Attraction* (London, 1972), pp. 175, 177.
27. Cf. above, pp. 156-8.
28. Cf. editors' discussion in Beecher and Bienvenu, op. cit., and Fourier (ed. Gide), op. cit.
29. Ibid., for an introduction to the extensive literature on these communities.
30. Beecher and Bienvenu (eds.), *The Utopian Vision of Charles Fourier,* Intro. and *passim*.
31. Lichtheim, *A Short History . . .*, pp. 49-64.
32. James Joll, *The Anarchists* (London, 1964), pp. 81-2.
33. Ibid., pp. 61-79.
34. Stewart Edwards (ed.), *Selected Writings of Pierre-Joseph Proudhon* (London, 1970), p. 255.
35. George Woodcock, *Pierre-Joseph Proudhon: His Life and Work* (New York, 1972), pp. 34-6.
36. Theodore Zeldin, *France, 1848-1945, Vol.I: Ambition, Love and Politics* (Oxford, 1973), pp. 458-66.
37. Juliet Mitchell, *Woman's Estate* (Harmondsworth, 1971), pp. 76-80.

38. Shlomo Avineri, *The Social and Political Thought of Karl Marx* (Cambridge, 1968), pp. 89-91, for a brief discussion of Marx's thought on this question.
39. These Marxist ethnographical studies included works by Kautsky and Lafargue. For their lack of impact, see Sowerwine, op. cit., pp. 71-5. Any Marxist theory of women's liberation must start at the level of general social theory, since it is impossible to get round the paucity of references in Marx's own work. Bebel's theory was only Marxist to a limited extent; Zetkin, who was more thoroughly acquainted with Marxism both as theory and as praxis, came closer to producing a genuinely Marxist theory of the emancipation of women. But essentially the task still remains to be carried out. The many recent discussions of Engels' *Origins of the Family* mainly serve to indicate its limitations in this respect.
40. E.g. Mitchell, op. cit., p. 80; Rowbotham, *Women, Resistance and Revolution* (Harmondsworth, 1974), pp. 80-4.
41. For Bebel's ideological development, see Hans Mommsen (ed.), *Sozialdemokratic zwischen Klassenbewegung und Volkspartei* (Frankfurt am Main, 1974), esp. p. 33.
42. August Bebel, *Die Frau und der Sozialismus* (61st ed., Berlin, 1964). An English translation of the second edition was published as *Woman in the Past, Present and Future* (London, 1885).
43. See W. Blumenberg (ed.), *August Bebels Briefwechsel mit Friedrich Engels* (The Hague, 1965).
44. For the impact of Bebel's book, see Hans-Josef Steinberg, 'Workers' Libraries in Germany before 1914', *History Workshop: A Journal of Socialist Historians*, Issue I (Spring, 1970), pp. 166-80.
45. I have attempted a more detailed analysis of Bebel's work in my *Sozialdemokratie und Frauenemanzipation.*
46. See Werner Thönnessen, *The Emancipation of Women. The Rise and Decline of the Women's Movement in German Social Democracy 1863-1933* (London, 1973), pp. 15-27.
47. See Chapter 2 of my *Sozialdemokratie und Frauenemanzipation*, which reconstructs the history of the Central Association from political police files in the Hamburg State Archives.
48. Reprinted in Clara Zetkin, *Ausgewählte Reden und Schriften* (East Berlin, 1957), Vol. I.
49. For a detailed analysis of this organisational structure, see Jacqueline Strain, 'Feminism and Political Radicalism in the German Social Democratic Movement 1890-1914' (PhD, California, 1964).
50. A full stenographic record of the proceedings of the *Frauenkonferenz* is attached to each relevant volume of the Party Congress Proceedings (*Parteitagsprotokoll*).
51. A detailed narrative of these disputes can be found in Jean Quataert, 'The German Socialist Women's Movement 1890-1918: Issues, Internal Conflicts and the Main Personages' (PhD, California, 1974).
52. For a detailed account, with full references, see Chapter 3 of my *Sozialdemokratic und Frauenemanzipation.*
53. The standard biography is Luise Dornemann, *Clara Zetkin. Leben und Wirken* (5th ed., East Berlin, 1973). There is a perceptive and illuminating account of Zetkin's career up to 1914 in Karen Honeycutt, 'Clara Zetkin: A Left-Wing Socialist and Feminist in Wilhelmian Germany' (PhD, Columbia, 1975).
54. Quoted in Honeycutt, op. cit., pp. 251 n.103, 287.
55. For the general background, see Carl E. Schorske, *German Social Democracy 1905-1917: The Development of the Great Schism* (Cambridge , Mass., 1955).

56. Accounts in Chapter 4 of my *Sozialdemokratie und Frauenemanzipation*. Dornemann, op. cit., and Honeycutt, op. cit.
57. Cf. Schorske, op. cit., drawing on the classic work by Robert Michels, *Zur Soziologie des Parteiwesens in der modernen Demokratie. Untersuchungen über die oligarchischen Tendenzen des Gruppenlebens* (2nd ed., Stuttgart, 1954).
58. Thönnessen, op. cit., p. 119.
59. Accounts of the party's policy on women can be found in the *Stenographische Berichte über die Verhandlungen des deutschen Reichstags* (esp. 1895-6) and in the section *'Frauenbewegung'* of the *Parteitagsprotokolle* (esp. in the last few volumes before the outbreak of World War I and the first volume issued in wartime). For Rosa Luxemburg, see J.P. Nettl, *Rosa Luxemburg* (2 vols., Oxford, 1966). For Zetkin's role in the party, see Dornemann, op. cit., and Honeycutt, op. cit. For a full analysis of the SPD's attitude towards women, see my *Sozialdemokratie und Frauenemanzipation*, ch. 5.
60. E.g. in Hamburg, 1905-6. Cf. *Stenographische Berichte über die Sitzungen der Bürgerschaft zu Hamburg im Jahre 1906*, 4. Sitzung, 24 Jan. 1906, p. 113.
61. Ulrich Linse, 'Arbeiterschaft und Geburtenentwicklung im Deutschen Kaiserreich von 1871', *Archiv für Sozialgeschichte XII* (1972), pp. 205-72. The views of Zetkin and Luxemburg are documented in Staatsarchiv Hamburg, Politische Polizei, S8897/IV: *Vorwärts*, 24 Aug. 1913, *Der Pionier*, 10 Sept. 1913 and *Hamburger Echo*, 31 Aug. 1913, and analysed in my *Sozialdemokratie und Frauenemanzipation*, Ch. 5.
62. See for example Friedrich-Ebert Stiftung, Bonn-Bad Godesberg/Archiv der Sozialen Demokratie: Nachlass Gerda Weyl, Lebenserinnerungen von Klara Weyl.
63. Thönnessen, op. cit., pp. 66-7.
64. August Bebel, *Aus Meinem Leben*, quoted in Quataert, op. cit., Ch. 8 (an interesting analysis of the SPD's views on sex roles).
65. Dieter Groh, *Negative Integration und revolutionärer Attentismus. Die deutsche Sozialdemokratie am Vorabend des Ersten Weltkrieges* (Berlin, 1974), p. 212 n.15.
66. Klaus Saul, *Staat, Industrie, Arbeiterbewegung im Kaiserreich. Zur Innen- und Aussenpolitik des Wilhelminischen Deutschlands* (Düsseldorf, 1974).
67. Quoted in Honeycutt, op. cit., pp. 206-22, 358-87.
68. This conclusion is reached on the basis of an extensive discussion of the available statistics in Chapter 4 of my *Sozialdemokratie und Frauenemanzipation*.
69. It was for this reason that the circulation of *Die Gleichheit* only began to increase rapidly after the introduction of special supplements for 'mothers and children'.
70. E.g. Ralf Lützenkirchen, *Der sozialdemokratische Verein für den Reichstagswahlkreis Dortmund-Hörde* (Monographien zur Geschichte Dortmunds und der Grafschaft Mark, Bd. 2, Dortmund, 1970), pp. 114-32.
71. Dornemann, op. cit., pp. 209-15.
72. *Die Gleichheit*, Vol. 17, No. 18, 2 Sept. 1907, pp. 150-1.
73. Thomas L. Hamer, 'Beyond Feminism: The Women's Movement in Austrian Social Democracy 1890-1920' (PhD, Ohio State, 1973); Hulda Flood, *Den Kvinnorörelsen i Sverige socialdemokratiska* (Stockholm, 1960); Ross Evans Paulson, *Women's Suffrage and Prohibition: A Comparative Study of Equality and Social Control* (Brighton, 1973), p. 147n.17; Per Schybergson, 'Barn- och kvinnoarbete i Finlands fabriksindustri vid mitten av 1800-talet', *Historisk Tidskrift för Finland* 59/1 (1974), pp. 1-17; Lennart Jörberg, 'The

Industrial Revolution in the Nordic Countries', in C.M. Cipolla (ed.), *The Fontana Economic History of Europe* (London, 1973), Vol. 4 (2), pp. 375-485; Gunnar Qvist, *Statistik och politik. Landsorganisationen och kvinnorna på arbetsmarknaden* (Stockholm, 1974); Jacques Droz (ed.), *Histoire Générale du Socialisme* (Paris, 1974), Tome II, 'Finlande'; G.D.H. Cole, *A History of Socialist Thought, Vol. III Part 2: The Second International 1889-1914* (London, 1956), pp. 677-708; Steven Koblik (ed.), *Sweden's Development from Poverty to Affluence 1750-1970* (Minneapolis, 1975), pp. 177ff.; information from Dr. David Kirby (SSEES, London).

74. Mari Jo Buhle, 'Feminism and Socialism in the United States 1820-1920' (PhD, Wisconsin, 1974); Elizabeth G. Flynn, 'Women in the American Socialist Struggle', *Political Affairs* (April, 1960), pp. 33-9.

75. Quoted in Buhle, op. cit., p. 264.

76. The two standard authorities on socialist history estimate the total strength of the American Socialist Party in 1912 variously at 150,000 and 118,000 (G.D.H. Cole, *A History of Socialist Thought, Vol. III: The Second International 1889-1914; Part III* (London, 1956), p. 775, and Jacques Droz (ed.), *Histoire Générale du Socialisme,* Vol. II (Paris, 1974), p. 495). In 1911, 35 branches reported a combined membership of 1,677 women; the total number of branches is uncertain. The Women's Committee estimated female membership at 10 per cent in 1911 and 15 per cent in 1912. In 1911, women were serving as secretaries to at least 158 branch committees. (Buhle, op. cit., p. 184.)

77. Buhle, op. cit.

78. *Die Gleichheit,* loc. cit.; Sowerwine, op. cit., pp. 244-6.

79. Sowerwine, op. cit., *passim.*

80. Marilyn Boxer, 'Socialism Faces Feminism in France 1879-1913' (PhD, California, 1975) is another informative account.

81. For Keufer, see Zeldin, op. cit., pp. 218-20.

82. Sowerwine, op. cit., pp. 294- 4; There is an extended account of the Couriau Affair in Boxer, op. cit.

83. Sheila Rowbotham, *Hidden From History. 300 Years of Women's Oppression and the Fight Against It* (London, 1973), pp. 77-107.

84. See Honeycutt, op. cit., for a brief critical resumé of Zetkin's later career.

85. The classic work on the Russian revolutionary movement up to 1881 is Franco Venturi, *Roots of Revolution. A History of the Populist and Socialist Movements in Nineteenth Century Russia* (London, 1960). For the general background, see Richard Pipes, *Russia under the Old Régime* (London, 1975), and Hugh Seton-Watson, *The Decline of Imperial Russia* (London, 1952). There is a collective biography of women revolutionaries in Robert H. McNeal, 'Women in the Russian Radical Movement', *Journal of Social History*, 5/2, 1971-2, pp. 143-63 (see also p. 32 above). See also Amy Knight, 'The *Fritschi*; A Study of Female Radicals in the Russian Populist Movement', *Canadian-American Slavic Studies* IX, 1 (Spring, 1975), 1-17; Cathy Porter, *Fathers and Daughters. Russian Women in Revolution* (London, 1976), pp. 116 56.

86. Barbara Engel, 'From Feminism to Populism. A Study of the Changing Attitudes of the Russian Intelligentsia 1855-1881' (PhD, Columbia, 1974), p. 76.

87. Quoted in Porter, op. cit., pp. 52-3.

88. Engel, op. cit., pp. 113-16.

89. Ibid., pp. 129-33.

90. Cf. Knight, art. cit.

91. Statistical analysis of 1,611 revolutionaries 1873-7 in McNeal, art. cit.; 244 of these were women. Eighty out of 525 prosecuted for political offences in

       1873-7 were women (Knight, art.cit.)
92.   Engel, op. cit., pp. 1, 287-307.
93.   McNeal, art. cit., p. 155.
94.   Ibid., pp. 157-9.
95.   Dale Ross, 'The Role of the Women of Petrograd in War, Revolution and
      Counter-Revolution 1914-1921' (PhD, Rutgers, 1973), p. 24.
96.   Richard Stites, 'Women's Liberation Movements in Russia, 1900-1930',
      Canadian-American Slavic Studies, 14, 1973, pp. 465-7.
97.   McNeal, art. cit., pp. 159-61.
98.   Stites, art. cit., pp. 468-70; Ross, op. cit., p. 25.

4 MILITANTS AND CONSERVATIVES

Retreat from Liberalism

The rise of socialism and the emergence of Social Democratic women's movements had profound and often unexpected consequences for bourgeois feminists. Some individual feminists indeed were so impressed by the socialist women's organisations that they abandoned middle-class feminism altogether and joined them. Sylvia Pankhurst in England and Lily Braun in Germany were two women who succeeded in crossing the barrier from bourgeois feminism to Social Democracy; there were many others less well-known. More common were what the German socialist women's leader Clara Zetkin called 'those female intellectuals who swing back and forth between feminism and Social Democracy'. Writing of one woman in particuar, the Hamburg radical feminist Regine Ruben, Zetkin remarked: 'She may stand inwardly nearer to the latter, but she is held back by material considerations, so that she feels unable to accept the consequences of her own train of thought.'[1] In some countries, indeed, the logic of the political situation pushed the entire radical wing of the feminist movement into cooperating with the socialists. After the Liberals came to power in Britain in 1905, for example, their continued refusal to grant women the vote alienated the suffragists, who sought closer links with the growing Labour Party; many of their leading members were active in the party, and the major female suffrage organisation, the NUWSS, officially endorsed the party in elections — a striking indication of the way in which the social infrastructure of liberalism in Britain was beginning to crumble even before the First World War.[2] In France, too, many of the more radical feminists such as Madeleine Pelletier put their faith in socialist parties, perceiving that the liberals had failed them.[3] Elsewhere, even if the feminists' links with socialists were not quite so close, some form of cooperation often became necessary in the final struggle for the vote.

More generally, the rise of socialist movements, with their aggressive tactics and intensive propaganda methods, had a marked effect on the way in which the feminists, particularly on the radical wing of the movement, went about trying to secure their aims. Mass demonstrations in the streets, banners and placards, slogans and colours, and the hard-hitting, aggressive approach to opponents, were all tactics pioneered by the socialist movement. They were increasingly adopted by radical

189

feminists in a number of countries after the turn of the century. Those feminists who used them soon came to be known as 'militants'. Militancy really meant four quite distinct things as far as the feminists were concerned, though the differences between them were not always apparent to outsiders. First, it simply meant the use of modern propaganda techniques, of street marches and processions, of banners and floats, of badges, colours and slogans, of headline-hitting publicity stunts, many of them quite innocuous and without any suggestion of violence or illegality. Militancy in this sense signified the adjustment of feminist propaganda techniques to the age of the mass circulation newspaper and the picture magazine. Secondly, militancy also meant, for a minority of its adherents, the use of civil disobedience in the pursuit of votes for women. The Women's Freedom League and the Votes for Women Fellowship in Britain and isolated feminists in other countries considered it justifiable to refuse to pay taxes or obey government orders as long as they were not represented in Parliament. This form of militancy was non-violent and passive in nature, though it was also, strictly speaking, illegal. It was a tactic that owed more to the example of nationalism than to that of socialism. Thirdly, militancy could mean an *active* form of non-violent defiance of government and the law, the heckling of politicians, the disruption of parliament sessions or official functions by shouting protests or throwing leaflets, and other forms of active civil disobedience and protest, including the refusal to pay fines or to eat in prison. Finally, for a tiny minority of feminists in one country – the suffragettes in Britain – militancy ultimately meant, not only all these things, but the use of physical violence, arson and destruction as well. These last, illegal forms of militancy had some affinities with the violent tactics pursued by the anarchists of the 1890s, as European contemporaries were quick to point out,[4] but most of all, they owed their inspiration to the Irish nationalist movement of the same period, as indeed the suffragette leader Emmeline Pankhurst admitted.[5] This was in fact a major reason why violent methods were adopted in Britain but not in other countries, where there had been no real equivalent of the Irish movement to confer legitimacy on them.

The story of the English suffragettes is too well-known to need more than a brief summary here. It began in Lancashire with a radical feminist movement, the Women's Social and Political Union, attempting in the familiar way to recruit working-class women to the suffragist cause. By 1905 its leaders had moved to London, where they began to disrupt political meetings and stage mass marches through the streets. These in turn were made the occasion for deliberately provoked clashes with the police, who often responded with a brutality that won the women hard-earned headlines in the press. The more the demonstrations continued, the larger became the number of women arrested on each occasion. By 1908 the scale of the WSPU's activities had become unprecedented. A great open-air meeting held in London in June 1908 attracted a crowd estimated at between a quarter and a half a million people; the WSPU march which had preceded it numbered 30,000. All this got the suffragettes nowhere. After the Prime Minister had refused to see a deputation in 1909, the suffragettes began a campaign of window-breaking in London, and refused to cooperate with the prison authorities when arrested and gaoled. Hunger strikes by suffragette prisoners became the rule; the sufferings of the victims of forced feeding attracted fresh sympathy in the press and more recruits to the cause. A period of 'truce' lasting from the elections of early 1910 until November 1911 (apart from one week of violence late in 1910) was followed by a renewal of the campaign. Suffragette marchers were brutally mishandled by the police, so the WSPU took to individual violence. Window-breaking on a massive scale began in 1911-12. Arrests and hunger strikes in prison followed, and the movement went underground. By 1913 the suffragettes were engaged in a full-scale campaign of arson and destruction, digging up golf courses, burning railway carriages and destroying property worth tens of thousands of pounds every month. This level of violence continued unabated until the beginning of August 1914, when the First World War broke out.[6]

By this time the WSPU was no longer the only militant suffragist society in Britain. In 1907 the first split occurred, when Charlotte Despard, Edith How-Martyn, Teresa Billington-Greig and others left the WSPU, taking the majority of its branches with them. They objected to the increasingly dictatorial attitude of the Pankhursts, who unilaterally annulled the WSPU's constitution on 10 September 1906. The secession claimed to be the legitimate continuation of the WSPU and tried to seize its funds, property and papers. The resulting quarrel was eventually settled in a compromise, and the secession adopted the name of the Women's Freedom League. It described its policy as one of 'constitutional militancy'. This involved measures of passive civil disobedience such as the refusal to pay taxes. The goods of those who followed this practice were seized and auctioned off by the tax authorities, and were usually bought up by suffragist sympathisers. The propaganda tactics employed by the League were daring and imaginative, but they stopped well short of the violence favoured by the WSPU. Four members of the League attempted to present a petition to the King as he was driving in his coach to the State Opening of Parliament in 1908; while this was going on, another member of the League was flying across London in a balloon, from which she scattered thousands of leaflets across the metropolis. Edith How-Martyn subsequently tried to present a petition to the King in the Royal Gallery of the House of Lords, and Muriel Matters, the balloonist of 1908, chained herself and two other members of the League to the grille of the Ladies' Gallery in the House of Commons and shouted 'Votes for Women!' until they were removed, still chained to the grille. After a number of its leading figures, including Charlotte Despard, had been arrested early in 1909, the League began to moderate its tactics and to concentrate on the peaceful picketing of the House of Commons. Though it increasingly disapproved of the Pankhursts' tactics, the Women's Freedom League continued to take part in the great processions and mass demonstrations organised by the extreme militants as long as these continued (i.e. until 1912), as indeed did the constitutional suffragist society, the NUWSS, led by Millicent Garrett Fawcett. In addition, apart from the period of the 'truce', to which it subscribed, the Women's Freedom League continued its campaign of civil disobedience; its members boycotted the census of 1911, and the policy of non-payment of taxes lasted right up to the outbreak of the First World War. Finally, while the WSPU withdrew from open demonstrations after 1912, the Women's Freedom League, which was numerically much stronger, cooperated with the NUWSS in further mass marches and parades, the most impressive of which was perhaps the one held in the summer of 1914 in London. In a sense, therefore, the tactics of the earlier phases of militancy, though not their violent undertones, had been absorbed into the mainstream of the British suffragist movement by the outbreak of the war.[7]

The suffragettes also had an impact on feminist movements outside Britain. In Germany, for instance, the German Union for Women's Suffrage, led by the radicals Anita Augspurg and Lida Gustava Heymann, began to use militant tactics after seeing the suffragettes at first hand during a visit to London to attend the International Woman Suffrage Alliance Congress of 1909. Disillusioned with the failure of German liberal politicians to support them, Augspurg and Heymann adopted the suffragette colours of green, purple and white in preference to the official international suffragist colours of white and yellow, issued frequent manifestos of solidarity with the Pankhursts right through even the final period of arson and destruction, opposed the liberal parties they had previously supported, and planned a march through the streets of Munich in 1912. Heymann also declared her unwillingness to pay taxes while she lacked the right to vote. But these tactics were too extreme, and too reminiscent of Social Democracy, for Augspurg and Heymann's followers; the march, which was eventually held in carriages rather than on foot, to emphasise the respectable, middle-class nature of the suffragist movement, attracted little support and was not repeated; and the suffrage movement itself split into a number of mutually hostile factions, most of which opposed the Augspurg-Heymann line.[8] The campaign waged by Rosika Schwimmer and her followers in the Hungarian radical suffragist movement clearly owed much to the example of the English suffragettes, perhaps transmitted through Schwimmer's friends the German militants Augspurg and Heymann.[9] Militant tactics were also adopted by the French radicals Hubertine Auclert and Madeleine Pelletier. Auclert gained notoriety for her refusal to pay taxes because she lacked the vote and adopted the practice, familiar among the radicals of other countries, of entering her name as a candidate in elections. After the turn of the century she became rapidly more militant. She tore a copy of the Code Napoléon to shreds in a demonstration held by feminists at the Vendôme Column to mark the Code's centenary in 1904. In 1908 she led twenty of her supporters into the Chamber of Deputies, throwing leaflets at the astonished politicians. Auclert's militancy was repudiated by the majority of French suffragists. But Madeleine Pelletier's magazine *La Suffragiste* carried articles repeating Christabel Pankhurst's views on the 'Great Scourge', claiming that most men were syphilitic and advising women to carry guns for self-protection. Pelletier, a qualified medical practitioner, at one time wore male clothing from the waist up, with bowler and tie, to symbolise her demand for sexual equality. She mounted several well-planned demonstrations against male supremacy. Pelletier succeeded Caroline Kauffman as secretary of *La Solidarité des Femmes*, the radical wing of the French suffragist movement, in 1905. She continued Kaufmann's occasional use of militant tactics. Already in 1904 at a banquet celebrating the centenary of the Code Napoléon, Kauffmann had thrown down from the gallery a number of huge balloons on which was written the slogan 'The Code crushes women; it dishonours the Republic'. When the man she paid to inflate the balloons ran out of breath, she shouted the slogan at the top of her voice until her arrest. Under Pelletier, the *Solidarité des Femmes* picketed elections. In 1907, Pelletier and Kauffmann staged a march through Paris and declared their intention of following the example of the English suffragettes. In fact, it was the English suffragettes who followed Pelletier, for the march consisted almost entirely of members of the WSPU staying in Paris. In 1908, Pelletier and Auclert entered a polling station, smashed the windows and overturned a ballot box. The almost total lack of support for these militant tactics in the French feminist movement condemned Pelletier to failure. Even a window smashing campaign along WSPU lines required if not mass support then at least a well-oiled organisation consisting of a few hundred women. Pelletier's support could be measured in dozens, not hundreds. In France, too, the repressive machinery of the state was more efficient, more ruthless and more intimidating than in England. Pelletier was an interesting figure; almost alone among militants, she did have real ties with anarchism, and her political affiliations lay with the socialist left, as we have seen. But women such as she remained isolated individuals. Their tactics were generally spontaneous and owed little to the example of others. Militancy in France never existed in the form of a concerted campaign. The English suffragettes never exercised any real influence in France.[10] It was only in a few countries that the militants managed to find emulators and to bring about a further radicalisation of the tactics of mainstream suffragist movements. Their greatest success was scored in America.

The cause of the suffragettes was popularised in America not only by Emmeline Pankhurst herself, who went on more than one speaking tour there, but also by two Americans who had become deeply involved in the WSPU's campaign while in London, Alice Paul and Harriet Stanton Blatch. Blatch organised a series of massive and elaborate suffrage parades through New York and Washington from 1910 onwards. These were eventually supported by the official female suffrage movement despite their use of the suffragette colours instead of the IWSA ones. Half a million people were said to have watched one parade in New York in 1912, with ten thousand marchers taking part. The NAWSA's support was rather grudging, however, and in 1913 Alice Paul seceded to form her own militant organisation, the Congressional Union for Women's Suffrage. Paul also opposed the NAWSA's concentration on state campaigns and proposed to move straight towards female suffrage on a federal basis by putting pressure on Congress rather than on state legislatures. These differences led to a complete rupture between the Congressional Union and the NAWSA in 1914. Freed from its ties with the mainstream suffrage movement, the Congressional Union now proceeded to take the same path as the English suffragettes. Just as militancy turned the English militants against the Liberal Party and the Germans against the left-liberal Progressives, so too it led Paul to oppose the party in power — the Democrats — and attempt to mobilise women who had the vote (mainly in the West) in favour of Republican candidates in Congressional elections. In pursuit of the Congressional Union's declared aim of securing female suffrage on a federal level through the passage of a Nineteenth Amendment to the Constitution, Alice Paul organised a series of spectacular publicity stunts, including a transcontinental 'suffrage drive' in an automobile, a special train called the 'Suffrage Special', further conventions and pageants, and the formation of a National Woman's Party to contest elections in the states where women possessed the vote. Other propaganda devices utilised by Alice Paul included motion pictures, magic lantern slides, a sophisticated press policy and constant use of the railway and the automobile to reach new areas of potential support.[11]

It was in 1916, however, that militancy in the classic suffragette mould came to America with the National Woman's Party campaign to prevent the re-election of Woodrow Wilson to the Presidency, a campaign based not on any realistic appreciation of Wilson's views on female suffrage — he was in fact coming slowly round to the idea that it would be a good thing if it were passed — but on blanket opposition to the party in power, the Democrats, to whom Wilson belonged. The campaign was a disaster for the National Woman's Party. Wilson carried ten out of the eleven states in which women had full voting rights. Disappointed and frustrated by their failure, the militants, directed by Alice Paul, whose word within the Congressional Union/National Woman's Party was law (there were no effective constitutional checks on her power), took to picketing the White House. The slogans they carried might almost have been deliberately calculated to arouse hostility, above all after America entered the First World War. The militants were not pacifists, but they did believe it was wrong for Wilson to tell the world that America was fighting to save democracy in Europe while women were still denied the vote at home. The picketing campaign turned into a personal vendetta against the President. Eventually, the militants, who had behaved with great decorum and had been well-treated both by the public and by the authorities, including the President himself, went too far. On 14 August 1917 they unfurled a banner outside the White House with the slogan: 'Kaiser Wilson, Have You Forgotten Your Sympathy with the Poor Germans Because They Were Not Self-Governed? 20,000,000 American Women Are Not Self-Governed. Take the Beam Out of Your Own Eye!' The pickets were attacked by a hostile crowd and quickly arrested. At this point the American militants escalated their tactics to a level of militancy just short of violence — the level of active defiance. The White House

pickets now courted arrest. Imprisoned, they went on hunger strike.
Forced feeding followed. There can be little doubt that the militants
were badly treated in gaol, as part of a concerted policy of repressing
internal dissent in wartime. The *New York World* spoke for most
Americans when it compared the militant suffragists to anarcho-syndicalist labour unions and other anti-war groups: 'No less offensive than
the IWW, the professional pacifists and the pro-German propagandists,'
it declared, 'they are serving the Kaiser to the best of their ability and
calling it a campaign for equal suffrage.' The moderate suffragists also
supported the government and condemned the militants' campaign as
counterproductive, though their leader, Carrie Chapman Catt, also
recognised that the militants made the NAWSA, which carefully
cultivated good relations with the President, appear all the more reasonable in comparison. The militants' campaign continued into 1918 with
'watch fires' being lit outside the White House and fuelled with copies
of Wilson's speeches, the burning of the President in effigy, further
riots, more arrests and continued hunger strikes. It ended only with the
passage of the Ninteenth Amendment, giving women the vote all over
the United States, in 1919.[12]

The American militant campaign seemed mild when compared with
its British counterpart. Nevertheless it went far beyond anything
attempted elsewhere. Alice Paul and the National Woman's Party, of
course, were hampered by the fact that their campaign reached its
height during wartime. Like the Pankhursts, and perhaps to an even
greater degree, Paul progressively shed support as her militancy increased, and became more and more dictatorial towards those who
remained under her control. Although the American militants were
repressed by the authorities, who believed them to be subverting the war
effort, they did not fare as badly as their militant colleagues in
Germany. The German militants Augspurg and Heymann were outspoken pacifists, and devoted most of their energies after July 1914 to
trying to organise middle-class women in opposition to the war. They
joined with feminists from other countries in forming the Women's
International League for Peace and Freedom at a conference in Holland
early in 1915. This organisation believed that women were naturally
pacifist, and that women's suffrage would help end war. Its members,
led by Jane Addams and the Hungarian feminist Rosika Schwimmer,
attempted to lobby governments and propagandise women in their
home countries. They met with total failure. In Germany, Augspurg
and Heymann lost most of their supporters; they were prevented from
speaking, their organisations were dissolved by the police, their printed

propaganda was censored, confiscated and banned, their correspon-
dence was put under surveillance and their political activities effectively brought to a halt.[13]

While the militants in Germany became pacifists during the war, the
English militants became super-patriots. On the outbreak of war, militant activity came to an immediate halt, ordered by the Pankhursts. At
the beginning of September 1914, Christabel Pankhurst returned to
England from her exile in France, and asserted that 'All — everything —
that we women have been fighting for and treasure would disappear in
the event of a German victory.' After all the abuse she had heaped on
the British political system, it was startling to hear her declare that
women were better off and enjoyed more rights in Britain and the
United States than anywhere else in the world. Emmeline Pankhurst
and her followers even asserted that the stewards who had brutally
ejected suffragettes from Liberal Party meetings before 1914 had been
'Huns' identifiable by their 'guttural accents'. Already before the war
the WSPU had broken with the labour movement (c. 1906), advocated
a property franchise and opposed the enfranchisement of all adult
males. The composition of the movement had become more upper-class,
its management increasingly dictatorial; and those who had resisted the
Pankhursts had been unceremoniously ejected. The cult of violence that
lay behind the campaign of arson and destruction had also been made
explicit at suffragette meetings, where a specially organised bodyguard
of thirty burly women had assailed the police with Indian clubs and
chairs whenever they had tried to arrest the suffragette leaders. Tactics
had become cynical, with the condemnation of violence in the police
but praise for it in the suffragette bodyguard, and with the deliberate
courting of arrest and imprisonment followed by attacks on the
authorities for doing what was really for them the only thing possible in
the circumstances. Ideology had become irrational and demagogic,
above all in the campaign against sexual contamination through the
'Great Scourge'. The suffragettes' behaviour in the war was the logical
culmination of this development towards fascism, not an unfortunate
aberration. The Pankhursts ended the war by founding the Women's
Party, a short-lived organisation aimed at increasing workers' productivity by employing 'engineering and organising experts' to run industry,
and by preventing strikes, pacifism and 'shirking', which the Pankhursts
believed were part of an international Bolshevik conspiracy. Indeed, the
potentiality for the suffragettes' evolution in the direction of fascism
had been there since their early days; for one of the chief characteristics
of early fascism in general was the attempt to mobilise working people

by socialist methods for middle-class ends.[14]

Before we move on to the wider context of these developments, we might perhaps ask why it was that militancy only reached the violent stage in England. One reason was the closeness of the prospect of victory. The House of Commons, after all, had been voting to enfranchise women for years. Victory seemed within the suffragettes' grasp in England, and when it failed to materialise, their rage and disappointment were all the greater. Elsewhere, matters did not seem so urgent, since the prospect of enfranchisement was more remote. Moreover, whereas in Sweden or Finland the suffragists, though repeatedly frustrated in their aims, received the full backing of the oppositional liberal politicians, who generally did their best to push through legislation when they were in power, in England these same liberal politicians were opposed to the suffrage. The English suffragettes were unusually isolated, and much of the responsibility for their evolution in the direction of extremism must be placed at the door of the Liberal Party and its anti-suffragist leaders.[15] A similar — and on the whole exceptional — failure by liberals to support female suffrage created a similar move towards militancy in the German suffragist movement. In America, the drift to militancy was the outcome of continued failure to achieve a victory that also seemed within the feminists' grasp. In both Britain and America, too, militant tactics possessed some legitimacy in the political system — through the example of the Irish in Britain, and the tradition of the Revolution in America. Police forces in continental Europe were also far more ruthless in suppressing disorder than their British and American counterparts, ungentle though these undoubtedly were. It is unlikely that militancy would have reached even the stage of active civil disobedience in Germany without mass arrests and an attempt to suppress the suffragist movement altogether.

The Decline of Feminism

The course taken by the English suffragettes was in fact a rather extreme symptom of a more general retreat of feminist movements from liberal beliefs towards conservatism at this time. In Italy, for example, where fascism originated, and came to power with Mussolini in 1922, the radical feminist movement was reduced to total insignificance by a split very similar to that which took place in Germany, as the left wing stuck to the ideals of pacifism and international cooperation which had inspired it in its early days and was rewarded with mass defections to the moderates during the First World War. The Italian moderates themselves were bitterly disappointed with the refusal of the Senate to ratify the enfranchisement of women voted on by the Lower House of Parliament in 1919, and disillusioned with the failure of Parliament to secure admission for women to the professions on equal terms with men despite the limited reform brought by the Sacchi Law in 1919. In 1922 the leader of the Italian National Council of Women, Countess Spalletti, referred to 'the low parliamentarism which poisons the life of the country'. All the major feminist associations supported fascism voluntarily in the early years of Mussolini's premiership, before a full fascist régime was imposed, led on by his promises to grant them the reforms which parliamentarism had failed to deliver, and reassured by the undoubted fact that he and his movement were crushing socialism, which they abhorred. They were rewarded with compulsory dissolution or repression in an atmosphere of increasing male chauvinism and discriminatory legislation and practice. The main moderate feminist society, the Association for Women (*Associazione per la Donna*), founded in 1898, was suppressed in 1925. The National Council of Women was allowed to continue; but after Mussolini concluded a Concordat with the Pope in 1929 it was obvious that its existence was largely without meaning.[16]

An even more dramatic move to the right was taken by the German feminist movement, which had become steadily more radical until in 1908 it found itself on the point of accepting the recommendation of a feminist Legal Commission, influenced by the ideas of the sexual libertarian Helene Stöcker and headed by the leader of the Federation of German Women's Associations, Marie Stritt, that German feminists should endorse the legalisation of abortion. This was too much for the moderates. In 1908 they seized their chance. They persuaded the large and extremely reactionary German-evangelical Women's League (*Deutsch-evangelischer Frauenbund*) to join the Federation and use its voting power to defeat the proposal to legalise abortion at the General Assembly in 1908. They followed this manoeuvre by ousting Stritt from the leadership in 1910 and replacing her with a conservative, Gertrud Bäumer. Stöcker's *Mutterschutz* League was refused admission to the Federation and a massive propaganda campaign was launched to discredit its aims. Under the strain of these events, the League broke up into a number of mutually hostile factions. The succession of accusation and counter-accusation which accompanied this process led to a series of sensational and scandalous court actions. At the same time, the female suffrage movement in Germany was also breaking up, as the majority of its members gradually abandoned the movement's original commitment to universal suffrage and opted for a limited property franchise instead. These developments left Bäumer and the moderates in command of the field. From 1908 to 1914, the German feminist movement as a whole carefully distanced itself from demands for universal suffrage, world peace, cooperation with the Social Democrats and the ideas of Stöcker's *Mutterschutz* League for sexual liberation. The fight against vice was transformed from a fight for the dignity of the individual woman to a campaign against racial disloyalty to the Germans.[17]

In 1899, Marie Stritt had told the International Council of Women that the lead in German feminism was being taken by the 'progressives' who were arousing in the 'moderate' and 'backward' elements an interest in the 'proper modern aspirations of women' and the 'economic, social and moral emancipation of the female sex'. A mere ten years later, in 1909, the International Council of Women was given a very different picture. This time the report was delivered by one of the leading conservatives, Alice Salomon. Like Stritt, Salomon reported that there were two different parties in the movement. But her estimation of them was a very different one.

> We know that there is a group of women — very small in number — who look upon our movement as a fight against wrong inflicted on women by men. To them the disqualification of the female sex is rather due to circumstances, to differences in education carried on through centuries, to suppression, and not to the difference in the natural gifts, talents and duties . . . They claim equality . . . on the ground of mere justice, with the idea of acquiring equal rights in every department of life . . . On the other hand there are the women claiming the vote — as they claim many other duties and rights for women — just because they believe in the difference of capacities and gifts of men and women. For them the advantage of women's suffrage does not lie in the doubling of the quantity of energy available for the service of mankind, but in the production of unique and new powers for public life that can never be given by men. These women ask for equal rights, not only on account of equal work in the professions, but also on account of the equal value of the women's share in the world's work, in their capacities as wives and mothers . . . Some are convinced that pioneer work must be done on educational, professional and social lines, before women themselves can be interested in the suffrage movement, and further because they believe that all rights are of importance only to those who know how to make use of them.[18]

Salomon was one of the leading conspirators in the plot to oust Stritt from the leadership of the German feminist movement, and she was perhaps exaggerating in 1909 when she claimed that the representatives of radical feminism — the first view she discussed in her speech — were only a tiny minority. A few years later, however, the German feminists would attempt to convey the impression that liberal individualist or radical feminism had never had any influence in their movement at all. And by 1914 the radicals had in fact been reduced to a position of impotence within the movement. The removal of legal restrictions on women's participation in politics in Prussia and elsewhere in 1908 facilitated a rapid expansion of the feminist movement which brought new social classes, particularly the respectable haute bourgeoisie of the Rhineland and North Germany and the industrial areas of the Ruhr and Silesia, into the movement, and helped push it further to the right. German universities were opened to women from 1902 (Baden) to 1908 (Prussia) onwards, and a new generation of feminist leaders came to the fore from the narrow, nationalistic background of German higher education, rather than (as had the radical leaders) from the cosmopolitan atmosphere of Zürich, Bern, Paris or London. Finally, as the votes of the Social Democrats grew in number with every election, so the middle classes became progressively more frightened at the prospect of social revolution which this process brought seemingly ever closer, and turned increasingly towards aggressive nationalism, militarism, anti-semitism, Social Darwinism and other right-wing ideologies.[19]

In the First World War the German feminists shed their left wing, a tiny group of pacifists led by the radicals Augspurg, Heymann and Stöcker, and moved further to the right. In the 1920s, the rise of Nazism presented them with more problems. The allegations of the pre-war anti-feminists were repeated with even greater vehemence by Adolf Hitler and the National Socialists, and this time many more people listened. 'The message of women's emancipation', wrote Hitler in *Mein Kampf*, 'is a message discovered solely by the Jewish intellect and its content is stamped by the same spirit.' Equal rights for women, Hitler declared, meant a deprivation of rights, since it involved women in areas where they would 'necessarily be inferior'. The feminist movement's response was to deny that it wanted equal rights at all. In attempting to refute Hitler's attacks it showed how the resurgence of anti-feminism could force women to abandon many of their feminist beliefs. The new 1919 programme of the Federation of German Women's Associations claimed that its aim was to 'unite German women of every party and world-view, in order to express their national solidarity and to effect the common idea of the cultural mission of women'. It declared housekeeping and child-bearing to be women's proper destiny, and rejected the idea that men and women were equal. It advocated 'eugenic' policies and the sterilisation of 'anti-social' elements, and actively tried to persuade women to have more children. It supported the legal requirement that women schoolteachers should not marry, and refrained from actively opposing the dismissal of married women from their jobs in the civil service and elsewhere. In the field of international politics, it supported the reconquest of territory lost by Germany in 1918, condemned the treaty of Versailles and refused to attend the International Council of Women after the war.

With views such as these prevalent, it is not surprising that the German feminist movement was neither willing nor able to campaign effectively for women's rights during the Weimar Republic. Most of its energy was taken up by working for stricter censorship of films, books and plays on moral grounds, and in campaigning for the abolition of state-regulated prostitution, which it finally achieved in 1927. The Federation lost its investments in the great inflation of 1923 and was never again able to afford large-scale lobbying, pamphleting and propaganda campaigns. By 1928 committee members were having to pay their own travelling expenses. The radical feminists had been ousted from the movement, were now a tiny, powerless coterie, and concentrated mainly on pacifism. The mainstream feminist movement faced a steady and, from 1929, a rapidly growing hostility to female emancipation on the part of the main political parties. It began to suffer from a conflict of interests between the economic pressure groups which came to dominate it after the gaining of the vote — professionals (who provided the leadership), white-collar workers, and housewives' associations. These conflicts reached their height in the social crisis of the depression, and the housewives' associations resigned from the Federation, reducing its membership by half. At the same time, the German feminist movement as a whole, like its American counterpart, had become predominantly middle-aged; at least three quarters of the women present at feminist meetings, remarked a newspaper in 1932, were aged forty or over.

In January 1933 Hitler became Chancellor and began by stages to erect the Nazi dictatorship of the 'Third Reich'. The feminist movement regarded these events with qualified approval. Disillusioned with parliamentarism, it welcomed the 'national revolution'. Despite a certain distaste for the Nazis' masculinist vulgarity, the German feminists applauded Hitler's belief that 'equal rights for women means that they experience the esteem that they deserve in the areas for which nature has intended them'. The feminists, as the President of the Federation remarked, could 'do nothing but approve of a nationalist government and stand by it', and offered to 'take up personal contacts with the best women in National Socialism'. In the last elections in which Germans enjoyed any freedom of choice at all, those of March 1933, the Federation gave considerable support to the Nazis, expressing the hope that Hitler would soon introduce a 'biological policy' to preserve the German family and a 'Law of Preservation' to protect it from 'asocial persons'. All this did not save the feminist movement, however much it may have been dictated by an instinct for self-preservation. In April 1933 it was ordered to join the mass women's organisation then being created by the Nazis. Gertrud Bäumer, the feminist movement's most influential figure, supported this move, even though it meant expelling the movement's Jewish members. She believed that the Nazi women's organisation was merely a larger version of the Federation, a 'new, spiritually different phase of the women's movement', and signified her desire to join it. But the Federation's constitution explicitly forbade it to join other organisations, and it therefore felt obliged to dissolve itself. With this came the end of the German feminist movement.[20]

Similar though less extreme developments occurred in America, where moderate and radical feminists alike in the early years had justified their claim for equal rights including the vote on grounds of the natural rights of the individual. Government was by consent of the governed; every individual had the inalienable right to develop his or her abilities to the utmost without any hindrances other than those posed by nature; the state should remove itself as far as possible from the active control of society — such were the beliefs that animated American feminists for the better part of the nineteenth century. From the 1890s these beliefs were gradually abandoned. Moral discipline seemed increasingly inadequate to control the lower orders, state intervention increasingly desirable. Morality could no longer be left to the individual. It was becoming a matter of public concern. Accompanying these changes was an influx of new members into the suffrage movement, particularly from 1905 onwards, and the growth of a new type of social reform, the settlement movement, in which middle-class women sought the active pacification of the lower orders by living among them. This kind of involvement brought with it a realisation of the need for state intervention and legislation to improve conditions in slum areas. Moreover, as urbanisation developed, municipal governments

legislated to an ever-increasing extent in matters concerning the home —
food quality, water, clothing, sanitation, education and so on. This
penetration of politics into the home led to the increasing use by the
feminists of the argument that women needed to be involved in politics
to protect their domestic interests. Politics in turn came to be seen as
a kind of 'enlarged housekeeping' for which women were in some ways
uniquely qualified. The natural rights of the individual receded as a
justification for female suffrage. Expediency and interest replaced right
and justice in the feminist vocabulary.[21]

At the same time, the feminists' assault on the liquor interest, the
city bosses and the party machines also brought with it an increasing
hostility towards those whom they regarded as the ignorant or willing
dupes on whose acquiescence these institutions rested: the labouring
masses and the new immigrants. As early as 1894, Carrie Chapman
Catt, one of the new and more conservative generation of feminist
leaders who succeeded the Stanton-Anthony old guard in the 1890s,
advanced the following rationale for giving women the vote:

> The Government is menaced with great danger . . . That danger lies
> in the votes possessed by the males in the slums of the cities, and the
> ignorant foreign vote which was sought to be brought up by each
> party, to make political success . . . In the mining districts the danger
> has already reached this point — miners are supplied with arms,
> watching with greedy eyes for the moment when they can get in
> their deadly work of despoiling the wealth of the country . . . There
> is but one way to avert the danger — cut off the vote of the slums
> and give it to women.

In addition to this danger, there was also the possibility that immigrants
from Catholic cultures (or, as the racist language of the day put it,
'Latin countries') would be uncompromisingly hostile to female equality.
Even Elizabeth Cady Stanton argued in favour of limiting the 'foreign
vote' and the 'ignorant native vote'. By 1903, only 5 out of the 150
delegates at the National American Woman Suffrage Association Congress opposed this policy.[22]

These developments were taking place at the same time as the rise of
a new racism which brought with it in the early twentieth century a *de
facto* disfranchisement of the American black voter. The female suffrage movement went along with this trend. The resurgence of white
politics in the American South of which this trend formed a part stimulated the growth of female suffrage movements organised on explicitly

white supremacist lines. Women's Suffrage Associations were formed in
Alabama in 1910, Arkansas in 1911, Florida in 1912 and Texas in 1908.
In Georgia female suffrage agitation was carried on continuously from
1899 onwards. With the growth of these organisations came the increasing representation of the South in the NAWSA. In 1903, the NAWSA
voted to allow state affiliates to determine their own entrance qualifications and to put forward their own arguments for the vote. This was
clearly designed to accommodate the new southern suffragist groups.
The leader of the Louisiana suffragists, Kate Gordon, a Corresponding
Secretary of the NAWSA from 1901-9 and a Vice-President in 1910,
wanted a 'whites only' clause attached to the female suffrage demand,
and opposed a federal amendment to the Constitution giving women
the vote because this might be used by the Republicans to oust the
white supremacist Democrats from their control of the South by enfranchising the blacks. Correspondingly, of course, in a state such as
Louisiana, where the white and black populations were about equal in
number, the enfranchisement of white women would give the whites a
permanent majority and the Democrats assured control of the state
even if black males did succeed in claiming their rights by registering as
voters. Gordon in fact eventually resigned when the NAWSA lent its
support to a federal Amendment, but most Southern suffragists remained within the organisation because they felt that they would never
persuade conservative Southern legislatures to enact female suffrage by
themselves. Their loyalty was well rewarded. Carrie Chapman Catt
referred to the migrant black vote in the North as 'purchasable' by the
political machines, and implied that it should be abolished. Like other
leaders, too, she assumed that female suffrage could not pass through
Congress without the assent of at least some Southern Democrats, and
that therefore some inducement had to be offered to these to support
the vote for women. At the 1903 NAWSA Convention, held symboli-
cally in New Orleans, Belle Kearney, a delegate from Mississippi, declared:

> Just as surely as the North will be forced to turn to the South for
> the nation's salvation, just so surely will the South be compelled to
> look to its Anglo-Saxon women as the medium through which to
> retain the supremacy of the white race over the African . . . Anglo-
> Saxonism is the standard of the ages to come. It is, above all else, the
> granite foundation of the South. Upon that its civilisation will
> mount; upon that it will stand unshaken.

The convention did not formally endorse these sentiments; but it did not repudiate them either.[23] On an international plane, a significant phase in the abandonment of liberal principles was marked by the accession of South Africa to the International Woman Suffrage Alliance in 1908. The South African Women's Suffrage Association consisted almost entirely of English-speaking women (rather than Afrikaners). It asked for equal voting rights in a petition of 4,000 signatures (including 2,000 from Cape Colony) sent to the South African Parliament in 1908. The petition claimed that

> Under existing qualifications, the intelligent white vote would be proportionately greatly strengthened, rather than weakened, by admitting women to citizenship, since the white vote would gain less than 5 per cent (roughly the white vote would benefit by 16 to 1). It was shown [in the petition] that masculine supremacy was in no way endangered in South Africa, as the women's vote would be well under 50 per cent of the men's and but 65 per cent should adult white suffrage be adopted.

The South African women complained that 'the claims of the "civilised" native, and of the lowest of the male population, are recognised and safeguarded, while those of the women, even as non-voting citizens, are contemptuously ignored'. These views seem to have been accepted without dissent when they were presented to the International Woman Suffrage Alliance Congress in 1909.[24]

The American feminist movement's move to the right was by no means halted by the war. As in other countries it split into a pacifist and a nationalist wing during the years 1914-18. The split continued into the 1920s, when the pacifist National Woman's Party, led by Alice Paul and supported mainly by business and professional women, decided to campaign for total equality, guaranteed by an amendment to the Constitution providing equal rights for women in every sphere. This measure would result in the repeal of special laws protecting women in certain kinds of employment. The militants argued that these laws were keeping 150,000 women out of jobs in New York alone. While the National Woman's Party mounted a vigorous campaign for equal rights legislation both at federal and state level, other feminist organisations, including the National League of Women Voters, organised widespread opposition, arguing that equal rights legislation would benefit only a small minority of professional women, and expressing the fear that irreparable damage would be done to hundreds of thousands of working women and their families. Representing the conservatism of small town women and housewives, the inheritors of the Progressive movement, and supported by philanthropists and women's trade union organisers, these organisations contended that 'The cry Equality, Equality, where Nature has created inequality, is as stupid and as deadly as the cry Peace, Peace, where there is no Peace.' This pointed to another division — between the pacifism of the militants and the support given to the war effort in 1914-18 by the moderates. This division continued into the 1920s. The militants also repeatedly disrupted women's conferences in the 1920s with their demands. Gradually they gained support. The conflict of interests and the social antagonisms that divided the feminist movement as a whole during the 1920s also led to the disintegration of the General Federation of Women's Clubs. By the end of the decade, one group of the Clubs had reformed in the General Federation of Business and Professional Women's Clubs, which lent powerful support to the Equal Rights Amendment proposed by the militants.[25]

Both factions of the American feminist movement in the 1920s espoused doctrines that in the circumstances of the time can only be described as conservative. But this did not save them from being smeared by the 'Red Scare' which swept the country in 1919-20. The central document of the scare was the notorious 'Spider Web Chart', which originated in the Chemical War Service of the War Department. It was widely publicised by the industrialist Henry Ford, and was inserted by conservative congressmen into the Congressional Record. The chart depicted a vast spider (Bolshevism) sitting at the centre of an enormous web of conspiracy connected to a large number of individuals and organisations. Among those who found a place in the web were Carrie Chapman Catt, Jane Addams, Florence Kelley, the National Council of Women, the National Woman's Party and other feminist individuals and organisations. All the various international women's organisations — the International Council of Women, the Women's International League for Peace and Freedom, the International Federation of University Women, the International Federation of Business and Professional Women's Clubs, the Pan-American Association for the Advancement of Women, the World Woman's Party, the International Alliance of Women for Suffrage and Equal Citizenship — were alleged to be fronts for Alexandra Kollontai's International Secretariat of Communist Women. By 1924 the Spider Web Chart had been expanded and refined to include the Woman's Christian Temperance Union and the Young Women's Christian Association. All these organisations were said to be steered by

Russian Communists, undermining America's defences by preaching pacifism and international cooperation. 'As for the Communists', declared one anti-feminist periodical, the *Woman Patriot*, in 1927, 'they are logically letting the Gold Dust Twins, Feminism and Pacifism, do their work . . . The pinks are all red sisters under the skin.'

The effect of these smears, crude though they were, was considerable. In the first place, they made it very difficult for the feminists to gain support, win members and influence legislatures. At the beginning of the 1920s, the moderate majority of the feminist movement helped to persuade Congress and state legislatures to pass a certain amount of legislation protecting women and children at work, providing maternity benefits, establishing women's prisons, altering nationality laws so that a woman would no longer automatically lose her American citizenship if she married a foreigner, and establishing and extending the scope of a Government-financed Children's Bureau. The feminists regarded their greatest achievement as the passing — after intensive lobbying — of the Sheppard-Towner Maternity and Infancy Protection Act (1921). This provided federal money for pre- and post-natal care, medical aid, hospitalisation, visiting nurses and consultation centres. It was described by its opponents, who included the medical profession, as 'inspired by foreign experiments in Communism . . . It strikes at the heart of our American civilisation'. In 1929 it was allowed to lapse and the programme was only continued on a smaller and more restricted scale, financed by some — though not all — of the states.

In other spheres, too, the feminists failed to push through the legislation they lobbied for after 1921. A Child Labor Amendment, which passed Congress in 1922, was rejected by the states (1924-6). The Spider Chart and the 'Red Scare' campaign were generally held responsible. The same factors also deterred many women from joining the feminist movement. Younger women stayed away. The leadership grew old and was not replaced — Carrie Chapman Catt continued to lead the League of Women Voters until 1947, Alice Paul led the Woman's Party even longer. Secondly, the campaign also forced women's organisations onto the defensive. They became more outspokenly conservative in order to prove that they were not 'red'. Some women's organisations, such as the Daughters of the American Revolution, which had been mildly progressive and supported the moderate feminist cause, became ultra-right wing after 1923 and started reprinting the Spider Web Chart themselves. Others, such as the National Federation of Business and Professional Women's Clubs, also moved to the right, though less dramatically. The 'Red Scare' formed the main talking point at the 1927

Congress of the National Council of Women. But all the Council could do to combat it was to move further to the right itself. Some organisations, including the National Consumers' League and the National Women's Trade Union League, lost members dramatically and almost ceased to function through lack of funds. The League of Women Voters was said to be very conservative by the mid-1920s; some of its branches opposed the provision of free schools for immigrants, arguing that the immigrants had no business being in America if they were not educated already. By the late 1920s, therefore, the American feminist movement was characterised by falling membership, political failure, financial decline and increasing conservatism.[26]

In other countries too the feminist movement declined after the First World War, victim of a growing polarisation of politics between socialists and conservatives in which the liberal principles that lay behind classical feminism had no place. In Finland, for example, the bitter and violent civil war of 1918, in which the middle-class liberals and conservatives emerged victorious, expressed a radicalisation of left- and right-wing politics in which the once strong feminist movement, already weakened by the granting of the vote in 1906, was deserted by the groups which had once supported it — bourgeois liberals who now regarded women's emancipation as dangerous and subversive. By 1926 the *Kvinnosaksförbunds Unionen* had a mere 218 members, the *Finsk Kvinnoforening* 1,300, the *Suomalainen Naisliitto* 1,730 and the Swedish-speaking Finnish women's movement 1,150. These were small figures in comparison to the widespread support enjoyed by Finnish feminism before the First World War. In East-Central Europe, right-wing dictatorships came into power in many countries between the wars, including Poland, Hungary and Yugoslavia, and they brought with them strongly anti-feminist policies and severe limitations on the feminists' freedom of action. Until we have some scholarly studies of women's organisations in these countries, the extent to which the feminists lent their support or offered opposition to dictators such as Pilsudski, Horthy and King Alexander must remain a matter for conjecture. But there can be no doubt that the rise to power of these men made things much more difficult for East European feminists.

The Bolshevik Revolution ended the short-lived liberal feminist movement in that country; it also brought to an end the separatist feminist movement of the Ukraine. Finally, the Nazi invasion of Austria and Czechoslovakia in 1938, Poland in 1939 and a number of other countries in 1940-1 brought not only the end of feminist movements in these lands but also the imprisonment and execution of many of their leading members. F. Plamnikova, the founder of Czech feminism, executed in a concentration camp in 1942, was probably the most distinguished of many victims. In Eastern Europe, the Communist seizure of power at the end of the Second World War prevented any recrudescence of liberal feminism.

In those countries where feminist movements were not suppressed, they continued to drift towards more conservative positions. A number of influences hastened the drift. With the rise of Bolshevism in the Russian and East-Central European revolutions of 1917-18, fear of revolution created a 'red scare' in the middle classes of many countries. Feminists were often directly affected. The obsession which many countries developed with the birth-rate after the slaughter of the First World War and with the continuing and seemingly irreversible downward trend of natality that had begun at the turn of the century with the spread of efficient means of contraception, also had an adverse effect on the feminists. In the industrialised countries, the declining birth-rate was widely attributed to the growing independence of women. The feminists were blamed, and not infrequently they were seen as part of a massive Bolshevik conspiracy to undermine the nation and destroy the family. In nearly all countries, feminists responded by trying to show that they were not responsible for the falling birth-rate, and indeed mounted strong campaigns to try and halt this trend. In coming to share this concern with the birth-rate, the feminists lost touch with the attitudes of younger women. In the 1920s and 1930s, feminists everywhere failed to recruit fresh blood to their cause. 'Modern young women', as the English feminist Ray Strachey observed, 'know amazingly little of what it was like before the war, and show a strong hostility to the word "feminism" and all which they imagine it to connote.' There were several reasons for this. After the First World War, feminism no longer held much appeal for radical young women, who responded to the more urgent demands of fascism or revolution. Political parties now actively sought female participation, and women who entered politics soon came to believe that women's emancipation was of minor importance compared with crises abroad and economic and political disasters at home. The prevailing ethos of youth culture was profoundly hostile to the moral authoritarianism of the feminists. Freudian ideology, contraception, economic independence, all combined in the 'roaring twenties' to make the feminists' ideas about alcohol, pornography and a single standard of moral self-restraint seem out of date and faintly ridiculous, representing the Victorianism of an older generation against whom the young were in revolt. Some feminist organisations, most notably National Councils of Women, became 'Establishment' discussion groups consisting of middle-aged aristocrats and philanthropists and women who had achieved eminence in politics or the professions. Others, such as the Woman's Christian Temperance Union, which were tied to more specific aims, found their support declining and the social status of their members falling as social drinking became acceptable among the middle classes. The movement for the repeal of Prohibition in America achieved far greater support from women at the end of the 1930s than the WCTU had done even in its heyday. Similarly, the idea that women could enjoy sex — something the feminists never admitted — also became generally accepted among the younger generation, and social purity organisations such as the Abolitionists lost support almost everywhere. In some countries (e.g. Germany) they had practically ceased to exist by the end of the 1920s. The feminists disapproved of all these tendencies. The German women spoke of a 'sexual crisis' signifying the collapse of moral standards and the endangering of the family; American feminists criticised the 'rebellion of the young'. Statements such as these simply separated the two generations even further. Ironically, these tendencies in fact denoted in the end a return to the home, hastened by the interwar obsession with the birth-rate and the hostility to female employment generated by the depression. They marked the defeat of feminism and the emergence of the 'feminine mystique' which was to govern women's lives in the industrialised countries of the capitalist world until the 1970s.[27]

Winning the Vote

So far in this chapter, we have seen that the decline of feminism was a long-term process with origins in the major social and political changes that were taking place in Europe and America from the turn of the century onwards. The First World War certainly played an important part in this process, but in those cases where enough evidence is available for a fairly detailed investigation — Britain, America and Germany — it seems that the process began well before 1914. The decline of feminism took place both on an internal and an external level. Internally, it consisted in the retreat of feminist movements from the demand for female equality into more conservative modes of thought, and externally, it consisted in the growth of anti-feminist forces which accused the feminists of being subversive and revolutionary, thus hastening the feminists' own abandonment of their more progressive principles. The feminists' move to a more conservative position in politics went hand-in-hand with their own decline. A pivotal position in this historical process was occupied by the winning of the vote, which is important enough to warrant special treatment in a section by itself.

Of course, it is a fairly obvious point that feminist movements were almost bound to be weakened by winning the vote. They had come to concentrate more and more on the franchise, and it served in many countries as a unifying focus on which feminists could concentrate. When it was won, many feminists felt there was little more to do. Unable to find a similar rallying point, feminists began to quarrel among themselves, and the differences between them were brought even further out into the open by their involvement in party politics after enfranchisement. Almost everywhere, radical feminism in particular collapsed when the vote was won. In 1909 it was reported that in New Zealand 'the women's societies had become extinct, because, equal voting rights having been granted, their work had been accomplished'.[28] In Germany, too, the suffrage movement dissolved itself, after victory, in 1919. 'The old-style women's movement', declared the radical feminist Minna Cauer, 'is finished.'[29] In some countries the suffragist organisations tried to convert themselves into political education societies. The NAWSA became the National League of Women Voters. In Britain, the NUWSS became the National Union of Societies for Equal Citizenship. But these organisations lacked a real cause. All that kept them going was institutional inertia — the unwillingness of their officials and leaders to abandon the organisational life, and their inability to find a role in conventional politics. Not surprisingly, these organisations enjoyed only a fraction of the support available to their predecessors. The Czech Society for Women's Political Rights, for example, numbered only 278 members by 1923.[30] The major disappointment for moderate and radical feminists alike was the failure of women to use their vote to further their interests as women; this after all had been one of the assumptions behind the feminist campaign. Instead, women voted the same way as men, along class rather than sex lines. Of course, feminists did try to secure adequate representation for women in the first post-suffrage legislatures. But only in a very few cases did they try to secure the election of women who would represent the female sex rather than a political party. The idea of a 'Women's Party' or (in countries with proportional representation) a 'Women's List' became more attractive as the male-dominated political parties failed to live up to the feminists' expectations; but many feminist movements, including that in Germany, where it was a constant subject of debate in the 1920s, realised in the end that the idea was impractical.

They were right. In Sweden, for example, the feminists, angered by

Social Democratic proposals to introduce laws restricting women's right to work in certain trades and disappointed by the generally hostile attitude to female involvement in the professions, formed a women's list in 1926-7 and contested the Stockholm City Council elections with it in the latter year. The attempt was a fiasco. The women's list received only 0.6 per cent of the votes cast. Mild support from the Liberals had meant nothing, for the Liberal voters voted Liberal, while the supporters of other parties were simply put off. The women's list — whose manifesto was restricted entirely to 'women's questions' — exerted even less appeal in the Riksdag elections of 1928, and the idea was then dropped.[31] In Denmark, a similar idea which had been tried out in 1913 also came to nothing.[32] Only in Iceland did a women's list succeed; after municipal enfranchisement in 1908 the Icelandic suffragists, led by Bríet Bjarnhedinsdóttir, angered by the reluctance of the parties to include women on their lists, put up four candidates for the Reykjavík City Council, and by personally canvassing all of the 1,100 female electors got all four elected to the Council. They were helped by the lack of deep party divisions, the fact that the election followed immediately on the granting of municipal suffrage, and the continued momentum of the suffragist campaign towards gaining full suffrage at the national level. The success was not repeated. In 1922 a woman was elected to the Althing, the Icelandic Parliament, on a non-party women's list, but she subsequently joined a political party, much to the chagrin of those who had sponsored her election.[33] Some success, though not of a practical nature, was also scored by the Australian feminist Vida Goldstein, who tried to secure her own election to the Australian Senate as a feminist, opposed to 'narrow and selfish party interests'. She was opposed by the WCTU, and despite the fact that she secured over 50,000 votes, she came fifteenth out of eighteen candidates and was not elected. Goldstein's opposition to party politics marked another stage in the progress of feminism to the right — she also opposed assisted immigration, advocated a white Australia policy and demanded the creation of an Australian navy. These post-suffrage feminists who argued that women should not participate in party politics found themselves of necessity adopting a position of hostility towards parliamentary democracy. 'It is impossible to work purely for ideals if attached to a party organisation', complained another Australian feminist in 1909.[34] How these ideals were to be achieved was perhaps suggested by the German feminists, who by 1932 had given up their faith in the parliamentary system altogether and were advocating a 'corporate State' on the lines of Mussolini's fascist Italy and demanding that one of the 'corporations' consist of women.[35]

But the connection between the winning of the vote and the progress of feminism towards conservatism and decline went deeper than this. In a paradoxical way, indeed, the enfranchisement of women was itself a symptom of this progress. A glance at a few concrete examples of enfranchisement may help to make this clear. Before the First World War, very few countries or states gave women the vote. If we discount the very limited franchises that existed in Bohemia, Austria and Germany, the first important instances of the enfranchisement of women are found in the American Midwest. In 1869 the territory of Wyoming enfranchised its women, though there was no feminist pressure for it; the territory consisted largely of the disorderly railhead towns of Cheyenne and Laramie, and the measure was intended both to attract women to migrate there and to impose order on the conduct of elections and court cases, where the presence of women, it was felt — correctly — would inhibit the drunkenness, corruption and disorder which characterised the territory's earliest days. In 1870 the territory of Utah also gave its women the vote, but here the polygamous Mormons mainly wanted to increase their voting strength over that of the 'Gentiles', mostly men searching for gold, who were threatening to upset it. In Colorado and Idaho, which enfranchised women in 1893 and 1896 respectively, the force that brought women to victory was Populism, a massive but short-lived political movement of established settlers and small farmers who blamed their economic troubles on what they saw as the selfishness and immorality of the East. The referenda on female suffrage owed their success to the Populists; the counties voting Populist gave the proposal massive support, in the belief that women voters would help tighten moral standards in politics, while the counties that stayed Republican or Democratic voted against. The collapse of Populism doomed female suffrage to failure for over a decade. Female suffrage enjoyed renewed success in the West with the rise of the Progressive movement, whose goals — moral reform, including prohibition, democratic control of city and party 'machines', and control of the elements of social disorder and political corruption symbolised by the influx of immigrants from southern Europe — were shared by the feminists. Indeed, the female suffrage movement was really part of the Progressive movement, a major constituent group that contributed much to its strength both in terms of individuals and in terms of organisation. To the supporters of Progressivism, giving women the vote thus seemed an easy way of securing a majority for referenda on the prohibition of alcohol and the introduction of a literacy test for immigrants. Immigration was at its height in these years – over a million immigrants entered the country each year in 1905-7, 1910 and 1913-14. Not surprisingly, resentment was most active in the areas least touched by it, above all, in the small towns of the West, where the big cities with their increasing and conspicuous wealth, their massive migrant population, their huge social problems and their corrupt machines became an object of hatred, fear and resentment. The votes of the white Anglo-Saxon Protestant women of the small towns of the West, they felt, could help counteract this influence at national elections and, above all, if it helped the Progressive Party to power, reassert the supremacy of traditional American virtues in the nation as a whole. In pursuit of these aims, women were enfranchised in Washington in 1910, California in 1911, Oregon, Arizona and Kansas in 1912, and Nevada and Montana in 1914. All these states were in the West; all were bastions of Progressivism.[36]

Broadly similar patterns and relationships may be observed in the cases of Australia and New Zealand, the first two countries in the world to give women the vote. In both countries, as we saw in Chapter 2, the cause of women's suffrage was championed by the Woman's Christian Temperance Union. The moral reform and social control impulses behind the drive for votes for women also animated those who secured its victory. The most dramatic illustration of this was perhaps in Western Australia, where women gained the vote in July 1899. A gold rush, beginning in 1893, had brought a huge influx of prospectors and upset the balance of the sexes in the population. By 1899 there were 70,000 adult males and only 20,000 adult females in Western Australia. The miners and prospectors were poised on the verge of taking over political power from the established landowners and middle classes, and the old governing party, led by the Prime Minister, Sir John Forrest, rushed through female suffrage in order to stop them. Although the great majority of women were in the older districts, this did not stop Forrest's party from being ejected from office shortly afterwards. In South Australia, the WCTU petitioned for female suffrage, and bills were introduced to enfranchise property-owning women in 1885 and 1889. This would have strengthened the position of the Country Party, representing established farmers. But the growth of Adelaide weakened the Country Party's hold on politics. In 1893 a Liberal-Labour coalition took power and passed measures redistributing constituency boundaries in favour of the centre of population. This was accompanied by female suffrage, passed by a narrow majority in 1894. The Country Party resisted both these measures strongly. But the furthest they could go towards safeguarding their interests was to insert an amendment allowing postal voting for women who lived more than three miles from a polling booth. The main support for female suffrage in South Australia came from the total abstinence societies, who saw it as a means of securing votes for prohibition. The point here, therefore, was to control the social upheavals generated by the expansion of the principal city, Adelaide. The political parties representing the city can in fact be seen as primary agents in controlling it; it was they after all, and not the Country Party, who had to run the city.

In 1901 the various states of which Australia was composed joined together in a federation; women in South and Western Australia automatically acquired the federal vote, and it was clearly anomalous to deny it to the women of New South Wales, Victoria, Queensland and Tasmania, so these were enfranchised too. This paved the way for the introduction of votes for women in state elections. In Queensland, where politics centred on a clash between established settlers and new mining communities, female suffrage was enacted in 1905 for much the same reasons as in Western Australia. New South Wales in 1902 followed the same pattern as South Australia. Tasmania gave women the vote in 1903 simply because they had it in federal elections. In Victoria, rate-paying women were automatically enfranchised in 1908; working-class women had to apply to get on the register. This qualification reflected the depth of social conflict in Victoria, where the influx of gold miners had been particularly heavy. Female suffrage was thus secured in Australia by a complex mixture of political, social, moral and institutional pressures. The dominant note struck by those who favoured it and welcomed its enactment was one of confidence that public order and morality would be the main beneficiary. It was the priority placed on social rather than institutional or political means of controlling disorder that explains why female suffrage was passed in Australia despite the absence of a large-scale feminist movement.[37]

In New Zealand, the first country to enfranchise women, female suffrage was enacted in 1894. Members of Parliament were divided, but there was a wide belief that, as Sir John Hall, the main advocate of votes for women, put it, female suffrage would 'increase the influence of the *settler* and *family* man, as against the loafing single man'. Giving the vote to women, said a conservative newspaper, was 'the only possible corrective to the evils attendant on universal manhood suffrage'. Another conservative politician said in 1892:

I do not deny for one moment that the country has been injuriously affected by the cities, and I have no doubt that the country will derive a certain proportion of assistance from the women, whose votes will to some extent counteract those of unthinking voters in the towns.

Passage of the measure was held up by a filibuster from the brewers' lobby. The WCTU sent in large petitions and mounted an extensive campaign outside Parliament. Ironically, the Government, which had been elected by the urban vote, was less than enthusiastic about the measure, and it only passed the Upper House by the manoeuvrings of the conservative opposition; women in New Zealand owed the vote not least to the fact that the female suffrage bill was going through Parliament at a time when the Government was weak and the political situation confused. Once the measure was passed, however, it was the Government which claimed and received most of the credit, not the opposition.[38]

Among all the complex alliances and alignments that surrounded the achievement of votes for women in these new societies, one thing at least is clear: the enfranchisement of women was seen, both by politicians and by the suffragists themselves, as a means of controlling society in the interests of the 'stable' part of the population, the middle classes. In the more complex societies of Europe, this is at first sight by no means so readily apparent. Yet *mutatis mutandis* it was true here as well. The main difference was that in Europe the enfranchisement of women was seen as a means of staving off a proletarian revolution. The only countries to enfranchise women before the First World War, Finland and Norway, provide interesting examples of the complexities in which this basic pattern was embedded. The development of Finland in the 1890s was dominated by an attempt by the country's Russian rulers to Russianise education and administration. Women took a leading part in the Finnish national resistance, and in the Russian Revolution of 1905 they seized their chance, and compelled the Tsar to concede a new constitution with universal suffrage for both sexes. This seems to have been the result of a compromise between the Social Democrats and the nationalist liberals, who had earlier supported the feminists' demand (advanced in a mass demonstration of a thousand women on 7 November 1904) for suffrage on equal terms with men (i.e. a limited suffrage). In effect, the Russians' anti-Finnish policy forced the socialists and liberals to bury their differences, and this continued throughout the reimposition of Russian authority after 1906 which had the effect of rendering the enfranchisement of women meaningless in practical political terms. It was only after the complete removal of Tsarist authority in 1917 that these differences at last came out into the open, resulting in a long-presaged civil war. In the Finnish case, therefore, though female suffrage was certainly followed by the enactment of prohibition and other moral reform legislation, the element of social control was not particularly obvious.[39]

It was rather more obvious in Norway, the other European country to give women the vote before the First World War. Here the prospects of female suffrage, seemingly remote in 1900, were transformed in 1905, when the prolonged crisis between Norway and the Swedish Crown was abruptly ended by a coup carried out by the Norwegian Government backed by the Storting sitting in a secret session. In a bloodless revolution, the Swedish king was deposed as King of Norway, and the question of the monarchy submitted to a plebiscite. Excluded from this referendum, women, organised by the suffrage movement, organised their own unofficial plebiscite. Such was the strength of national feeling that 300,000 female votes were cast (compared with 400,000 male votes), and when the result was submitted to the Storting, all the members present in the House rose to their feet. The 'women's plebiscite' demonstrated the national reliability of the great mass of Norwegian women to the politicians. It gave the suffragists invaluable organisational experience and showed the parties that they could be efficient. In 1906 the suffragists worked for the Radicals in the election, opposing the anti-suffrage Conservatives and Agrarians. The victory of the Radicals paved the way for a women's suffrage bill, which passed by 93 votes to 23, after only 2 hours' debate, on 14 June 1907. It enfranchised all women who already possessed the municipal suffrage, which had been granted on a property qualification in 1901 (i.e. about 300,000 women). The immediate effect of this was to rob the major suffragist organisation of three large branches and 'many hundreds' of women, for all those who favoured a property franchise now left the movement since they had achieved their aim. A rump continued the struggle in alliance with the group which had previously broken away in favour of universal suffrage. However, not surprisingly, the first election in which these propertied women voted, in 1909, returned a conservative-dominated government, which proved predictably hostile to any further extension of the franchise.

The general election of 1912 once more brought the Radicals to power, and in 1913, despite the opposition of the Conservatives and a minority of the Liberals, women's suffrage became universal in 1913.

Here, as in Finland, the enfranchisement of women was followed by a series of moral reform and social control laws.[40]

Far more obvious connections between female suffrage and fear of proletarian revolution can be seen in the widespread enfranchisement of women at the end of the First World War, when bourgeois anxiety about socialism and Bolshevism reached fresh heights. Of course, the winning of the vote seemed to many radical feminists to be no more than the just reward of a long campaign to convince men of the rationality of giving women the vote. Many historians, in contrast, have noted that with a very few exceptions countries tended to enact female suffrage at the end of the First World War, and they have concluded that women were given the vote as a reward for their participation in the war effort. It is certainly true that in many countries feminist campaigns provided the immediate stimulus for the granting of female suffrage. By the time they were mounted, however, the feminists themselves had become sufficiently conservative to reassure governments that they were not giving in to any really revolutionary pressure, though giving the vote to women certainly still appeared progressive enough for middle-class liberals and reformist Social Democrats to hope that it would assuage the passionate desire of the masses for equality. Because of the relatively conservative political opinions of the majority of women, it was obvious that the enfranchisement of the female sex would have a stabilising effect on parliamentary democracy. The need for such a stabilisation was all the more apparent because many of these liberal-Social Democratic alliances only came to power at the end of the First World War on the collapse of conservative-authoritarian political systems, and the situation in which they took power was one of extreme political confusion and tension in which it was of paramount importance to them to secure the general acceptance of the legitimacy of parliamentary democracy at the earliest possible moment. It was considerations such as these, and not, as we shall shortly see, any desire to 'reward' women for the part in helping the war effort, that were uppermost in the minds of legislators at the end of the First World War.

One example of this situation was to be found in Russia, where women were enfranchised after the February Revolution of 1917. The Provisional Government, faced with the danger of further unrest after the collapse of the Tsarist régime, was in precisely the kind of situation in which the enfranchisement of women seemed a sensible concession to make. The Revolution provided the opportunity for the Russian League of Equal Rights for Women, which had spent most of the war in patriotic work, to campaign once more for the vote. Led by Dr

Praskoviya Shishkina-Yavein, the League demanded full equality in every sphere 'in the interest of progress, in the interest of the prosperity and culture of our native land'. The Provisional Government was lobbied, and a large street demonstration was organised on 19 March (Old Style), in which the old revolutionary Vera Figner as well as the feminists participated. All supporters of the Provisional Government considered themselves revolutionaries and radical tactics such as demonstrations were regarded as legitimate, even by the Mutual Benefit Society, now led by Anna Shabanova. Clearly, when all Russian men were being given equal rights, the feminists were outraged that 'only we women, outcast of the outcasts, living as slaves of yesterday's slaves, are waiting for the government frankly and openly to put forward a declaration of our rights'. Their wait was not long. On 21 March-3 April the President of the Provisional Government, Prince Lvov, assured a deputation of feminists who included Shabanova, Shishkina-Yavein, Anna Milyukova, Ariadna Tyrkova and the revolutionary Vera Figner, that women would be granted the vote. Shishkina-Yavein was appointed to represent women on the Council of 61, charged with the task of drawing up a constitution, and laws were passed on 15 April (New Style) giving women over twenty full voting rights. In the next few months women were also given access to the civil service, the legal profession and all elective bodies on an equal basis with men. These legislative measures had little practical effect. The political parties were dominated as before by men, and although some women voted and were elected in municipal elections, the Bolshevik Revolution made the bodies to which they were elected irrelevant. The feminist an end, this time against the background of the spread of Bolshevism. In Britain too, then, female suffrage was also enacted to maintain stability in the face of increased threats of disorder and revolution.[43] tion.[41]

Female suffrage was granted in many countries which underwent revolutions in 1918. The Habsburg Empire was overthrown at the end of the First World War, and most of the new nations which succeeded it gave women the vote. The Karolyi government in Hungary, for example, whose leader had been converted to the idea of female suffrage before the war, included some members of the Liberal Democratic Party, the group most closely associated with Rosika Schwimmer's suffragist movement. Schwimmer had become a pacifist and opposed the war. This did not endear her to the conservative wing of the nationalist movement, which came to power in a bloody 'White Terror' after overthrowing a Bolshevik revolution which in turn had briefly displaced the Karolyi régime. The counter-revolution in Hungary disfranchised women. In 1920 it gave them back the vote, but after 1921 restricted it to women over thirty years of age who fulfilled certain educational and economic qualifications. In Poland, once stability had been established, women obtained the vote in 1921. Although Poland was a Catholic country, the influence on its policy of the Allies and the League of Nations, whose creation it really was, the close involvement of women in the nationalist movement, and the initial dominance of nationalist liberals, ensured that female suffrage would become a reality. Similarly, in Czechoslovakia, once independence was obtained, it was highly unlikely that women would be denied the vote. They obtained it in the constitution of 1919-20. In the new Austrian Republic, women were given the vote by the Provisional National Assembly at the end of 1918. Of all the successor states, in fact, only Yugoslavia denied women the vote. The constitution of 1921, which reflected Serbian influence, was based on manhood suffrage. This was surprising, since a national Women's Suffrage Association had existed in Serbia since 1906, and its leaders had made 'national ideals' the first point on their programme. Women's part in the nationalist movement had been recognised by the opening of the University to them in 1888. But in the mid-1900s the Serbian Radicals, who led the nationalist movement, became markedly more conservative, and this may well account for their rejection of female suffrage in 1921. The same Assembly, for example, also made the Communist Party illegal and gave wide powers to the King. Yugoslavia was an overwhelmingly agricultural country, and the feminist movement was weak. The Catholic Church had a strong hold on the main national minority, the Croats, and the Serbs may have been reluctant to strengthen its influence by giving women the vote. Finally, Serbia had existed as an independent state long before 1918, and there was thus a greater measure of continuity with the past than in states such as Austria, Czechoslovakia, Poland and Hungary. Unlike these countries, Yugoslavia was not born in a revolution. In general, the enfranchisement of women in the successor states was a part of the process of stabilisation after the fall of the Habsburgs and the defeat of Bolshevism.

The revolutions of 1918 also had an impact in Sweden, where economic crisis, food rioting and dissensions between supporters of the allies and the Central Powers created widespread fear of a Bolshevik Revolution or Civil War in 1918. To preserve stability, all reformist and constitutional parties agreed to strengthen parliamentary democracy in 1919 by introducing ministerial responsibility and female suffrage, among other measures; these were finally ratified in 1921. Similarly in Germany, female suffrage was seen by the post-revolutionary moderate Social Democratic government as a means of dissuading the advocates of a Soviet or Council system from opposing the calling of a National Assembly on parliamentary lines. Kurt Eisner, the Bavarian revolutionary, told the government on 25 November 1918 that the National Assembly should not be generally elected on parliamentary lines, but should consist of representatives of the revolutionary workers' and soldiers' councils, which (incidentally) contained scarcely a single woman. The government spokesman replied:

> The attitude that Herr Eisner had adopted towards the Constituent Assembly was incomprehensible to him [the speaker]. For decades Social Democracy has been demanding votes for women, and in the very hour in which this goal has been achieved, women are to be told: 'now you can't vote!' That means nothing other than putting the question on the shelf again.

Ironically, therefore, German women owed the vote not only to the Revolution, but also to the fact that it was defeated; for while there was no prospect of female suffrage being enacted by the Kaiser's government, whatever women's services to the war effort, and least of all had Germany actually won the war, there was little chance of women playing a role in a system controlled by workers' councils either.[42]

In all these countries, female suffrage was achieved during or shortly after the First World War, but it owed little to the direct influence of the war on the position of women in society. The same may be said of the gaining of the vote in Britain (1918). It has often been asserted that British women obtained the vote in recognition of their services to the national war effort. This is a myth. Very few of those Liberal and Unionist MPs who supported female suffrage in 1917 had opposed it before the war (some 8 per cent, in fact). Other factors were responsible for the changed circumstances. Before 1914, many Unionists abstained in female suffrage votes in the House of Commons in order to throw the onus of defeating it onto the Liberals. By 1917, however, the Liberal leader Asquith had been replaced as Prime Minister by Lloyd George, whose prejudices against giving women the vote were far less marked, and there was a coalition government. Before the war, the Irish MPs had opposed female suffrage so as not to annoy Asquith at a time when Home Rule was at a critical stage. In 1917 circumstances had changed and they supported it. Moreover, an election was due in 1915, and although the life of the Parliament was repeatedly prolonged, the instability of the coalition's support made another election a distinct possibility. In order to accommodate this, a franchise reform had to be passed to enable troops to qualify at short notice. This opened up a whole new area for debate — if troops could vote, then why not munitions workers, for example? In order to avoid dissension, the Government appointed a special conference chaired by the Speaker of the House of Commons, who happened to be a supporter of female suffrage and appointed a majority of pro-suffrage members. The compromise arrived at on female suffrage by the conference, whose recommendations covered many aspects of electoral reform, gave the vote to women over the age of thirty. This satisfied both those Liberals who objected to the property qualifications stipulated in pre-war bills and those Unionists who were frightened of giving all women the vote. The House of Lords, which had on more than one previous occasion defeated suffrage bills passed by the House of Commons, was fearful of losing all its powers if it clashed with the Commons again, as it had done (with disastrous consequences for its own freedom of action) in 1910, and was unwilling to reject a bill approved by the coalition. In 1917, there was almost no pressure exerted by the feminists, who were almost entirely engrossed in supporting the war effort. This, along with the Government's decision to allow a free vote on the female suffrage clause, gave MPs a freedom of choice that many had felt they lacked when the Parliament was being coerced by the suffragettes before the war. Most important of all, perhaps, there was a widespread fear that if at least some measure of female suffrage were not granted, suffragette violence would break out with redoubled force once the war came to an end, this time against the background of the spread of Bolshevism. In Britain too, then, female suffrage was also enacted to maintain stability in the face of increased threats of disorder and revolution.[43]

In other countries where women gained the vote in the period 1914-18, the influence of the First World War operated, if it operated at all, in a similar way: indirectly, through its effect on the general political situation, rather than directly, by affecting the position of women in society. In Denmark and Iceland, for example, where women got the vote in June 1915, the new constitutions which contained the women's suffrage provision had already been approved before the war in the summer of 1914. The outbreak of war delayed rather than hastened their final implementation. In both countries, women owed the vote to the advent of Liberal governments to power in 1914 rather than to the special circumstances of the war, and a good deal as well to the influence of the Social Democrats.[44] The same can be said of the achievement of female suffrage in the Netherlands (1919), which, like these other countries, remained neutral in the war. In belligerent Belgium, by contrast, despite the fact that women played a greater part in the war effort than anywhere else, and were actively involved in resisting the German occupation, they did not get the vote after the war. Even more unusual was the fact that they had the Social Democrats to blame for this. The Catholics came to power with the Social Democrats and Liberals in 1919, and were certainly not ill-disposed to the idea of female suffrage, which they were aware would bring them a major electoral advantage. The Social Democrats, whose strength had been greatly increased by the introduction of universal manhood suffrage at the end of the war, were unwilling to give up their newly acquired electoral power to the Catholics and rejected the idea of female suffrage above the communal level.[45] In Canada, where women achieved the vote during the war, female suffrage did at first glance appear to be related to wartime conditions. In 1917 the Government enfranchised women with close relatives at the front. But this was in fact an excuse. The Conservative Government introduced it purely in an attempt to stave off defeat in the forthcoming elections. The point was that the Government's electoral strength lay in the East, which supplied the great majority of troops. In the West, conscientious objection to military service was widespread, and there were large numbers of recent immigrants, many of them from enemy countries, who could not be conscripted. Women who had not been born British citizens were also disfranchised. The measure created a storm of disapproval, but it passed, and the Government was duly re-elected. In 1918 it proved unable to resist the mounting pressure to enfranchise all women, exerted not only by the female suffrage movement, which had been revitalised by the controversy, but also by the irate Liberal Party. At the same time, female suffrage at the federal level had become difficult to resist since a number of provinces had already enfranchised women — the Prairie Provinces of Manitoba, Saskatchewan and Alberta in 1916, and British Columbia and Ontario in 1917. The conservative Maritime Provinces followed more slowly (Nova Scotia 1918, New Brunswick 1919, Prince Edward Island 1922, Newfoundland 1925), and Catholic Quebec did not give women the vote until 1940. This chronological pattern reflected the fact that by 1910, when the suffrage movement really got under way in Canada, Canadian politics was beginning to feel the impact of American Progressivism. The main proponents of female suffrage in the Western states of Canada were the Farmers' Associations, who, like the Progressives in the United States, saw in female suffrage an opportunity to reassert traditional liberal virtues against the growing dominance of the big cities. In Ontario and British Columbia female suffrage reflected the growing power of the Liberals, who were broadly comparable to the Progressives and believed that giving the vote to women would help defeat corruption, alcoholism and immorality. In all this, clearly, the war itself only played a relatively minor part.[46]

Finally, much the same may be said about the enfranchisement of women in the United States. Already in the states which had given women the vote in 1910, the suffrage movement had gathered its strength in running referendum campaigns and bringing them to a successful conclusion. An even more prominent role was played by the suffragists in the final struggle of 1916-18. The militants under Alice Paul seized the initiative and swung round the campaign from its concentration on individual states to a focus on the securing of a federal Amendment to the Constitution once more. In 1915 the inefficient, Anna Howard Shaw retired from the Presidency of the National American Woman Suffrage Alliance and was succeeded by Carrie Chapman Catt. Catt was an organiser of genius. When she took over in 1915 the membership of the NAWSA stood at 100,000. By 1917 she had raised it to more than two million. She constantly lobbied the President, Woodrow Wilson, and by 1917 had converted him to her views. She devised an elaborate, secret 'Winning Plan' which the state leaders of the suffrage movement signed in 1916. The 'Winning Plan' envisaged the winning of female suffrage in at least one Eastern and one Southern state and the adoption by as many states as possible of the 'Illinois Law' which in 1913 had granted women Presidential suffrage by act of the legislature without consulting the electorate. 1917 saw the first woman elected to Congress, Jeannette Rankin of Montana, and the appointment of Committees on Woman Suffrage in the Senate and the House. While the militants continued to keep press attention focused on the issue, the suffragists maintained a steady pressure on Congress through ceaseless lobbying and organising, and continued to fight for the vote at state level. In 1917 North Dakota, Ohio, Indiana, Rhode Island, Nebraska and Michigan adopted potential female voters. On 9 January 1918 President Wilson formally committed himself to active support of the suffrage. On 10 January the House passed the Constitutional Amendment giving women the vote. It secured exactly the two-thirds majority required. It took unexpectedly long to secure the passage of the Amendment through the Senate and obtain its ratification by the states. Catt and the suffragists therefore maintained their pressure for both these objectives. Helped by the influence of the President and favourable decisions by the United States Supreme Court, the struggle was brought to a triumphant conclusion in August 1920.[47]

The fact that all this took place during the First World War is of little significance. The suffragists, of course, could not resist using the war to bolster their arguments. Carrie Chapman Catt remarked in 1917 for example that 'an enormous number of slackers in war but actors in voting have been revealed in the German counties of South Dakota — the counties which defeated women suffrage on referendum in 1916'. But the war did not by itself materially alter the suffragists' prospects of success. To begin with, its impact on the American economy was not very great, and in any case those women who were drawn into war production were either black or working class and so of little concern to either the suffragists or the government. A Committee on Women's Defence Work was set up in 1916 under Anna Howard Shaw, and proved very active. But much of its work was purposeless (for example, registering women, most of whom were never asked to work). The Government attached little importance to the Committee. It was simply a way of keeping middle-class women occupied. Moreover, the feminist movement itself was deeply divided over the war. In 1915 Jane Addams, inspired by a speaking tour undertaken in America by the Hungarian feminist and pacifist Rosika Schwimmer, formed a Women's Peace Party, with aims including a 'Concert of Nations', an international police and an early cessation of hostilities. By 1916 it had 25,000 members. It failed to stop America entering the war. But it remained a strong pacifist influence within the feminist movement until the Armistice. Moreover, the militant Woman's Party, led by Alice Paul, argued that the war was absurd and immoral so long as women in America lacked the vote. The publicity it attracted — above all, in the notorious 'Kaiser Wilson' demonstration — tarred the NAWSA with the pacifist brush. No matter how hard Catt tried to dissociate herself from the militants' actions, no one could escape the fact that the NAWSA shared their views on the point at issue. A NAWSA document declared too that President Wilson should begin setting the world right for democracy by giving women the vote. This argument certainly had some influence on the President. But to Americans in general it helped contribute to the unpatriotic image of the feminist movement which was to prove so disastrous for it after the war.[48]

Moreover, as an argument, it had the distinct disadvantage of glossing

over the undemocratic aspects of female suffrage. As a Senator from
Idaho asked his colleagues during one of the final debates,

> Does anybody suppose that this amendment is anything but a white
> amendment? . . . Do you propose to put the South under Federal
> Control as to elections? . . . Nobody intends that the two and a half
> million Negro women of the South shall vote, unless . . . party ex-
> pediency compels action for the sheer purpose of party advantage.[49]

Democratic control of the South would ensure that only white women
registered as voters. This was in fact only part of a wider pattern of
political change that lay behind the victory of the suffragists in 1918-20.
In the South, for example, the growth of a female suffrage movement
occurred just after the passage of alcohol prohibition laws in a number
of states (Alabama 1907-9, Georgia 1907, Mississippi 1908, North
Carolina 1908 and Tennessee 1909). Prohibition was seen as a means of
controlling and ordering the black population. In 1913, the reorientation of the temperance movement which this signified culminated in
the conversion of the Anti-Saloon League from a policy of securing
local options and state prohibition to a federal Prohibition Amendment.
In 1914, five states adopted prohibition, in 1915 five more, and in
1916 an additional four. The campaign achieved victory in 1919 with
the passage of the eighteenth Amendment enforcing Prohibition throughout America. This sequence of events is of course almost an exact
parallel of the development of female suffrage in the same period. The
geographical distribution of support for the two measures was also very
similar. Both were associated with Populism and Progressivism. Both
represented an attempt by middle-class white Anglo-Saxon Protestants
to control the blacks, the immigrants and the big cities. They were a
response to what was felt as a growing threat to the supremacy of
American values. They achieved victory in the war not least because
with the conflict against Germany and − to an immeasurably greater
extent − the Bolshevik Revolution of 1917 and the revolutions in
Central Europe at the end of the war, the fear of the subversion of the
values represented by the Protestant middle classes reached panic proportions.[50]

   Female suffrage, then, was not only a cause of the decline of feminism, it was also a symptom; for without the retreat from liberalism
that had already begun before the First World War, the feminists would
not have found it so easy to get the vote. The enactment of female
suffrage had a stabilising effect on political systems − though in some

cases this was short-lived. The very stabilisation which it helped bring about then ensured that it would have little meaning in terms of helping women secure more equal rights. Because the abandonment of radicalism by the feminists themselves was part of this process of stabilisation, the chances of pushing through more radical feminist legislation after suffrage were further reduced. These developments were not at all what the feminists themselves expected, and they were bitterly disappointed with the fruits of enfranchisement. 1920 marked the end of the era of feminism. In the countries where women possessed the vote, feminist movements continued to decline or were eventually suppressed; while elsewhere, no other European country enfranchised women until the end of the Second World War.[51]

Notes

1. Institut für Marxismus-Leninismus beim ZK der SED, East Berlin: NL 5/15: Zetkin to W. Blos, 27 December 1905.
2. Constance Rover, *Women's Suffrage and Party Politics in Britain 1866-1914* (London, 1967), pp. 66-7.
3. See above, pp. 172-3.
4. E.g. 'There is a close connection between the ideas of the suffragettes who follow the banner of Mrs Pankhurst and the anarchist terrorists who, half a generation ago, taught the doctrine of propaganda by the deed' (Staatsarchiv Hamburg, Politische Polizei, S9001: *Vorwärts*, 25 February 1913).
5. Andrew Rosen. *Rise Up, Women! The Militant Campaign of the Women's Social and Political Union 1903-1914* (London, 1974), p. 84. See also the sustained comparison in Teresa Billington-Greig, *The Militant Suffragette Movement. Emancipation in a Hurry* (London, 1911), pp. 200-3.
6. Rosen, op. cit., is now the standard account of the suffragette campaigns: the account in this paragraph is based on Rosen's book.
7. Roger Fulford, *Votes for Women – The Story of a Struggle* (London, 1957), pp. 164-300.
8. Richard J. Evans, *The Feminist Movement in Germany 1894-1933* (London, 1976), pp. 87-93.
9. See above, pp. 100-1.
10. Theodore Zeldin, *France 1848-1945, Vol. I: Ambition, Love and Politics* (Oxford, 1973), p. 348; Charles Sowerwine, 'Women and Socialism in France 1871-1921: Socialist Groups from Léonie Rouzade to Louise Saumoneau' (PhD, Wisconsin, 1973), pp. 233-41; Patrick K. Bidelman, 'The Feminist Movement in France: The Formative Years 1858-1889' (PhD, Michigan, 1975), pp. 267-71.
11. Sidney R. Bland, 'Techniques of Persuasion: The National Woman's Party and Woman Suffrage' (PhD, George Washington University, 1972) is the most detailed and thorough account. See for the events recounted in this paragraph esp. pp. 9-12, 26-76. There is another account of American militancy in Ruth F. Claus, 'Militancy in the English and American Woman Suffrage Movements' (PhD, Yale, 1975).
12. Bland, op. cit., pp. 77-137.

13. Evans, op. cit., pp. 214-23.
14. Rosen, op. cit., pp. 54, 103, 176-7, 182-3, 203-13, 226-8, 268-71;
    Billington-Greig, op. cit., pp. 5, 30, 73, 81, 87, 115; Fulford, op. cit., p. 243;
    F.M Leventhal, 'The Petticoat Vote', *Times Literary Supplement* 19 Sept.
    1975, p. 1045. Characterisations of Fascism are innumerable; among the
    more widely known are F.L. Carsten, *The Rise of Fascism* (London, 1967),
    S.J. Woolf (ed.), *European Fascism* (London, 1969) and Eugen Weber,
    Varieties of Fascism (Princeton, 1964).
15. David Morgan, *Suffragists and Liberals* (Oxford, 1974) is the most recent
    account of the history of female suffrage legislation in Edwardian England.
16. Alexander de Grand, 'Women under Italian Fascism', *Historical Journal*
    19/4 (1976), pp. 947-68.
17. Evans, op. cit., pp. 130-70.
18. ICWT 1909, pp. 212-13.
19. Evans, op. cit., Chapters 3-6; Fritz K. Ringer, *The Decline of the German
    Mandarins. The German Academic Community 1890-1933* (Cambridge,
    Mass., 1969); Agnes von Zahn-Harnack, *Die Frauenbewegung-Geschichte,
    Probleme, Ziele* (Leipzig/Berlin, 1928).
20. Most authors have followed the misleading account given in Clifford
    Kirkpatrick, *Nazi Germany: Its Women and Family Life* (New York, 1938),
    which portrays the feminist movement as irreconcilably opposed to every-
    thing the Nazis stood for (e.g. Kate Millett, *Sexual Politics* (New York,
    1969) and Jill Stephenson, *Women in Nazi Society* (London, 1975)). The
    conclusions presented in the above account rest on extensive unpublished
    documentation from the archives of the feminist movement (see Chapter 8
    of my book *The Feminist Movement in Germany* for references). I have
    attempted a more general discussion of the extent of German women's
    support for Hitler in my article 'German Women and the Triumph of Hitler',
    Journal of Modern History, Vol. 48, No. 1, March 1976. The most stimula-
    ting account of women and the Nazis is Tim Mason, 'Women in Germany
    1925-1940: Family, Welfare and Work', *History Workshop: A Journal of
    Socialist Historians* Nos. 1-2, March-Sept. 1976.
21. Aileen S. Kraditor, *The Ideas of the Woman Suffrage Movement 1890-1920*
    (London, 1965), p. 66-73; J. Stanley Lemons, *The Woman Citizen. Social
    Feminism in the 1920s* (Urbana, 1973), pp. 1-4; John P. Rousmanière,
    'Cultural Hybrid in the Slums: The College Woman and the Settlement
    House 1889-1894', *American Quarterly* Vol. XXII (Spring, 1970), pp. 45-
    66; Jill Conway, 'Women Reformers and American Culture 1870-1930',
    Journal of Social History Vol. 5, No. 2, 1971-2, pp. 164-77; Eleanor Flexner,
    'Cultural Hybrid in the Slums: The College Woman and the Settlement
    (Cambridge, Mass., 1966), pp. 203-15; William L. O'Neill, *Everyone Was
    Brave. The Rise and Fall of Feminism in America* (Chicago, 1969), pp. 34-5,
    148-50, 160-1; Allen F. Davis, *American Heroine. The Life and Legend of
    Jane Addams* (New York, 1975); Lois Banner, *Women in Modern America.
    A Brief History* (New York, 1974), pp. 1-72, 88-102. One aspect of these
    new ideas was 'domestic feminism'; see above p. 39n.1.
22. Kraditor, op. cit., pp. 125, 138 for the quotations in this paragraph.
23. Ibid., pp. 202-3, for Gordon, Catt and Kearney. See also Lee N. Allen,
    'The Woman Suffrage Movement in Alabama, 1910-1920', *Alabama Review*
    Vol. XI (April 1958), pp. 83-99, and the following articles by A. Elizabeth
    Taylor: 'The Origin of the Woman Suffrage Movement in Georgia', *Georgia
    Historical Quarterly* XXVIII, No. 2 (June 1944), pp. 63-79; 'Revival and
    Development of the Woman Suffrage Movement in Georgia', *Georgia His-
    torical Quarterly* XLII (December 1958), pp. 339-54; 'The Last Phase of the

Woman Suffrage Movement in Georgia', *Georgia Historical Quarterly*
XLIII (March 1959), pp. 11-28; 'The Woman Suffrage Movement in Texas',
Journal of Southern History XVII (May 1951), pp. 194-215; 'The Woman
Suffrage Movement in Florida', *Florida Historical Quarterly* XXXVI (July
1957), pp. 42-60; 'The Woman Suffrage Movement in Arkansas', *Arkansas
Historical Quarterly* XV (1956), pp. 17-52.

24. IWSAC 1909, pp. 118-20; IWSAC 1911, p. 128.
25. J. Stanley Lemons, *The Woman Citizen, Social Feminism in the 1920s*
     (Urbana, 1973), pp. 43-52, 181-204.
26. Ibid., pp. 118-221; C.A. Chambers, *Seedtime of Reform: American Social
     Service and Social Action 1918-1933* (Minneapolis, 1963), pp. 61-83;
     William H. Chafe, *The American Woman: Her Changing Social, Economic
     and Political Roles, 1920-1970* (New York, 1972), pp. 25-47; Alice S.
     Rossi, *The Feminist Papers* (New York, 1974), pp. 131-59. Compare German
     antifeminist smears (Evans, op. cit., Ch. 6).
27. Marie-Hélène Lefaucheux (ed.), *Women in a Changing World. The Dynamic
     Story of the International Council of Women Since 1888* (London, 1966)
     for general information on the suppression of feminism in various countries.
     The Ray Strachey quotation is taken from Sheila Rowbotham, *Hidden
     From History* (London, 1973), p. 163. See also Jane Lewis, 'Beyond
     Suffrage: English Feminism during the 1920s'. *The Maryland Historian* 6/1
     (1973), pp. 1-17; Banner, op. cit., pp. 141-54; Joseph R. Gusfield, 'Social
     Structure and Moral Reform: A Study of the Woman's Christian Temperance
     Union', *American Journal of Sociology* Vol. 51, No. 3 (Nov. 1955), pp. 221-
     32; Evans, *The Feminist Movement in Germany*, pp. 237-8; Betty Friedan,
     The Feminine Mystique (New York, 1963); IWSAC 1923, p. 28; IWSAC
     1926, p. 216 (for figures of Finnish feminist societies' membership).
28. ICWT 1909, p. 61.
29. Quoted in R.J. Evans, 'The Women's Movement in Germany 1890-1919'
     (D.Phil., Oxford, 1972), pp. 326-8.
30. William L. O'Neill, *The Woman Movement: Feminism in the United States
     and England* (London, 1969), pp. 89-92; IWSAC 1923, p. 161.
31. Jarl Torbacke, 'Kvinnolistan 1927-1928 – et kvinnopolitiskt fiasko',
     Historisk tidskrift 1969, pp. 145-84.
32. WSP, p. 80.
33. IWSAC 1909, pp. 130-1; Laufey Valdimarsdóttir, *A Brief History of the
     Woman Suffrage Movement in Iceland* (London, 1929), pp. 6-8; Inge
     Dahlsgård (ed.), *Kvindebevaegelsens hvem-hvad-hvor* (Copenhagen, 1975),
     p. 284.
34. Norman Mackenzie, 'Vida Goldstein: the Australian Suffragette', *Australian
     Journal of Politics and History*, 6/2 (1960), pp. 190-204: IWSAC 1911, p. 78.
35. Evans, *The Feminist Movement in Germany* pp. 247-8.
36. Alan P. Grimes, *The Puritan Ethic and Woman Suffrage* (New York, 1967),
     pp. 27-77, 95-144; Banner, op. cit., pp. 93-101; Lemons, op. cit., *passim*;
     Flexner, op. cit., pp. 248-75; Andrew Sinclair, *The Better Half: The
     Emancipation of the American Woman* (London, 1966), pp. 300-1. See
     also B. Beeton, 'Woman Suffrage in the American West 1869-1896'
     (PhD, Utah, 1976).
37. William Pember Reeves, *State Experiments in Australia and New Zealand*
     (London, 1902), Vol. I, pp. 126-35; S. Encel, N. Mackenzie, M. Tebbutt,
     Women and Society: An Australian Study (Melbourne, 1974), pp. 222-36;
     Dianne Scott, 'Woman Suffrage: The Movement in Australia', *Journal of
     the Royal Australian Historical Society* 53/4 (Dec. 1967), pp. 299-322.
38. Patricia Grimshaw, *Women's Suffrage in New Zealand* (Wellington, 1972),
     pp. 64-5, 86-94.

39. WSP, pp. 55-6; Hugh Seton-Watson, *The Decline of Imperial Russia* (London, 1952), pp. 242-3.
40. WSP, pp. 66-9; T.K. Derry, *A Short History of Norway* (2nd ed., London, 1968), pp. 194-206.
41. Dale Ross, 'The Role of the Women of Petrograd in War, Revolution and Counter-Revolution 1914-1921' (PhD, Rutgers, 1973), pp. 167-72; Richard Stites, 'Women's Liberation Movements in Russia 1900-1921', *Canadian-American Slavic Studies*, Vol. 7, No. 4 (1973), pp. 460-74.
42. Dahlsgård (ed.), op. cit., pp. 125-8, 141, 143-4; IWSAC 1909, pp. 133-4; IWSAC 1923, p. 183; Ross Evans Paulson, *Women's Suffrage and Prohibition: A Comparative Study of Equality and Social Control* (Brighton, 1973), p. 109 n.15; Martha Braun *et. al.* (eds.), *Frauenbewegung, Frauenbildung und Frauenarbeit in Österreich* (Vienna, 1930), pp. 80-1; Hugh Seton-Watson, *Eastern Europe Between the Wars 1918-1941* (London, 1962); C.A. Macartney, A.W. Palmer, *Independent Eastern Europe: A History* (London, 1966); Ingvar Andersson, *A History of Sweden* (London, 1955), pp. 414-30. The German government's debate with Eisner can be read in *Die Regierung der Volksbeauftragten 1918/19*, eingeleitet von Erich Matthias, bearbeitet von Susanne Miller unter Mitwirkung von Heinrich Potthoff (Quellen zur Geschichte des Parlamentarismus und der politischen Parteien, I. Reihe, Bd.3, Düsseldorf, 1969), pp. 179-93. Cf. Evans, *The Feminist Movement in Germany*, Chapter 7, for the failure of female suffrage before the Revolution.
43. Martin D. Pugh, 'Politicians and the Woman's Vote, 1914-1918', *History* 59/197 (October 1974), pp. 358-74. See also Brian Harrison, *Separate Spheres: The Opposition to Women's Suffrage in Britain* (London, 1978), pp. 202-27, for the most recent account of the impact of the First World War on women's suffrage in Britain.
44. Dahlsgård (ed.), op. cit., p. 200; IWSAC 1920, pp. 167-72. For the political background, see above pp. 80-1, 89-90.
45. V. Mallinson, *Belgium* (London, 1969), pp. 96-7; Dahlsgard (ed.), op. cit., pp. 269-71. For a contrast between the strong female suffrage movement in the Netherlands and its weak counterpart in Belgium, see above, pp. 134-5.
46. Catherine Cleverdon, *The Woman Suffrage Movement in Canada* (London, 1950).
47. Flexner, op. cit., pp. 276-324; Banner, op. cit., pp. 119-28.
48. Kraditor, op. cit., pp. 7-10.
49. O'Neill, *Everyone Was Brave*, pp. 169-222; Flexner, op. cit., p. 304.
50. Paulson, op. cit., pp. 137-42, 157-60, 165, 171-3; Joseph R. Gusfield, *Symbolic Crusade: Status Politics and the American Temperance Movement* (Urbana, 1963), pp. 100-10. For feminism and the 'red scare', see above, pp. 207-8.
51. Spain enfranchised women briefly during the Republic of the 1930s; Franco's victory in the Civil War of 1936-9 disfranchised them once more. For further disfranchisements due to the collapse of constitutional political systems, see above, pp. 199, 203, 209-10. Sweden did not of course enfranchise women until 1921, but in fact the enactment of female suffrage had been decided upon in 1919; it was held up for two years by constitutional technicalities.

CONCLUSION

By the 1930s classical feminism in Europe, America and Australasia had come to the end of its historical trajectory. In the century or so since its first emergence as an organised force it had undergone several crucial changes in its *aims*, its *ideology*, its *political orientation* and its *social base*. The *aims* of feminist movements were initially primarily economic in character. The early feminists demanded access for unmarried women to the professions and the right of married women to control their own property. They backed up these demands by fighting for improvements in girls' secondary education and the admission of women to universities, in order to secure the qualifications necessary for engagement in professional activities and to attain the level of education necessary to manage their own domestic and financial affairs. As these demands were conceded, and middle-class women began both to move into the professions, above all into teaching, in substantial numbers, and to extend their domestic role in society through charitable activities, the aims of feminist movements underwent the first of their major reorientations. They developed a moral dimension, extending to include the abolition of state-regulated prostitution and the elimination of drunkenness, both to be achieved through moral suasion and the mobilisation of public opinion against sexual and alcoholic libertinism. This generally led on to the demand for the vote, which feminists initially saw as an important addition to the techniques of moral reform which they were developing. Female suffrage was enacted earliest where its moral function was most evident and most socially appropriate – in Australasia, for example, or in the American Midwest. Elsewhere, the female suffrage movement gradually broke away from its origins and formed a separate, radical wing of feminism. This gained rapidly in strength once it was established; and it soon forced the majority of moderate feminists to endorse at least some of its aims in order to prevent the further erosion of their support relative to that of the radicals. Gradually, the energies of the feminist movement came to centre on the unifying symbol of the vote. This hastened a further reorientation of the feminists' aims, in which greater emphasis came to be placed on the limited nature of the suffrage demanded, and the exclusion of large sections of the population from its benefits. Once this adjustment had been made, the way to victory was open. With the

enactment of fer   the aims of the feminist movement
became contradictory, as movement split into mutually hostile
factions; radical feminists lost support, turned to pacifism or collapsed altogether, while the moderates continued to develop in the conservative direction in which they had begun moving before.the winning
of the vote.

These successive changes in aims and policies corresponded to a
more long-term reorientation of the feminists' *ideology*. The feminists
began as liberal individualists. Their claim to equal rights for women
was based on the notion that the world consisted not, as feudal apolo-
gists believed, of fixed and immutable social categories – nobles, clergy,
the 'third estate' of commoners, serfs and villeins – but rather of free
individuals all endowed with reason and all equal in the sight of God.
Society, they argued, should be led by the most industrious and most
able, not by an hereditary caste of nobles with no qualification other
than a pedigree. To allow this to happen, legal restrictions on the
ability of individuals to compete with one another on the basis of equal
opportunity should be removed. Early feminist ideology consisted
fundamentally in the extension of these ideas and demands to women:
though early organised feminism was also logical enough to extend
them to other groups oppressed by reason of birth, such as blacks,
serfs and slaves, and national minorities. With the development of
radical feminism an attempt was also made to include the 'lower orders'
in the list as well. It soon became apparent, however, that the lower
orders resisted being helped to escape from their lot as individuals and
wanted instead to improve their position as a class. This setback helped
bring about the disintegration of the liberal individualist synthesis by
revealing the falsity of the premises on which it rested. The feminists
abandoned their original position of asserting the absence of any
innate differences in reason or ability between men and women and
retreated to a position in which innate differences were not only accepted but were also made the basis for feminist demands. The argument
had long been present in feminist propaganda that women's moral
behaviour was superior to men's. The original consequence for the
feminists had been the demand that men should improve their behaviour to match the standards which women had achieved. Now however it was accepted that they were constitutionally unable to do this.
Women's moral superiority was now thought to be inborn, a consequence of their function as mothers. The suffrage was demanded so
that women could help curb immorality and disorder not by education
and moral suasion but by legal enforcement and government coercion.

The acceptance of the existence of innate differences in reason and moral constitution between human beings was crucial for the feminists. When applied to men and women, it opened the way to the acceptance of woman's primary role as housewife and mother and the consequent abandonment of demands which rested on a denial of these differences, such as the right to abort or the right of married women with children to work outside the home. More generally, it also opened the way to racism and Social Darwinism, and the belief that inborn and immutable differences in character and intellect existed not only between men and women but also between whites and blacks or between the middle and upper classes and criminals, alcoholics, illiterates, immigrants and the 'lower orders' in general.

Feminist movements did not, of course, exist in a political vacuum; their changing *political orientation* and the relationships they enjoyed with political parties and governments played an important part in influencing their development. Almost invariably they began as part of wider movements of liberal social and political reform, from which they gradually freed themselves organisationally but not ideologically. Feminism and liberalism coexisted somewhat uneasily; the feminists were in essence applying the liberal creed with a consistency and logicality which liberal parties and movements could not but sympathise with but felt unable to follow in practice for reasons of political expediency. Despite these differences and ambiguities at the day-to-day political level, the alliance with liberalism remained central to the politics of feminism — a fact which has perhaps been obscured by the notorious experience of the English suffragettes, whose exceptional militancy was in part provoked by a hostility to feminism on the part of liberal politicians that was itself unusual, though not wholly without parallel in other countries. The major backing for feminism in nearly every country — including Britain for most of the late nineteenth century — came from liberals, even if the support they gave was sometimes less than wholehearted. Feminist movements in different countries took on the colouring of the liberals around them, whether they were anti-clerical, as in France or Italy, nationalist, as in Finland or Bohemia, or moderate and rather timid, as in Germany and Russia. Corespondingly, the main opposition to feminism came from the same conservative, agrarian or aristocratic groups that opposed middle-class liberalism.

When liberals themselves began to change, so too did the feminists. At the political level, indeed, the feminists' retreat from liberalism was in fact part of a general change in the nature of liberalism itself, so that it would be more accurate to describe it as a retreat *with* liberalism from the individualist tenets and progressive ideologies of an earlier era. At this time, liberalism in many countries was undergoing a reorientation that took it away from individualism and towards a greater belief in state interventionist and collectivist solutions to social problems in order to preserve social peace and pre-empt the more far-reaching solutions advocated by the left. The Progressive movement in America, the policies of Asquith's government in Britain, the neo-liberalism of Friedrich Naumann in Germany, the reforms of the Giolitti era in Italy, all these were part of this realignment of liberal politics. As industrial society reached maturity, liberalism became a Janus-faced political ideology, demanding equality from entrenched élites but denying it to the lower classes. Feminism shared these characteristics. Its stress on moral probity, for instance, involved a direct criticism of the moral laxity both of the allegedly effete aristocracy and of the supposedly promiscuous, drunken and disorderly lower classes. The feminists were increasingly concerned with the problem of social control, and this included the upper classes, who (it was believed) were setting the proletariat a bad example. The way in which problems of social control featured in the actual granting of female suffrage illustrates the extent to which the feminists owed what many of them saw as their crowning victory to these more conservative implications of the liberal creed. At the same time, the growing collectivism and conservatism of the liberals constituted part of an attempt to adjust to the growing social and political tensions that eventually pulled them apart. Liberalism itself collapsed as the rise of socialist and (after 1917) communist movements on the left caused the middle classes to desert it for more conservative political movements and parties. The decline of feminism was in fact part of this general decline of liberal beliefs and values in the first three decades of the twentieth century. Liberal political parties have never recovered from it; nor have feminist movements, now, where they still claim some continuity with the past, conservative or establishment groups with little appeal for the young and little general impact even on the women of the classes from which they once drew their support.

In the broadest sense, as we have seen, the gradual metamorphosis and eventual collapse of liberalism and feminism reflected the changing alignments and antagonisms of aristocracy, bourgeoisie and proletariat as industrial society progressed towards maturity. The feminists' political orientation was conditioned by their *social base* in the middle classes. More specifically, economic and social change also had particular implications for the ideology and practice of the feminists in its effect on the economic and social position of women *within* the middle classes. Early industrial society brought a narrowing of the opportunities open to middle-class women to achieve economic independence by introducing educational qualifications for a number of professions which women were unable to attain because of the poor provision of education for girls. Partly as a result of pressure from economic feminists, the employment of middle-class women in some professions, above all in teaching, then underwent a rapid increase. At the same time, married women were benefiting from improved secondary education for girls. These developments provided the social foundations both of an increase in the participation of women in moderate feminist movements and of the rise of moral reformist feminism. These in turn led to the emergence of radical feminism. The struggle for equal voting and other rights that followed also embodied a struggle for equality within the professions and within marriage. Already, however, the situation was beginning to change; the rapid growth of employment opportunities for women in the professions was coming to an end. Not only were equal pay and promotion resisted by men, but even before the First World War an anti-feminist counter-attack began which soon had professional women on the defensive; by the 1920s most of them were agreeing that women could not marry and have children and pursue a career at the same time. In addition to this, the expansion of the tertiary sector of many advanced economies, with the vast accompanying growth of white-collar and secretarial jobs for women, was rapidly devaluing the achievement of the feminists in opening up the professions. Female employment in non-manual jobs became commonplace, as did the involvement of married women in public affairs, for as the state became more involved in the home through sanitation, food and drugs and other legislation, married middle-class women began to see politics as a means of protecting their interests as housewives.

These developments began by moving feminism away from the doctrines of individual equality towards an acceptance of sex-role divisions in society. Feminism became ideologically defensive. As these social changes continued, however, they undermined, then finally destroyed the rationale of feminism altogether. Above all after enfranchisement, it was to political parties, not to feminist movements, that women turned for the protection of their interests, both as housewives and as professional or white-collar employees. The feminists were unable to compete because they were not institutionalised in the political system as were the political parties. In their effort to retain some function for themselves, feminist movements concentrated more and more on economic problems, and to an increasing extent, as the examples of America and Germany in the 1920s indicate, they became the playthings of economic pressure groups. The feminists had come full circle, and ended as they had begun, with a predominantly economic set of aims which they sought to achieve within the existing political system. Feminist history was repeating itself when the feminists of the 1920s, despairing at ever getting their aims accepted by the political systems of the day, extended their programme to encompass the reform of politics themselves; this time, however, they did not seek to extend or rationalise parliamentary constitutions as they had done before the First World War, but rather they now came to seek their abolition altogether. Moreover, by the 1920s, deep contradictions had emerged between the economic interests of the social groups of which the feminist movement consisted — business and professional women, white-collar workers and housewives. As these contradictions worked their way through to their conclusion, the feminist movement underwent its final disintegration and collapse.

Not every feminist movement followed this precise historical trajectory from beginning to end or at the same speed. The reasons for the variations between feminist movements and the nature and pace of these movements' developments are very suggestive of the forces operating for or against feminist movements in general. These too can be divided into a number of interrelated categories or levels. At an intellectual or ideological level, the most striking contrast is between Catholicism and Protestantism, the one a major obstacle to feminism, the other an almost essential precondition of its emergence. At the political level, it is clear that feminist movements flourished only in liberal, constitutional states which offered them the freedom in which to organise and the means through which they could secure the acceptance and implementation of their proposals. These states reflected the predominance of the middle classes, of which the feminists themselves formed a part. Since many of the feminists' ideas and aims would benefit the middle classes as a whole, it followed that they tended to develop most rapidly and secure most acceptance where the middle classes were strongest. The widely varying patterns of interaction between these factors produced different forms of feminist movement from country to country. In France, for example, a bourgeois democracy undergoing industrialisation but predominantly Catholic in religion, organised feminism began relatively early (in the late 1860s) but never succeeded either in making a full transition to radicalism or in breaking out of the narrow confines of Protestantism and anti-clericalism. In America, which was both Protestant and democratic, feminism developed along classical lines, emerging very early and in due course undergoing massive and irreversible radicalisation. In Germany, by contrast, which although predominantly Protestant and industrial was also strongly influenced by feudal and authoritarian structures inherited from its past, feminism developed quite early, remained unusually limited and conservative, and radicalised only briefly, though in a sharp and rapid way, before retreating equally rapidly into a new and more permanent version of its former conservatism.

Moreover, the political situation of the middle classes also affected the degree to which feminists were able to escape from the larger liberal reformist movements in which they generally had their origin to establish a separate existence of their own. In states struggling for national self-determination, such as Finland and Bohemia, the feminists often subordinated their own aims to those of the parent nationalist movement. It was only when these parent reform movements gained some measure of success, as with the nationalist movement in Finland in 1884 or the anti-slavery movement in the United States after the end of the Civil War, that the feminists felt justified in breaking away. In a country such as Hungary, where nationalism was the vehicle of a class of feudal landowners, the situation was even more complicated, and feminism seemed bound to remain narrowly moderate in its orientation without the emergence of an urban middle class. In due course the Jewish-German bourgeoisie of Budapest did provide the social basis for a radical feminist movement in Hungary, which enjoyed a brief and very active existence but experienced a total lack of success in achieving its aims. In some countries, additional complexities and paradoxes could emerge, with a limited female suffrage becoming the vehicle of Magyar nationalism in Hungary, for example, or with universal female suffrage perceived as likely to benefit Catholicism and so being rejected by anti-clerical liberals in France. In whatever combinations they worked themselves through, however, the influences operating for or against the feminists were relatively few in number. In favour were Protestant religion, liberal polity, bourgeois society, against were Catholic Church, authoritarian constitution, feudalism and aristocracy. That profoundly ambiguous political force, nationalism, could be found in both camps. Victorious, and jealous of its own privileges, as in Germany or Hungary, it could act as a barrier to feminist progress; where it still sought to achieve fulfilment, as in Bohemia or Finland, it was the very motor of feminism. Where its main enemy was the Catholic

Church, as in France or Italy, its effects were the most ambivalent of all, simultaneously inspiring the feminists and denying them victory because they were imprisoned within the barriers of an anti-clericalism which most women, still loyal to the Catholic Church, would undoubtedly use the vote to destroy.

However much the feminists differed from country to country, they all shared a common fate in the interwar years. Yet the decline of feminism was neither total nor final: nor, despite the confusion and disappointment it engendered in those who had fought hardest for it, did enfranchisement signify unambiguous defeat. The meaning of the feminists' ideas and achievements for women in general, and middle-class women in particular, are complex and difficult to unravel. Much further empirical research is needed before we can generalise about the significance for the everyday life of ordinary women of the vote, of professional and economic independence and opportunity, of moral repression and other reforms fought for and partly achieved by organised feminism: and we need a more elaborate and comprehensive theory of women's liberation itself before we can adequately measure these reforms by any absolute theoretical standard. Certainly, it is a fairly obvious point that the removal of formal legal barriers to economic opportunity failed altogether to bring real economic equality to women; and the feminists themselves were already realising by 1930 that the vote was no short-cut to political equality either. Women in top political, business or professional jobs are still everywhere a minute, insignificant minority. Economic growth, above all in the tertiary sector, has brought employment to women, but it is subordinate, supportive employment, in nursing, secretarial jobs, primary rather than secondary education, replicating women's continued subordinate role within the family. Even in the feminists' own terms, in other words, success has proved elusive, equality little more than symbolic.[1]

Yet in some ways symbolic equality was enough to satisfy all but the most radical and perceptive of the feminists. One of the major drives behind feminism was the need felt by middle-class women to reassert their superiority of status over socially or racially 'inferior' men to whom political and social change was bringing rights, and thus status, which they were still denied. To a degree, as above all the history of female suffrage indicates, feminism was about status equality, not about sex equality. Viewed in these terms it was remarkably successful. In a more general sense, the feminists provided an indispensable means through which millions of middle-class women were brought into public life, given a political education and helped to adjust to the rapidly changing conditions of the industrialising societies in which they lived, both in a political and in an economic and social sense. In however limited a way, therefore, the feminists helped women to enter the modern world. The feminists played an important role in the process of social change as a whole, aiding the reduction of violence and the establishment of middle-class dominance and social control in newly settled or rapidly growing centres of population. Female suffrage also helped stabilise bourgeois constitutionalism in many lands after the collapse of political systems of feudal origin and under the threat of proletarian revolution, even if this stabilisation was in many cases little more than temporary. All these were achievements of some historical importance.[2]

In some ways, too, time has brought many of the reforms which the feminists failed to achieve themselves except in a very limited number of countries. The inter-war years may have seen the negation of many of the feminists' policies, but since 1945 their ideas have been vindicated more widely than they themselves ever dared hope. In 1945 a whole range of countries granted women the vote, bringing the total up to 40. By the 1970s the states in which women enjoyed full equality of political rights numbered over 100, and only traditionally-oriented Moslem states continued to resist the idea of female suffrage. Marriage laws were reformed not only in countries such as France, Belgium and Italy, where the male supremacist Napoleonic Code had long seemed impervious to any attempts at amendment, but also in other, more backward countries as well. The proportion of women in universities everywhere rose dramatically after the Second World War, and continued to do so right into the late 1960s. Both at national and at international level, legislation of a general kind, attempting a comprehensive equalisation of women's rights with those of men, became increasingly frequent. A series of United Nations declarations on equal rights was accompanied by Equal Rights legislation in many countries, including America, where an Equal Rights Amendment to the Constitution was finally passed in the 1970s. A feminist of the turn of the century surviving into the 1970s would have been surprised and gratified by the extent to which ideas derided as absurd in 1900 had become generally accepted not only in European societies but also all over the world seventy years later.[3]

The spread across the world of classical feminist notions of female equality (i.e. the idea that women should have formal, legal equality of status and opportunity) owed at least something to the activities of the feminists themselves after 1920. For although the inter-war years saw the decline of feminist movements in those countries where they had emerged before 1914, it would be mistaken to conclude that there was a decline of feminism on a global scale in this period. Feminists might have been frustrated in their own countries, but with the end of the war and the establishment of the League of Nations they saw a major opportunity to broadcast their message to the rest of the world. Already in 1913, Carrie Chapman Catt devoted her Presidential speech at the International Woman Suffrage Alliance Congress to the need to emancipate the women of Asia, where she had gone on an extensive tour with the Dutch feminist leader Aletta Jacobs, attempting to interest women in the question of equal rights. The next task of women, she said, lay in awakening the East to the feminist message.[4] After 1918, a major part of the efforts both of the International Council of Women and of the International Woman Suffrage Alliance (renamed International Alliance of Women for Suffrage and Equal Citizenship) was devoted to extending the feminist movement to what is now known as the 'Third World'. To some extent, of course, this signified that the feminists were seeking compensation for failure in their own countries. An increasing number of the officers of these international women's organisations had little or no connection with feminist movements in their own lands. This trend was accentuated by the tendency of National Councils of Women to coopt women who had reached positions of eminence in public life, whether they were feminists or not, and by the growing enmeshment of international women's organisations in the international bureaucracy created by the League of Nations and its satellite organisations such as the International Labour Office. The international women's movement, apart from its work on an international level, which was mainly concerned with moral reform (above all, the suppression of the 'white slave trade', which was now held responsible for prostitution in most countries), exerted a steady pressure on non-European countries to create women's organisations. International congresses and individual contacts gave encouragement and help to feminist leaders in colonies and in emerging nations. By the eve of the Second World War there were National Councils of Women in twenty-three European and sixteen non-European countries. Even this greatly exaggerated the preponderance of European countries in the worldwide women's movement by 1938, since there were feminist movements in many other countries than these. In fact, the real driving force behind the emergence of feminism outside Europe was not the encouragement of European and American women, but the growth of nationalist movements aiming to throw off the yoke of European colonial domination altogether. The 1920s saw the real beginnings of bourgeois nationalism in many Asian and Middle Eastern countries. As in Europe, it brought with it the growth of feminist movements. This final phase of feminism, its spread to the 'Third World', did not work itself out until the triumph of nationalism and the collapse of the great colonial empires in the 1960s.[5]

By this time, however, the concept of women's emancipation which bourgeois feminism embodied was already beginning to be superseded; for it was the 1960s which also saw the birth of the Women's Liberation Movement, whose intellectual roots lay in theories which the feminists themselves had rejected. The first of these theories was socialism. On the face of it, of course, the experience of the inter-war years had not been encouraging for the socialist concept of women's emancipation. Immediately after the Bolshevik Revolution of 1917, attempts were made to implement socialist ideas of female emancipation in Russia. Doctrines of sexual freedom and female independence were propagated by the Bolshevik women's leader Alexandra Kollontai, and the state began to take over some of the functions of the family and to relieve women of the burden of child-rearing through communal households and *crèches*. But this had not gone very far, even in Moscow and Leningrad, before Stalinisation brought a reaction. An obsession with the birth-rate and a growing moral repressiveness led in the 1930s to the reintroduction of many laws abolished in the revolution, including the outlawing of homosexuality (1934) and abortion (1936, 1944). Communist parties everywhere sang the praises of the family, which they alleged capitalism was seeking to destroy. Divorce law was tightened up in Russia, illegitimacy penalised, the authority of the father strengthened, the mothers of large families given bonuses and decorations. Sexual indulgence was stigmatised as counter-revolutionary. These policies were certainly anti-feminist in the broad sense of the word, though bourgeois feminists and even some pre-1914 socialist women might indeed have approved of a few of them. But the Social Democrats in Russia had been comparatively indifferent to women's emancipation before the Revolution. And in other countries, such as Germany, the socialist women's movement had been concerned to strengthen the proletarian family; Clara Zetkin and Rosa Luxemburg had even advocated larger working-class families and opposed contraception. The essence of the socialist approach to female emancipation lay in fact not so much in the theories of sexual freedom advanced by Kollontai (or before her by Fourier), as in the insistence that the state should help working women gain equality by intervening actively to ensure that they were on equal terms in competing with men for jobs, and by relieving them of the burden of child-rearing and housekeeping through maternity benefits, *crèches* and communal households. It was the abandonment of many of these schemes that constituted the real setback for the socialist advocates of female emancipation between the wars. Only after Stalin's death did they emerge once more; though it is arguable that without the industrialisation brought about under Stalin's leadership they might not have been possible on a widespread scale anyway.[6] Among Social Democratic women there was also something of a reaction in the 1920s, as the old left wing of the Socialist Women's International, including Clara Zetkin, split off to join the Communist Party. Social Democratic parties took a more conservative attitude towards women, above all in the era of mass unemployment during the Depression, when they generally supported the dismissal of married women workers to save men's jobs. Only in the long term did Social Democratic governments such as those of the Scandinavian countries create equal opportunities for women in a systematic way. In general during the inter-war years, Social Democratic women's movements suffered the same fate as feminist movements; they were suppressed along with the parent party in right-wing dictatorships, and declined, moved to the right or failed to exert any real influence in the liberal democracies.[7] The question of which wing of the women's movement, the socialist or the feminist, offered the better chance of emancipation and equality, still awaited an answer.

It is clear, however, that of the two only the socialist theory of women's emancipation possessed the possibility of further development, for the Women's Liberation Movement has used or modified many of its elements in developing a theory of female emancipation appropriate to the advanced industrial societies of the late twentieth century, while universally rejecting the feminist concept of equal rights as inadequate. Allied to the socialist elements in women's liberation ideology is another body of theory which the feminists rejected — the theory of sexual freedom and fulfilment. Those women who advocated sexual freedom were always given short shrift by the feminists, and the 'new morality' which they advocated was seen as a new immorality by the advocates of women's rights. Yet although they were not feminists as understood by their contemporaries, and were indeed eventually expelled or excluded from feminist organisations altogether, women such as Margaret Sanger, Victoria Woodhull, Marie Stopes and Helene Stöcker were more significant in the long run than the feminists imagined. With the spread of efficient means of contraception, the advocacy of sexual freedom was ceasing to be wholly harmful to the interests of women, though the established women's organisations proved unable to recognise this fact. The spread of Freudian ideology hastened the obsolescence of feminist sexual attitudes. Despite their limitations, the apostles of sexual freedom pointed the way beyond feminism to the liberation of women. Even Freud's ideas, though profoundly anti-feminist, eventually proved to have a generally liberating effect.

It is the combination of socialism — though in a multitude of forms, some of them barely recognisable — and sexual liberation, that distinguishes the ideology, the beliefs and the aims of the present-day Women's Liberation movement from those of the feminists of the nineteenth century. The tendency for supporters of Women's Liberation to look to feminists of the past for legitimation for their efforts has obscured the fact that in many respects the advocates of Women's Liberation reject the aims and beliefs of the feminists and operate on a very different set of assumptions about the nature of society and the purpose of political action. The employment of a new political vocabulary by the Women's Liberation Movement is revealing: 'liberation' instead of 'equal rights', stressing the inadequacy of the mere legal equality which was the principal aim of the feminists; 'consciousness-raising', deriving from the ideology of Marxism with its emphasis on the need for the oppressed to liberate themselves as a group rather than — as the feminists thought — as individuals; 'sexism', deriving from the concept of 'racism', signifying rejection of ways of thought which the feminists themselves eventually came to share. Another difference lies in the Women's Liberationists' avoidance of the large formal organisations so dear to the feminists. Like the feminist movement, it is true, the Women's Liberation movement started as part of a wider movement of social and political protest, this time in association with the student and civil rights movements of the 1960s. Even more remarkably, perhaps, its geographical spread is not dissimilar to that of the old feminism: the Women's Liberation movement is strongest in the United States, where it has gained its most striking success, and developed concepts and ideas which have formed the|basis for Women's Liberation in other countries, and in Great Britain, where it has developed an extensive network of groups; and in Denmark, Sweden and Iceland the Redstockings, in Norway the Women's Front, in Holland the Dolle Minas, have all reached considerable prominence. In contrast, organised Women's Liberation movements have been slower to make an impact in those countries, such as Germany, France and Italy, where the old feminism was notoriously weak. In most countries, the old feminists and their successors have reacted with thinly disguised hostility to the ideas of the Women's Liberation movement.[8] The new feminists are building their movement on the ruins of the old, but for all the superficial resemblances, their ideas are really very different to those of their predecessors. Only time will tell whether they will gain as wide an acceptance.

Notes

1. Evelyne Sullerot, *Women, Society and Change* (London, 1971); Lynne B. Iglitzin and Ruth Ross (eds.), *Women in the World: A Comparative Study* (Oxford, 1976). These are two more or less arbitrary selections from a vast and rapidly growing literature.

2. See David Pivar, *Purity Crusade: Sexual Morality and Social Control 1868-1,900* (London, 1973), esp. p. 48 n.36, for the feminists as a modernising élite; Alice S. Rossi, *The Feminist Papers. From Adams to de Beauvoir* (New York, 1974), p. 271, for feminism as status politics; and Ross Evans Paulson, *Women's Suffrage and Social Control* (Brighton, 1973), *passim*, for female suffrage as social control.

3. Sullerot, op. cit.

4. IWSAC 1913, pp. 184-94.

5. For the rise of feminism in the Third World, a subject barely studied by historians as yet, see Cora Vreede-de Stuers, *The Indonesian Woman: Struggles and Achievements* (The Hague, 1960); David Marr, 'The 1920s Women's Rights Debates in Vietnam', *Journal of Asian Studies* XXXV/3 (May, 1976), pp. 371-90; Daw Mya Sein, 'Towards Independence in Burma: The Role of Women', *Asian Affairs* 59/3 (1972), pp. 288-99; Dahlsgard, op. cit., Lefaucheux (ed.), op. cit. A study of the feminist movement in Egypt, based on extensive research into primary sources, is being completed by Margot Badran (St Antony's College, Oxford). There is some material on the effects of colonial rule on women in Iglitzin and Ross (eds.), op. cit. see also Charlotte Beahan, 'The Women's Movement and Nationalism in Late Ch'ing China' (PhD, Columbia, 1976). A number of 'Third World' countries, including some of the Latin American republics, enfranchised women in the inter-war years.

6. See, among a considerable literature, Michael P. Sacks, *Women's Work in Soviet Russia* (New York, 1976); Fannina W. Halle, *Women in Soviet Russia* (London, 1935); and W.M. Mandel, *Soviet Women* (New York, 1975).

7. Some examples in Inge Dahlsgård, *Kvindebevaegelsens hvem-hvad-hvor* (Copenhagen, 1975); for Germany, see Werner Thönnessen, *The Emancipation of Women. The Rise and Decline of the Women's Movement in German Social Democracy 1863-1933* (London, 1973).

8. Dahlsgård, op. cit.; Maren Lockwood Carden, *The New Feminist Movement* (New York, 1974); S. Encel, N. Mackenzie, M. Tebbutt, *Women and Society: An Australian Study* (Melbourne, 1975); Mitchell, op. cit.; Iglitzin and Ross (eds.), op. cit. The impact of Women's Liberation movements in different countries can be gauged not only by the spread of groups and the scale of publications, but also by access to mass media, the construction of women's studies courses in universities and so on, and in these respects the geographical division discussed above is still strong, though becoming less so.

APPENDIX: INTERNATIONAL FEMINIST MOVEMENTS

Reference has been made in the course of the book to a number of international feminist organisations. Some explanation of the origin and nature of these organisations is necessary, and it is the purpose of this appendix to supply it. It also seems useful to suggest a few comparisons with the Socialist Women's International, discussed in Chapter 3.

International contacts and influences played an important part in stimulating the growth of feminist movements in many countries. The immediate translation of feminist classics such as John Stuart Mill's *The Subjection of Women* into a number of foreign languages was an important stimulus to the growth of feminist sentiment. Personal contacts were even more influential. Radical migrants from Britain helped foster feminist ideas in Australia and New Zealand, while the initial impetus for the foundation of the German feminist movement came from a Hungarian converted to feminist ideas in New York. It was not surprising, therefore, that most feminists felt themselves to be part of a vast international movement carried on by the tide of history towards an ultimate goal which was the same for every nation in the world. Feminists in every country paid especial attention to the progress of feminist movements in other parts of the globe, seeing them as pursuing essentially the same goals as themselves, and indeed it is remarkable how similar were the aims and beliefs of feminists in lands widely separated by geography and political culture.

Feminists frequently sought to gain prestige for themselves by organising international congresses on the 'woman question'. The emerging radical feminist movement in Germany held one such congress in Berlin in 1896, for example, and the French feminists Léon Richer and Maria Deraismes were indefatigable organisers of international gatherings. These meetings often played a major role in stimulating the growth of feminist movements in the host country by calling the attention of the press to what might otherwise have passed unnoticed as little more than small and ineffectual organisations on the fringe of politics. But nothing could disguise the fact that congresses of this kind were not truly international, however successful they were in local terms. Relatively few foreigners attended the German Congress of 1896. And the International Women's Rights Congress organised by Richer and Deraismes in Paris in 1878, though attended by 220 people from eleven different countries, was less impressive than it seemed at first sight. Only half of all the delegates were women, and the backwardness of the French feminist movement was revealed by the fact that only 45 per cent of the French delegates were female, compared with 83 per cent of the British and American delegations. Like many such congresses subsequently organised by the French feminists, it was international in name only, since 168 of the delegates were French, and the only other countries represented in force were Britain, with thirteen delegates, and the United States, with sixteen. There were no delegates from Germany, despite the existence of a large and well-organised women's movement there. In fact, in so far as the congress was international at all, it was as a meeting between the British supporters of Josephine Butler's campaign against the state regulation of prostitution and those they hoped to recruit in France for the extension of their crusade to the continent. In 1889 Richer organised a second international congress in Paris. Only seventeen foreigners were present among the 200 delegates, but at least this time there were three times as many women as men in the French delegation. This was largely because the bulk of the French delegates were not so much feminists as upper-class women active in Jewish and Protestant philanthropy. There were no socialist or working-class women present, not least because of the high entrance fee.[1]

Such efforts can best be regarded as attempts of the feminists of one country to gain prestige in their own land by giving their movement an air of internationalism. More serious perhaps was the earlier venture launched by the Swiss feminist Marie Goegg in 1868, the International Association of Women (*Association Internationale des Femmes*), based in Geneva. Goegg was almost an international feminist movement in herself. Born in Geneva in 1826, she had married a German from the liberal state of Baden, and lived in London for many years after her husband was exiled from Germany for his part in the liberal revolution of 1848. In 1867, she attended a Peace Congress organised by one of the many pacifist societies of the era, the International League of Peace and Liberty. She was inspired to form the International Association of Women as a result. The Association held a meeting during the Pacifist League's next congress, and Goegg published a letter in its magazine, the *United States of Europe*, inviting women to join. By the time of the Association's first congress, held on 27 March 1870, it counted fifteen member associations. Most of these represented individual Swiss cantons, but there were also member groups from England, America, Germany, France, Italy and Portugal. The movement cooperated with Josephine Butler in opposing the Contagious Diseases Acts in Britain and also won the support of a number of prominent individuals including Elizabeth Cady Stanton in America and Henriette Goldschmidt and Luise Otto-Peters in Germany. Petitions were sent to the Spanish Cortes asking for women's suffrage and to the Italian Chamber of Deputies demanding lay education for girls. In 1871 a Danish branch was formed, which in due course became the Danish Women's Association.[2]

Despite its vigorous and active growth, the International Association of Women collapsed at the end of 1871. The political tensions created in Switzerland by the Franco-Prussian War of 1870-71 had already forced Goegg to resign; but what finally destroyed the Association was the international police repression engendered by the revolutionary uprising of the Paris Commune in 1871. The blame for the Commune was laid by many governments on the International Working Men's Association, in which Marx and Bakunin played a leading role, and an immediate attempt was made to repress all voluntary associations with the word 'International' in their title. Goegg's movement was doubly suspect because it had actually tried to cultivate contacts with the International Working Men's Association. Member groups such as the Danish branch, frightened at the prospect of government repression, severed contacts. Deprived of Goegg's leadership, the International Association of Women was effectively dead by the end of 1871. Goegg's subsequent activities were largely restricted to the narrower field of Swiss feminist organisations.[3] During the rest of the 1870s the only form of international movement possible was one that gave the appearance at least of being politically neutral and charitable in orientation. Even this, as we have seen, was not sufficient to prevent the German branch of Josephine Butler's British, Continental and General Federation for the Abolition of the State Regulation of Vice, founded in 1875, from being suppressed by the police in 1885. In fact, international feminism did not revive until the end of the 1880s, and this time it was the Americans who took the lead. After the way had been shown by Frances Willard's foundation of the immensely successful World's Woman's Christian Temperance Union in 1884, the initiative was taken up by the Stanton-Anthony wing of the American Women's Suffrage Movement. Elizabeth Cady Stanton had already conceived the idea of an International Woman Suffrage Movement in 1883 while visiting her son in France and her daughter in England, and in fact a conference attended by forty-one people including Stanton, Susan B. Anthony, the French radical feminist Hubertine Auclert and a number of British feminists at Liverpool in November 1883 had already resulted in the establishment of an organising committee. Stanton and Anthony did not however take any further positive steps until 1887, and by this time the close connection of Anthony herself with temperance reform and social purity movements had suggested a widening of scope to include not just suffrage societies but feminist movements of all kinds. With the encouragement of Frances Willard and May Wright Sewell, a pacifist and social purity worker, a conference was eventually called in Washington in March 1888 to celebrate the fortieth anniversary of the Seneca Falls Declaration by founding a permanent International Council of Women.[4]

To some extent, the Washington Congress, like its counterpart in France in the following year, was intended mainly to enhance the prestige of its organisers, in this case the Stanton-Anthony faction of the American suffrage movement. The occasion was dominated by the Americans; England, France, Denmark, Norway, Finland, India and Canada sent representatives from abroad. Some of these women were attending merely in an individual capacity. The Danish Women's Association had responded enthusiastically, but the General German Women's Association had refused to attend on the grounds that the proceedings would be dominated by radicals.[5] The Constitution of the International Council of Women provided for the affiliation only of National Councils of Women, thus encouraging the formation of such councils in individual member nations. Predictably, the sole member council was the American one, founded in 1888. No other national councils were founded until the formation of one in Canada in 1893, though there was an abortive attempt to establish one in France in 1892. For the first five years of its existence, therefore, despite the nominal presence on its Committee of a number of foreign representatives, the International Council of Women was in effect a purely American organisation. Its domination by the Americans was re-affirmed at the World's Congress of Representative Women, held in conjunction with the Chicago Exposition of May 1893, and organised by the International Council of Women. All women's organisations were invited. 126 sent representatives, but these came from only four-teen countries. Nearly half the organisations – 56 – were American. 34 were British, 9 German, 7 French, 6 Canadian, 3 Swedish, 2 Finnish, 2 Danish, 2 Norwegian, 1 Belgian, 1 Italian, 1 'South American, 1 Swiss and 1 Australian. Since most of the foreign societies sent only one representative, while each of the American groups sent many, the over-whelming majority of the 600 participants were American. Another consequence of American domination was the fact that the largest group of societies present was concerned with civil and political reform; 30 were religious, 17 philanthropic, 15 concentrated on 'moral and social reform', 11 on education, 6 on industry, 5 on art and literature, 4 on science, and 4 on 'miscellaneous' subjects. All these subjects formed the main topics for debate, along with 'the Solidarity of Human Interests', at the Congress's seventy-six sessions.[6]

It was only after this that the Council became truly international. National Councils were established in Germany 1894, Britain 1895, Sweden and New Zealand 1896, Italy and the Netherlands 1898, Denmark 1899, Switzerland and Argentina 1900, France 1901, Austria 1902, Hungary and Norway 1904, Belgium 1905, Bulgaria and Greece 1908, Serbia 1911, South Africa 1913, Portugal 1914 and the various states of Australia over a period stretching from 1896 to 1911. The list gives a rough idea of the global distribution of feminist movements before the First World War. All the National Councils were in effect moderate feminist in their political complexion, not least because they included many societies which were more philanthropic than feminist. Its diversity inevitably weakened the International Council's sense of purpose. The President of the Council from 1900 onwards, the Countess of Aberdeen, whose election was a symptom of the emancipation of the Council from its American origins and its capture by the 'establishment', attempted to make a virtue of this.

It will be asked [she said] how in the world can such a conglomeration of associations existing in so many different countries, and formed for so many various objects, some actually opposed to one another, and comprising hundreds of thousands of women of different religions, different races and upbringing, have an intelligible purpose and work together for a practical end? And yet we claim that in the very variety of opinions and ideas and methods of work which exist among us lies our *raison d'être*, the centre and kernel of our being. For the unity which it is our aim to seek does not lie in identity of organisation or identity of dogma, but in a common conservation to the service of humanity in the spirit of love which we hail as the greatest thing in the world.

Nevertheless, this could not disguise the fact that the Council had to allow member councils complete freedom of action and ideology, and formed little more than a forum for the exchange of opinions. Its most important function apart from instigating the formation of National

Councils was to satisfy, as the Countess of Aberdeen put it, 'those who were anxiously concerned to see so large an undertaking, entirely offi- cered by women, carry out its business in a business-like way'.[7] The International Council had a staggeringly elaborate structure, adhered punctiliously to the forms of parliamentary procedure, and tried to legitimise women's involvement in politics in the eyes of male society by making its congresses as long, as detailed and as comprehensive as possible – the published account of its proceedings in 1899, for ex- ample, runs to seven volumes.

The moderate feminist domination of the International Council did not satisfy those who wanted it to press more vigorously than it was willing to do for the aim of female suffrage. As early as 1899, the American suffragists declared their intention of setting up a separate International Woman Suffrage Alliance. The split was formalised at the 1904 Congress of the International Council, which was held in Berlin in recognition of the fact that the German feminist movement was the largest and best-organised in the world after those of America and Britain. Despite the fact that the Council voted in 1904 that 'strenuous efforts be made to enable women to obtain the power of voting in all countries where a representative government exists',[8] and set up a Standing Committee on Women's Suffrage led by Anna Howard Shaw, the radicals went ahead with their plans and founded an International Woman Suffrage Alliance. Its leader was Shaw's great rival in the American suffragist movement, just ousted by her from the move- ment's leadership, Carrie Chapman Catt, who may well have seen in international activity an outlet for the energies she was no longer able to employ on the American scene, and a welcome opportunity to save face. The new Alliance comprised the suffrage societies of America, Canada, Germany, Britain, the Netherlands, Norway and Sweden. In 1906 they were joined by suffrage societies in Hungary, Italy and Russia, in 1908 by those of Bulgaria, Denmark, Finland, South Africa and Swit- zerland, in 1909 by those of Belgium, France and Serbia, in 1911 by those of Iceland, Portugal and Romania. In addition there were affiliated com- mittees in Austria and Bohemia (1909) and Habsburg Polish Galicia (1911), and in Australia, where women already had the vote, the Women's Political Association became a member in 1904. The International Woman Suffrage Alliance represented radical feminism on an interna- tional level. Not surprisingly, perhaps, it was even more dominated by the Americans than was the International Council of Women. Despite the fact that it was more single-minded than the Council, and despite its greater sense of mission and its confidence that it was riding on the crest of a wave of progress and evolution to rapid victory, the Alliance faced rather more serious internal problems than the Council, due to the fact that many member countries had more than one suffrage society. All attempts to force national suffrage societies to unite failed. The Alliance itself only managed to avoid being split on the issue of limited versus universal suffrage by allowing wide latitude to member associations on this point, and by stipulating that all associations in all countries could join, but the voting at Congresses would be divided by countries, not by member societies. Every Congress was preceded by elaborate and sometimes disputatious constitutional discussions. The greater sense of urgency that characterised the Alliance was marked by the fact that it held a Congress every other year, while the Council only met every five years. It represented the dynamic side of feminism; the Council, increasingly dominated by aristocrats and patronised by governments, represented its official, 'establishment' aspect. The Alliance was a minority movement. Only seven of the member countries in 1911 — Austria, Britain, Germany, Sweden, the Netherlands, the USA and Denmark — had suffrage movements over 2,500 strong.[9]

Neither organisation was in reality much more than a means of establishing contact between different national feminist movements by the holding of congresses. Leading officers of these international organisations did tour foreign countries, and especially in Asia they helped bring feminist societies into existence. As far as established feminist movements were concerned, however, they did not even go as far as the Socialist Women's International in trying to lay down specific programmatic points to which all had to adhere; their few generally declared aims were vague in the extreme. It was left to moral reform societies such as Frances Willard's World's Woman's Christian Temperance Union (1884) or Josephine Butler's British, Continental and General (later, International) Federation for the Abolition of the State Regulation of Vice (1875) to draw up a firm programme of definite, precisely formulated demands; and even here, noticeable differences between constituent national groups were emerging by the turn of the century. Still, all these international organisations, including the socialist one, gave their members a sense of belonging to a great and irresistible current of world opinion, however much a minority they might be in their own country. This gave them confidence in themselves and belief in the inevitability of ultimate victory. It was for this reason that they considered international organisations of such importance, however meagre the results of their establishment were in practical terms.

Notes

1. Patrick K. Bidelman, 'The Feminist Movement in France: the Formative Years 1858-1889' (PhD, Michigan, 1975), pp. 172ff.,304ff; R. Schoenfliess *et al*. (eds.), *(Der) Internationale Kongress für Frauenwerke und Frauen-bestrebungen* . . . (Berlin, 1897).
2. Barbara Schnetzler, *Die frühe amerikanische Frauenbewegung und ihre Kontakte mit Europa (1836-1869)* (Bern, 1971), p. 114; Theodore Stanton, *The Woman Question in Europe* (New York, 1884), pp. 378-81; see also above, p. 76.
3. Annie Leuch-Reineck, *Le Féminisme en Suisse* (Lausanne, 1929).
4. Maire-Hélène Lefaucheux, *Women in a Changing World: the dynamic Story of the International Council of Women since 1888* (London, 1966), pp. 9-13.
5. See above, p. 104.
6. May Wright Sewell (ed.), *The World's Congress of Representative Women 15-22 May 1893* (Chicago, 1894), pp. 1-5.
7. ICWT 1899, Vol. I, p. 47.
8. Lefaucheux, op. cit., p. 27.
9. Information drawn from IWSAC reports. For the Women's International League for Peace and Freedom, founded 1915, see above, pp. 196-7, 206. For the International Abolitionist Federation, see above, pp. 35-6, 52-3, 77, 104, 106, 130-1. For the World's Woman's Christian Temperance Union, see above, pp. 35-7, 53-4, 60-62, 83, 151, 171, 207, 211, 213, 215.

A NOTE ON FURTHER READING

In a book of this nature, there seems little point in listing all the various sources and publications consulted, the more so since they can be found without too much difficulty in the notes. It may be useful, however, to mention some of the more easily accessible published studies of feminism. The most useful general survey is Inge Dahlsgård (ed.) *Kvindebevaegelsens hvem-hvad-hvor* (Copenhagen, 1975), a comprehensive handbook with especially valuable information on feminism in the Nordic countries. Léon Abensour's *Histoire générale du féminisme dès origines à nos jours* (Paris, 1921) is a very general survey beginning in classical times. The *Lexicon der Frau* (Zürich, 1953) is perhaps the best work of reference. The historical chapters of Kate Millett, *Sexual Politics* (New York, 1969) are essential reading. Sheila Rowbotham, *Women, Resistance and Revolution* (London, 1972) is a selective but geographically wide-ranging account of women's involvement in revolution since the seventeenth century. On a more official level, the published congress proceedings and official historical manuals of the International Council of Women and the International Woman Suffrage Alliance are important sources of information. Feminist ideology is covered in Alice S. Rossi (ed.), *The Feminist Papers: From Adams to de Beauvoir* (excellent introductory and linking commentaries) and Miriam Schneir (ed.), *Feminism: The Essential Historical Writings* (New York, 1972). These collections are heavily biased towards America: Europe is represented in Rossi's anthology, for example, only by socialist writers. Viola Klein, *The Feminine Character: History of an Ideology* (London, 1946) and Vernon L. Bullough, *The Subordinate Sex. A History of Attitudes Towards Women* (Urbana, 1973) are historical accounts of ideas (mostly men's) about the nature of women and their place in society. As yet most work on feminist movements outside the United States is available only in the form of articles or unpublished dissertations. Their appearance can be monitored in *Dissertation Abstracts* and in journals such as *Feminist Studies*, the *Journal of Interdisciplinary History*, the *Journal of Social History*, and *Signs*. Some of the articles are usefully reprinted in anthologies such as Berenice A. Carroll (ed.), *Liberating Women's History: Theoretical and Critical Essays* (Urbana, 1976) and Lois Banner, Mary Hartman (eds.), *Clio's Consciousness Raised: New Perspectives on the History of*

254

Women (New York, 1974). There are few books on individual feminist movements. For America, Eleanor Flexner, *Century of Struggle: The Woman's Rights Movement in the United States* (Cambridge, Mass., 1966), William L. O'Neill, *Everyone Was Brave: The Rise and Fall of Feminism in America* (Chicago, 1969) and Aileen S. Kraditor, *The Ideas of the Woman Suffrage Movement 1890-1920* (London, 1965) are probably the most comprehensive. There is no scholarly study of British feminism, though more than one is in preparation. On the suffragettes, the standard work is Andrew Rosen, *Rise Up, Women! The Militant Campaign of the Women's Social and Political Union 1903-1914* (London, 1974). The antipodean feminists are comparatively well served in S. Encel, N. Mackenzie and M. Tebbutt, *Women and Society: An Australian Study* (Melbourne, 1975) and Patricia Grimshaw, *Women's Suffrage in New Zealand* (Wellington, 1972), both works of sound scholarship and stimulating ideas. For France, the best introduction available in any language is the chapter on 'Women' in Theodore Zeldin, *France 1848-1945, Vol. 1: Ambition, Love and Politics* (Oxford, 1973). The history of feminism in the Nordic countries is best approached through Dahlsgård, op. cit., and the various publications produced by Gunnar Qvist and the Women's History Archive at the University of Gothenburg. On Germany, Margrit Twellmann, *Die deutsche Frauenbewegung im Spiegel repräsentativer Frauenzeitschriften. Ihre Anfänge und erste Entwicklung 1843-1888* (2 vols., Meisenheim am Glan, 1972) and Richard J. Evans, *The Feminist Movement in Germany 1894-1933* (London, 1976) span the history of the feminist movement from beginning to end. Martha Braun, *Frauenbewegung, Frauenbildung und Frauenarbeit in Österreich* (Vienna, 1930) is an official history of Austrian feminism, packed with information. For Russia, see Richard Stites, *The Women's Liberation Movement in Russia: Feminism, Nihilism and Bolshevism 1860-1930* (Princeton, 1977). On Italy, the most accessible studies are: Pieroni Bortolotti Franca, 'Femminismo e Socialismo dal 1900 al primo dopoguerra', *Critica Storia* vii (1969), pp. 23-62, and Alexander de Grand, 'Women under Italian Fascism', *Historical Journal* 19/4 (1976), pp. 947-68. Finally, Brian Harrison's *Separate Spheres: The Opposition to Women's Suffrage in Britain* (London, 1978), is not only a fully-documented study of its own subject, but also has a great deal of interest on feminism and female suffrage as well.

INDEX